Latinx Experiences
in U.S. Schools

Race and Education in the Twenty-First Century

Series Editors: Kenneth J. Fasching-Varner, University of Nevada, Las Vegas; Roland Mitchell, Louisiana State University; and Lori Latrice Martin, Louisiana State University

This series asks authors and editors to consider the role of race and education, addressing questions such as "how do communities and educators alike take on issues of race in meaningful and authentic ways?" and "how can education work to disrupt, resolve, and otherwise transform current racial realities?" The series pays close attention to the intersections of difference, recognizing that isolated conversations about race eclipse the dynamic nature of identity development that play out for race as it intersects with gender, sexuality, socioeconomic class, and ability. It welcomes perspectives from across the entire spectrum of education from Pre-K through advanced graduate studies, and it invites work from a variety of disciplines, including counseling, psychology, higher education, curriculum theory, curriculum and instruction, and special education.

Recent Titles in Series

Latinx Experiences in U.S. Schools: Voices of Students, Teachers, Teacher Educators and Education Allies in Challenging Sociopolitical Times, edited by Margarita Jiménez-Silva and Janine Bempechat

Implications of Race and Racism in Student Evaluations of Teaching: The Hate U Give, edited by LaVada Taylor

Technology Segregation: Disrupting Racist Frameworks in Early Childhood Education, by Miriam B. Tager

Surviving Becky(s): Pedagogies for Deconstructing Whiteness and Gender, edited by Cheryl E. Matias

Latinx Curriculum Theorizing, edited by Theodorea Regina Berry

Intersectional Care for Black Boys in an Alternative School: They Really Care About Us, by Julia C. Ransom

Culture, Community, and Educational Success: Reimagining the Invisible Knapsack, edited by Toby S. Jenkins, Stephanie Troutman, and Crystal Polite Glover

Whiteness at the Table: Antiracism, Racism, and Identity in Education, edited by Shannon K. McManimon, Zachary A. Casey, and Christina Berchini

The Classroom as Privileged Space: Psychoanalytic Paradigms for Social Justice in Pedagogy, by Tapo Chimbganda

Latinx Experiences in U.S. Schools

Voices of Students, Teachers, Teacher Educators, and Education Allies in Challenging Sociopolitical Times

Edited by
Margarita Jiménez-Silva
and Janine Bempechat

LEXINGTON BOOKS
Lanham • Boulder • New York • London

Published by Lexington Books
An imprint of The Rowman & Littlefield Publishing Group, Inc.
4501 Forbes Boulevard, Suite 200, Lanham, Maryland 20706
www.rowman.com

6 Tinworth Street, London SE11 5AL, United Kingdom

Copyright © 2021 The Rowman & Littlefield Publishing Group, Inc.

All rights reserved. No part of this book may be reproduced in any form or by any electronic or mechanical means, including information storage and retrieval systems, without written permission from the publisher, except by a reviewer who may quote passages in a review.

British Library Cataloguing in Publication Information Available

Library of Congress Cataloging-in-Publication Data

Names: Bempechat, Janine, 1956- editor. | Jiménez-Silva, Margarita, 1969- editor.
Title: Latinx experiences in U.S. schools : Voices of Students, Teachers, Teacher Educators, and Education Allies in Challenging Sociopolitical Times / edited by Janine Bempechat and Margarita Jiménez-Silva.
Other titles: Latinx experiences in United States schools
Description: Lanham, Maryland : Lexington Books, 2021. | Series: Race and education in the twenty-first century | Includes bibliographical references and index. | Summary: "In this edited volume, Latinx students, teachers, teacher educators, and education allies in Latinx communities share the ways in which hateful anti-immigrant rhetoric in today's sociopolitical context has impacted Latinx educational experiences. This book emphasizes acts of courage, community organization, and transformation as these stakeholders have risen into leadership positions"— Provided by publisher.
Identifiers: LCCN 2021035558 (print) | LCCN 2021035559 (ebook) | ISBN 9781793611871 (cloth) | ISBN 9781793611895 (paperback) | ISBN 9781793611888 (ebook)
Subjects: LCSH: Hispanic Americans—Education—Social aspects. | Hispanic Americans—Education—Political aspects. | Discrimination in education—United States. | Culturally relevant pedagogy—United States. | Community and school—United States.
Classification: LCC LC2669 .L396 2021 (print) | LCC LC2669 (ebook) | DDC 371.829/68073—dc23
LC record available at https://lccn.loc.gov/2021035558
LC ebook record available at https://lccn.loc.gov/2021035559

We dedicate this work to our former, present, and future students who inspire us daily and remind us that equity work is a collective and moral imperative.

Contents

List of Figures and Tables — xi

Introduction — xv
Margarita Jiménez-Silva and Janine Bempechat

SECTION I: VOICES OF STUDENTS — 1

Introduction: My Experience at the City Council Meeting — 3
Joseph Luevanos

1. "I Don't Like the Way He Acts With Mexicans:" An Analysis of Opinion-Augmentative Writing Sessions with Emergent Bilingual Learners — 7
Evelyn C. Baca

2. "What Do You Mean, You *Feel* Latina?" Use of Pan-Ethnic Identity Labels among Middle School Bilingual Youth — 25
Jenny E. Jacobs

3. "Why Isn't Cinco de Mayo 365 Days a Year!": Culturally Sustaining Practices in an Age of Distrust — 47
Orlando Carreón

SECTION II: VOICES OF TEACHERS — 65

Introduction: The Making of a Radical Educator — 67
Melody Esqueda

4. Rising Up to Lead in the Post-Truth Era: A Teacher's Path from the Classroom to City Hall — 71
Laura Gomez and Ruth Luevanos

5 Unshifting Practices and Perspectives: Disrupting the Cycle through Anti-Racist Pedagogy 87
Christine Montecillo Leider, Molly Ross, and Megan Schantz

6 A Funny Thing Happens on the Way to the Classroom: Positioning Latinx Students, Families, and Teachers as Knowers while Promoting Cultural Competence for Culturally Relevant Pedagogy through Study-Abroad in Chile 109
Kenneth Fasching-Varner

SECTION III: VOICES OF TEACHER EDUCATORS 125

Introduction: The Journey from Student to Teacher to Teacher Educator: A Cry for Change 127
Ofelia Castro Schepers

7 Educating Teachers to Work with Latinx Children and Families in Challenging Sociopolitical Contexts and Times 131
Eleonora Villegas-Reimers

8 What Counts as Official Knowledge? Pursuing Accreditation in a Post-Truth Era 153
Jaclyn Caires-Hurley, Andrea M. Emerson, Anne Ittner, and Carmen Cáceda

9 Preparing Bilingual Teachers through a Bilingual Undergraduate Teacher Corps: Nidos de Lengua y Comunidad 173
Nadeen T. Ruiz, Margarita Jiménez-Silva, and Samantha A. Smith

SECTION IV: VOICES OF EDUCATION ALLIES 191

Introduction: Passion, Resilience, Community, and Education: Core Values as Educational Allies 193
Karen Kay

10 Undocu-Ally Trainings: Reducing Stigma and Prejudice via Educational Interventions 195
Jesus Cisneros

11 Voces Unidas: Advocating for Emergent Bilinguals while Navigating Arizona's Sociopolitical Context 211
Ashley Coughlin, Margarita Jiménez-Silva, and Karen Guerrero

12 Preparing Teachers to be Allies in Addressing Mental Health with K-12 Students 223
Gabrielle Luu

Conclusion: Educational Movimientos: The Imperative to
Sustain Relationships and Build Community 239
Patricia D. Quijada Cerecer and Leticia Alvarez Gutiérrez

Index 247

About the Editors and Contributors 255

Conclusion: Educational Movimientos: The Imperative to
Sustain Relationships and Build Community 239
Patricia D. Quijada Cerecer and Leticia Alvarez Gutiérrez

Index 247

About the Editors and Contributors 255

List of Figures and Tables

FIGURES

Figure 3.1 Tweet 1: August, 2016: *Staff Discussing Facundo the Great and Humanizing a Person's Name*. [The principal snapped this picture of the assistant principals teaching and watching *Facundo the Great* with his entire staff in the school library.]   56

Figure 3.2 Tweet 2: August 17, 2016. *Students in Mrs. L's English Class Learning How to Spell and Pronounce Each Other's Name*. [The picture shows a teacher at the front of the classroom leading an assignment where students spent time learning the importance of pronouncing each other's name correctly. This lesson was taught on the first day of school—an action that connotes value and importance.]   57

Figure 3.3 Tweet 3: March 30, 2017: *Santi, Mari, Jose, Kathy, Christina Sharing with English Department Community Responsiveness*. [Here the principal tweets a picture of a student panel conducted at one of our CRSH trainings. The principal mentions "community responsiveness," a nod to the discourse of our trainings that emphasized the importance of teachers becoming ethnographers of their communities.]   58

Figure 3.4 Tweet 4: April 5, 2017: *Teacher's Working on Their Identity Crest as Part of Plaza CRSH Week*. [The principal's tweets a picture of the staff filling out their identity crest as part of plaza CRSH week. Plaza

	CRSH week refers to a week-long activity where students and faculty express their identity through various themes and forms. Each day of the week corresponding to a unique identity theme. CRSH plaza week was created and led by a student ambassador team created after the previous Cinco de Mayo event. In this tweet I also noticed that "CRSH" had entered the common school discourse and was being used to name their traditions (i.e., CRSH week). Finally, this activity was not designated for a particular content team; rather, all teachers (and students) were responsible for the activity.]	58
Figure 3.5	Tweet 5: April 5, 2017—A Rainbow of Colors Celebrating the Cultural Wealth #crushedit. [The picture is of approximately 80 teachers and students (mostly students) standing proudly and looking up at the camera. The teachers and students stood in clusters most visibly distinguished by the color of their t-shirt. From left to right, the clusters of t-shirts were represented by the colors purple, blue, green, yellow, red, in that order. Each color represented an aspect of the teacher/student's identity. Here I notice the discourse of CRSH morphed into a verb and picked up a social media signifier as represented by the hashtag #crushedit.]	59
Figure 3.6	Picture Taken Using my iPhone Video Camera: Cinco de Mayo 2017. [The picture illustrates brown and white students dancing to a popular Mexican song that is fast-paced and intended to be danced in uniform. In the distant background is the umbrella of a street vendor selling various fruits in a plastic cup with lime and red chili powder. Across the sky, the bright colors of "papel picado" blow gently across the campus, connected by a single string.]	60
Figure 5.1	A Cycle of Unshifting Perspectives and Practices	97
Figure 5.2	Anti-Racist Practices and Pedagogy as a Disruption	99
Figure 12.1	Themes and Subthemes Found	229

TABLES

Table 2.1	Summary of Participants	31

Table 6.1	Program Participants over Time	112
Table 8.1	Examples of Transformational Resistance	164
Table 9.1	Corps Students' Rating of the California Mini-Corps Experience	180
Table 9.2	Conversation and Formal Language Self-Ratings by Corps Students	181
Table 9.3	Conversation and Formal Language Self-Ratings by Corps Students	181
Table 12.1	Constructs Identified	228

Introduction
Margarita Jiménez-Silva and Janine Bempechat

The journey of assembling this book has been both professional and personal for us. Margarita, as a child of Mexican immigrants, entered the school system labeled as an English learner and was part of the 1970s forced school busing movement intended to desegregate Los Angeles schools. Janine is a Jewish refugee immigrant whose family was expelled from their home country and resettled in Canada, where she was raised. We began conceptualizing this book shortly after the election of former President Trump in November 2016. We were both alarmed and fearful that the anti-immigrant rhetoric prevalent during the presidential campaign would now impact policy. We were thus motivated to reach out to colleagues with an invitation to contribute their voices to this volume. Since proposing this book, we have experienced a polarizing administration, endured the COVID-19 global pandemic, and witnessed a national racial reckoning that has profoundly affected all who work for social justice, including the adults in whose hands we place students everyday—our children's teachers.

Since the 2016 presidential race, our country has seen a rise in increasingly divisive rhetoric about race, ethnicity, and social class. The Southern Poverty Law Center (SPLC) reported that between November 9, 2016 (the day after the election) and November 14, 2016, it received over 437 reports of hateful intimidation and harassment, the majority of which occurred in K-12 school settings (SPLC, 2016). The SPLC recently reported that the number of hate groups in our country is at an all-time high, with Latinx communities having been subjected to a range of humiliations from misinformation about co-ethnic group members to blatant racism (SPLC, 2019). Beutel (2018), in his analysis of the overlap between Trump's tweets and anti-Muslim and anti-Latinx hate crimes, wrote that "Words matter. Heated political rhetoric, especially derogatory language toward groups of people, can create all kinds of unintended consequences, including sometimes physical violence."

Words do indeed matter, and the ways in which derogatory and hateful speech are received, interpreted, and internalized by children, youth, and young adults demand attention. In this book, we have chosen to focus on Latinx communities for a variety of reasons. We note that we are using the term Latinx as the gender-neutral alternative to Latino and Latina. It is a term increasingly used by scholars, activists, and the general public, as well as growing number of journalists. We use the term Hispanic interchangeably with Latinx when referring to statistics provided by government agencies, which use the label Hispanic to describe this community.

The Latinx community is the largest and second fastest growing minority group in the United States, comprising 60.6 million (18% of the U.S. population) individuals (Pew Research Center, 2020). Furthermore, 29% of our country's preK-12 population is Hispanic (National Center for Education Statistics, 2019). We know that Latinx students face educational challenges, often resulting from a broken education system that underfunds schools, devalues our communities' cultural wealth, and demoralizes teachers. Although we recognize that evidence of learning goes beyond test scores, it is worthy to note that the National Assessment of Educational Progress (NAEP) achievement data in 2019 revealed that only 23% of fourth-grade and 22% of eighth-grade Hispanic students scored at or above proficient in reading (NCES, 2019a), and only 28% of fourth-grade and 20% of eighth-grade Hispanic students scored at or above proficient in mathematics (NCES, 2019b). Recent figures show that the Hispanic high school dropout rate is 8.6%, (Bauman, 2017), and their college completion rate is 53% (Musu-Gillette et al., 2016).

Regrettably though, too often, conversations centered on Latinx communities focus on underachievement and approach solutions from a deficit or remedial perspective. This book presents Latinx communities from an asset-based perspective, focusing on their strengths and resilience. We recognize that the Latinx community is not a homogenous group, and that its members vary in geographic origins, immigration histories, political ideologies, and socioeconomic status. The central argument that we propose is that the derogatory characterization of Latinx communities, painted with a broad brush by the previous administration, continues to have a profoundly negative impact on students and educators across the education landscape, affecting both identity and sense of belonging in our society.

OVERVIEW OF THIS VOLUME

This book is unique in that it provides a platform for Latinx students (Section 1), their teachers (Section 2), teacher educators (Section 3), and education allies who work closely with Latinx communities (Section 4) to share ways in which the rise in hateful speech is having negative impact on preK–Higher Education communities. In the final integrative chapter, prominent Chicanx scholars Patricia Quijada Cerecer and Leticia Alvarez Gutiérrez provide a synthesis of the issues raised by the contributors and present an agenda for moving forward. This book is intended to serve a wide variety of audiences and includes introductions to each of the four sections contributed by emerging scholars. We have purposefully reached out to early- and mid-career researchers and practitioner-scholars who are actively engaged in or with Latinx communities in order to present authentic and often overlooked perspectives.

Section I, *Voices of Students*, begins with the reflection of Joseph Luevanos, a high school freshman whose pro-immigrant stance at a city council meeting was met with overt anger and derision from anti-immigration adults in the room. He recounts his frustration with the hostility he encountered, as well as the satisfaction he experienced from persisting and making his voice heard in this formal setting.

In Chapter 1, Evelyn Baca presents findings from an ethnographic project on language policy and its impact on Latinx student identities. In this chapter, Baca led a series of pre-writing sessions with a group of bilingual Latinx fifth-grade students as they brainstormed and selected topics for an argumentative writing task. Drawing from both LatCrit and New Literacy Studies perspectives, she analyzed how the students drew from their situated knowledge as they discussed and selected a range of social justice–related topics to address. By contrasting the students' rationales for selecting topics with the dominant standards-based perspectives on argumentative writing, Baca highlights the ways the pre-writing activity galvanized student interest in the writing task by engaging the students in issues of social justice faced by their local and the global communities. She concludes with a discussion of implications for practice and future research on argumentative writing in the upper elementary grades.

Jenny Jacobs examines the discourse around ethnic identity labels in Chapter 2, noting that identity politics that play out in society are often mirrored in schools, and that dual language programs, designed to uphold linguistic equality, can also provide unique spaces for positive ethnolinguistic identity development for young people. In the study she reports here, six Spanish/English bilingual middle school youth participated in interviews and group discussions and co-constructed the meaning of three social identity labels: Hispanic, Latino/a, and American. Findings show that, indeed, Latinx and their white peers constructed the label "Latino/a" as positive, in contrast to dominant anti-immigrant rhetoric. Nevertheless, many of the students, all U.S.-born, struggled to accommodate their immigrant heritage with the label "American." Jacobs recommends including more curriculum exposing Latinx youth to ethnic studies and positive representations of immigrants in U.S. history, as well as youth-centered pedagogies such as youth participatory action research and photovoice.

In chapter 3, Orlando Carreón describes research he conducted with Chicanx/Latinx students in Hope Valley, CA. As a scholar-activist in his own community, he weaves together stories from his experiences as a community member, researcher, activist, and consultant. It is from this vantage point that he retells his experiences of an incident that occurred on Cinco de Mayo, 2016, when Latinx students brought their Mexican flags to school to express their identity. A confrontation between administrators and students prompted a police presence on campus and resulted in the local media falsely reporting the event as a school riot. His narrative serves as a point of departure on how one school, its administrators, teachers, and students responded by learning how to pronounce students' names. He uses postcolonial theory to frame the sociopolitical context in which Latinx students have experienced schooling, including pedagogical frameworks that are discussed in the literature as useful in the education of Latinx youth. He asserts in this chapter that in an era of increased negative rhetoric, equitable educational experience for Latinx students begins with a pedagogy of trust, centralizing student voices, and a collective response by administrators, teachers, and students.

Section II, *Voices of Teachers*, begins with novice teacher and first-generation college and Masters graduate Melody Esqueda's reflection on her evolution as a "radical" educator. She describes her passion to empower her low-income students to see themselves as worthy and deserving of an exemplary education.

In chapter 4, Laura Gómez and Ruth Luevanos share the latter's personal journey from classroom teacher to city hall councilmember. Through the use of *testimonio* as a methodological tool (Delgado, 2013; Aleman, 2010), the authors explore the social, political, cultural, and educational contexts that shaped Luevanos' experiences as an educator from and of underrepresented communities in the greater Los Angeles area to her election as a city councilwoman. Her testimonio reveals her personal and political struggle for education equity and social justice as a leader-teacher and advocate for the inclusion of historically marginalized groups.

In chapter 5, Christine Montecillo Leider, Molly Ross, and Megan Schantz challenge the grit narrative, the notion that hard work can overcome all obstacles and lead to success. The authors argue that this narrative erases the lived experiences and personal challenges that many bilingual and (im)migrant families face(d). The reality, they maintain, is that our current systems have been built to serve White middle-class and White upper-middle-class individuals and as such, we cannot expect an ever diversifying student population to simply "work hard enough" if the system was not designed to be responsive to their needs. In this chapter, teachers who have worked in these increasingly diverse districts provide both insights into the challenges they face and also offer recommendations, particularly with regard to supporting Latinx students as they experienced Trump administration rhetoric.

In chapter 6, Kenneth Fasching-Varner provides analysis of empirical data from a 15-year longitudinal research project focused on a study-abroad teacher education program in Chile. Varner's research highlights the extent to which U.S. participants were transformed by their experiences as outsiders, challenged by their own beliefs and their own perceptions of difference. Varner demonstrates how this study-abroad experience focused on seeing Latinx students, families, and teachers as whole, complete, and a value-added set of partners to U.S. educators. That recognition comes from positive and meaningful sustained interaction over multiple weeks, as well as through dialogue to position Latinx students, their families, and teachers as knowers and power brokers.

Ofelia Castro Schepers opens section III, *Voices of Teacher Educators*, with a deeply moving account of witnessing her elementary school Latinx students regularly "othered" and demeaned by her White, affluent colleagues, behaviors that became more acceptable after the 2016 presidential election. As she reflects on this and similar experiences in her own education, she recounts her decision to become a teacher educator to recruit, retain, and support Latinx teachers who can strive to make our public schools open and welcoming to students of color.

In Chapter 7, Eleonora Villegas-Reimers picks up Schepers's call. She argues that the need to prepare effective teachers to work with Latinx children and families in the United States should be priority for all teacher preparation programs, not only because the number of Latinx children continues to increase in the United States but also because indicators of their success in school show that their academic performance is, on average, at the lowest rates when compared with any other group of students. This trend has been going on for many years, but it has intensified in the current sociocultural context, in which Latinx individuals are constantly labeled as not belonging, being social deviants, and a burden to society, wherein children are experiencing higher levels of stress due to constant bullying, insults, threats to their security, and fears that their relatives will be deported with no warning. Villegas-Reimers describes the current sociopolitical context and educational experiences and outcomes of Latinx students and explores best teacher education preparation practices to educate effective teachers to work with Latinx children and families.

In Chapter 8, authors Jaclyn Hurley, Andrea Emerson, Anne Ittner, and Carmen Cáceda describe the tensions inherent in determining what constitutes official knowledge as they sought re-accreditation of their university's teacher preparation program. They juxtapose their mandate to ascertain how to maximize their program's diversity while at the same time aligning outcomes for curriculum, clinical experiences, and recruitment and retention to predetermined standards. The authors document the process of identifying the knowledge, skills, and dispositions that their students will need to teach in a diverse PK-12 school system in a way that meets mandated standards, but at the same time reflects and honors their students' diverse ways of knowing and learning. Culturally responsive pedagogy, for many, is an elusive construct. The authors argue that preparing culturally responsive teachers requires, at its core, an understanding that individuals cannot put down their cultural and historical consciousness as they enter institutionalized spaces in pursuit of standardized ways of knowing and learning.

In Chapter 9, Nadeen Ruiz, Margarita Jiménez-Silva, and Samantha Smith describe how a critical shortage of Latinx bilingual teachers in California, coupled with the impact of past English-only policies and explicit anti-Latinx sentiment in MAGA constituencies have impacted teacher education programs' ability to recruit and retain Latinx bilingual teachers. They share a mixed-methods study that informs teacher education programs about how teacher educators can build on California's Mini-Corps efforts to create a pipeline of bilingual teachers who are supported by a Latinx community beginning in students' first year of college. The counter-messages these students received as Mini-Corps participants served to build resilience and provided navigational support as they considered a teaching career.

Section IV, *Voice of Education Allies*, begins with Karen Kay's depiction of her social justice awakening at the realization of the damage to communities of color done by the hateful rhetoric and outcome of the 2016 presidential election. Kay recounts how her introduction to the Tutors for Incarcerated Youth program at the University of California, Davis has empowered her to commit to community-based actions for change.

In Chapter 10, Jesus Cisneros notes that campus personnel play a critical role for undocumented students seeking support and information, yet there are few professional development opportunities that prepare campus personnel to work with these students. In his chapter, Cisneros features the implementation of educational interventions across institutions of higher education that acknowledge the important role of campus personnel for responding to the presence and needs of undocumented students. This chapter highlights viable examples of culturally responsive practices that educational institutions can and should employ to improve the campus climate for undocumented students.

In Chapter 11, Ashley Coughlin, Margarita Jiménez-Silva, and Karen Guererro relate the effort they spearheaded in Arizona to address the deeply restrictive language policy—Proposition 203—that all but prohibited access to bilingual instruction for emergent bilinguals. The result of their work was the Teachers of Language Learners Learning Community (TL3C) Consortium. As the authors explain, this consortium was conceived and developed as a response to the need for strength through community, networking of resources, and a refusal to stay silent regarding restrictive language policies and the lack of support for teachers and families of emergent bilinguals.

Gabriella Luu, in Chapter 12, shares results from a survey of 190 preservice teachers that probed their knowledge about possible causes, symptoms, and treatments of depression in children and youth. These preservice teachers further discussed what they believed to be their roles supporting students who may be exhibiting signs of depression. Luu presents compelling literature about the impact of the current sociopolitical climate on Latinx students' mental health. Teachers can serve as allies in identifying, referring, and supporting students who may be exhibiting signs of depression or other mental health distress. Luu reminds us of the need for teachers to consider how stigma within Latinx communities surrounding mental health issues and disparity in access to mental health services can impact families' abilities to support their children.

In the book's conclusion, Patricia Quijada Cerecer and Leticia Alvarez Gutiérrez powerfully weave the themes presented across this book's chapters. They remind us of the negative impact on children and families of past and current education practices and policies while also highlighting the strength and hope within our communities. The authors emphasize the power teachers have to help students become "researchers, theorists and activists, critiquing power structures and disrupting colonial student-teacher hierarchies and adult-centric categories that often limit what youth can do."

The 2020 election results shifted the conversation within many of our communities to one of hope, with the election of President Joseph R. Biden and Vice President Kamala Harris. Days after the election, CNN reporter Van Jones emotionally shared that under the Trump administration, "too many of us have felt like they can't breathe," echoing George Floyd's final words of "I can't breathe." Our hope with this work is that we shift from just breathing to helping our communities thrive. Throughout this book, we emphasize acts of courage, community organization efforts, and the transformation of educators who, viewing the political landscape, are rising into leadership roles to ensure that the next generation of Latinx students is provided opportunities to thrive.

REFERENCES

Bauman, K. (2017). School enrollment of the Hispanic population: Two decades of growth. U.S. Department of the Census. https://www.census.gov/newsroom/blogs/random-samplings/2017/08/school_enrollmentof.html.

Beutel, A. (2018). How Trump's nativist tweets overlap with anti-Muslim and anti-Latino hate crimes. Retrieved from https://www.splcenter.org/hatewatch/2018/05/18/how-trump's-nativist-tweets-overlap-anti-muslim-and-anti-latino-hate-crimes.

Flores, A. (2017). How the U.S. Hispanic population is changing. Fact Tank: News in the Numbers. Pew Research Center. http://www.pewresearch.org/fact-tank/2017/09/18/how-the-u-s-hispanic-population-is-changing/.

Musu-Gillette, L., Robinson, J., McFarland, J., KewalRamani, A., Zhang, A., and Wilkinson-Flicker, S. (2016). *Status and trends in the education of racial and ethnic groups 2016* (NCES 2016-007). U.S. Department of Education, National Center for Education Statistics. Washington, DC. Retrieved [date] from http://nces.ed.gov/pubsearch.

National Center for Education Statistics (2019). *National Assessment of Educational Progress NAEP reading report card for the nation and the states.* Washington, DC: National Center for Education Statistics, Office of Educational Research and Improvement, U.S. Dept. of Education.

Pew Research Center (2020). Hispanic population surpassed 60 million in 2019, but growth has slowed. Fact Tank: News in the Numbers, July 7. Washington, DC.

Southern Poverty Law Center (2016). The Trump effect: The impact of the 2016 presidential campaign on our nation's schools. https://www.splcenter.org/20160413/trump-effect-impact-presidential-campaign-our-nations-schools.

Southern Poverty Law Center (2019). The year in hate: Rage against change. https://www.splcenter.org/fighting-hate/intelligence-report/2019/year-hate-rage-against-change.

Section I

VOICES OF STUDENTS

Introduction

My Experience at the City Council Meeting

Joseph Luevanos

It was 2018 in the middle of the summer. I had only finished my first year of high school a month prior and had nothing much to do on a Monday in the middle of July. My mom had heard about a city council meeting that intended to address a recent controversy over immigration within California. A few hours later I was in the car heading toward the city chambers equipped with a bag of Jolly Ranchers and my laptop. My mom and I arrived around 3:30 p.m., a whole three hours before the meeting even began, so we could get seats inside in case the meeting was completely packed. We were the first ones there by a solid 20 to 30 minutes. The extra time also gave the chance to do some research beforehand regarding the main topic of the meeting, Senate Bill 54.

SB54 was fairly simple for something that caused so much contempt. The sanctuary state law, as it was commonly referred to, prevented local and state law enforcement from assisting federal immigration agencies. The bill was passed in 2017, but a few cities led by Huntington Beach were suing the state saying it was unconstitutional. The meeting that evening was meant to determine whether Simi Valley would join in with Huntington Beach to assist with their lawsuit.

I was there to make my case to protect SB54 and was determined to present my case using data and evidence. I did not walk in with the intent to provoke anything but, rather, to share information and my perspective. I would at least be able to say to myself, "I at least tried." When my mom and I entered the city chambers, we were told the order of the public opinions would be determined by who got there first once all the other items on the agenda were settled. A small wave of relief fell over me. I figured I could share the data I found, refute counterarguments I anticipated being made, and would get to wait patiently until the meeting was over. I thought things may get a little tense, but that it would still be a generally calm ordeal. I also thought that a bag of Jolly Ranchers would last until I was able to speak. I was wrong.

As more and more people started to enter the chamber and the time inched closer to 6:30 p.m., the room became very charged very quickly. Those who were pro-SB54 decided to dress in white and those who were against SB54 wore MAGA hats. As signs rose, so did voices. Chants grew louder and more off-rhythm as the seats were filled and walls were lined. Amid the growing chaos, I decided to open Google slides and make my own little sign. It read "Pro-SB54" and was held up not very high. It was the lone Pro-SB54 signs among a sea of cartoony letters saying dicey things at best and xenophobic chants at worst, with multiple "Love it or leave it" signs polluting the airspace. A lanky man who appeared to be in his fifties was parading around the front of the room with one of these signs before he caught a glimpse of my laptop. He walked over and looked briefly at me with a face that implied that he was thinking "stupid kid" before returning back to his march. I lowered my laptop and changed my presentation so that all the letters were rainbow and that I could flicker between a slide that said "Pro-" and another that said "SB54." The man walked past me again so I showcased my updated "sign." He walked over to me and said in his attempt at a menacing tone, "You're going to be the first one on the buses when they deport all the Mexicans." My mom who was sitting next to me gave him the stare of death and the man scuttled away as if he saw a ghost. Out of all the things I could feel after that moment, the best I can describe it as I remember is "ok boomer" and a little chuckle at the end.

The meeting started and the room grew quiet as all the other items on the agenda were discussed first. A very uncomfortable-looking businessman left the premises after talking about energy with a face that said, "Nope." That night, there were over 100 people who submitted speaker cards, so the time was reduced to a minute and a half per person. I was one of the first people to submit a speaking card, so I was getting ready to speak but I never was given my opportunity. Person after person spoke before a 20-minute recess was called. It was 10:00 p.m. I was lied to by the person selecting the speaker cards. I was down to five Jolly Ranchers, my legs were numb from sitting, and the yelling and jeering from the people in the MAGA hats was weighing on me. Despite these things, I still had some energy left in me because no one really supported their arguments with raw data and numbers but, rather, with personal anecdotes, Bible verses, or conspiracy theories. After listening to many arguments against SB54 ranging from fear mongering to the Illuminati, the question arose about how one of those MAGA hat people would respond to my argument and any counterclaims to theirs. I found a MAGA hat person who appeared to be more restrained than the others during the sequence of speakers, a woman who appeared to be in her fifties. I asked why she was against SB54 and she quickly began a rant that was very off-topic about her parents who she claimed to be prisoners at one time somewhere in Eurasia. I then asked what that had to do with SB54. She then repeated herself in a more mocking tone, as if she thought I had lost one too many brain cells. I then asked if I could share my take on SB54. She said yes. So I began sharing data on the benefits to sanctuary cities including an immigrant population that feels it is safe. She proceeded to interrupt and give her argument again as if she was explaining to a toddler. After she spoke, I would continue with my points until I got interrupted again. This process repeated four times and she got progressively louder each time until she had to hold her throat from screaming so loud. A crowd began to form around us and an officer who was in the room intervened and split the crowd and the "discussion" if you could even call it one. There is a picture of this happening if you type "Simi Valley city council meeting" into Google. This woman sued a newsperson who Tweeted that picture for libel, lost, and then was blasted on social media for punching a young protester at another event. My mom was in the bathroom when most of this happened and learned about the whole debacle shortly after.

The recess was eventually over and I finally got to speak and give my points at around 11:20 p.m. and, by then, the city council members seemed to be uninterested. After all the speaker cards were called, the four present city council members voted unanimously to join the lawsuit despite knowing that it was a losing battle. After the meeting, all the people wearing MAGA hats joined for a group photo like they had just won their little league game. I later learned that a considerable portion of the anti-SB54 people was not from Simi Valley but was part of an organization that goes around to different city council meetings to cause trouble and misrepresent the population.

Out of all things, that meeting left me feeling hungry because I did not eat the entire time aside from a few too many Jolly Ranchers. Looking back at that night, I was still primarily feeling hunger, but I now realize that I felt fulfillment for using my voice, perspective, and data to try to make a difference.

Chapter 1

"I Don't Like the Way He Acts With Mexicans"

An Analysis of Opinion-Augmentative Writing Sessions with Emergent Bilingual Learners

Evelyn C. Baca

INTRODUCTION

As the largest minoritized population in the United States (U.S. Census Bureau, 2019), the Latinx population includes a diverse array of individuals from both multigenerational and more recent immigrant families. Throughout this long history, Latinx communities have been subjected to various waves of nativist, anti-immigrant rhetoric and discrimination (Acuña, 2015). In its most recent manifestation, there has been a surge in overtly xenaphobic speech, policies, and violence directed at both Latinx and other minoritized immigrant populations (Ortmeier-Hooper, 2017). For our nation's immigrant and linguistically diverse youth, this means many students are navigating their learning in the midst of reports of racial violence, family separations at the border, political threats of mass deportation in their communities, and both subtle and not-so-subtle forms of discrimination (Flores & Schachter, 2019; Lutz, 2019).

Yet, students from culturally and linguistically minoritized backgrounds continue to shape the growth trajectory of public schools across the United States (Nieto & Bode, 2018). Within this increasingly multicultural landscape, the U.S. Census Bureau (2015) anticipates that the number of students of color and students who speak a language other than English at home will continue to rise over the next 30 to 40 years (U.S. Census Bureau, 2015). In fact, the most recent estimates indicate that approximately 20% of the school-aged population speaks a language other than English at home, of whom over 70% are Spanish speakers (U.S. Census Bureau, 2015). Researchers, educational practitioners, and communities must therefore come together in an effort to transform historical cycles of inopportunity in our growing K-12 population (Ladson-Billings, 2013). In this chapter, I argue for transformation from the perspective of critical literacy scholars who approach literacy development by identifying the interconnected relationship between academic development, student identities, and the diverse sociocultural contexts in which students go about their everyday lives (Moll et al., 1992; Paris & Alim, 2017; Vasquez, 2007; Vygotsky, 1967). In doing so, I examine how two fifth-grade Latinx emergent bilingual learners[1] (EBLs) with varying levels of official English proficiency negotiate their identities through an argumentative, *identity-text* writing task. Cummins (2006) defines *identity texts* as "the products of students' creative work or performances ... (written, spoken, visual, musical, dramatic, or combinations in multimodal form) that then hold a mirror up to students in which their identities are reflected back in a positive light" (p. 60). From a critical literacy perspective, I examined the unique ways the argumentative writing process became a window into the sociocultural-historical experiences of the focal students, while simultaneously providing an opportunity for the young learners to reflect on their role as agents of positive social change in their communities.

STUDY CONTEXT

Data collection for this study took place during the spring of 2017. This time period was central to this study because the argumentative writing task prompted the students to write a letter to the president of the United States (or another individual of their choosing) on an issue of importance to them (see the methods section for greater detail). The president at the time, Donald J. Trump, was inaugurated on January 20, 2017, and the focal students' writing analyzed herein was reflective of this particular point in our nation's history. That is, as Mexican American EBLs both Jeff (pseudonym) and Danny (pseudonym) chose to write about the recent political discourse surrounding the expansion of the U.S.-Mexican border wall. There is evidence that the concerns of both focal students throughout the argumentative writing process were common in schools across the United States at this time (Costello, 2016; Osorio, 2018). The focal students' writing choices, therefore, reflected the broader anxieties and experiences of Latinx youth and communities following the 2016 election.

At the same time, it is important to highlight that the first part of the twenty-first century in Arizona was a time in history marked by a number of policies and policy efforts openly hostile to individuals and children from Latinx and immigrant backgrounds (Powers & Williams, 2012; Gándara & Orfield, 2012). In education, the passage of Proposition 203 in 2000 (also known as "English for the Children") had an immense influence on the trajectory of EBL instructional programs throughout the state. The law was further reified by House Bill 2064 (H.B. 2064), which, contrary to established research and theory in the field (Krashen, MacSwan, & Rolstad, 2012; Rolstad et al., 2005), mandated the grouping of all EBLs into Structured English Immersion (SEI) classrooms where teachers were expected to focus on discrete English grammar and language skills for four hours a day. The goal, however misguided, was to facilitate the acquisition of English as rapidly as possible (i.e., in an unrealistic one-year time frame). At the same time, Proposition 203 sought to eliminate bilingual programs and limit the use of home language supports in the classroom (Arias & Faltis, 2012). Although the law had a provision allowing parents to obtain waivers under specific circumstances, few parents successfully obtained waivers and most bilingual programs serving EBLs across the state closed (Mahoney et al., 2010). Educators at schools where bilingual programs survived, at times sought to help parents obtain waivers for EBLs who were at least 10 years old or who passed oral/aural portions of the state English language proficiency assessment (Baca, 2021). This policy is relevant to the present study because the EBL focal students, Danny and Jeff, were classified as English language learners (ELLs) and required by state law to enroll in an SEI classroom. However, Danny's mother advocated for him to receive a waiver at the start of his fifth-grade year (because he met the requirement to be 10 years old for a waiver). For this reason, during the 2016–2017 academic year Danny was able to enroll in his first year of dual language bilingual education, whereas Jeff was enrolled in the SEI classroom. Prior to presenting my findings from the writing sessions, I outline the literature, conceptual framework, and methods I drew from to inform my work with Danny and Jeff.

LITERATURE REVIEW

There is a long history of scholarship examining the importance of critical literacy. Within this tradition, scholars have argued for educational approaches that focus not only on the acquisition of functional literacy skills (e.g., demonstrating basic reading comprehension) but also on the importance of engaging students in critical literacy experiences that expand their understanding of the sociocultural-historical and political contexts of their local, national, and global communities (Freire, 1970; Luke, 2012; Vasquez, 2007). The focus, then, is often on addressing issues of power and injustice in society by providing opportunities for students to analyze and critique what counts as "official knowledge" as they closely examine the "the norms, rule systems, and practices governing everyday life" (Luke, 2012, p. 22). Historically, this was an approach to schooling that grew out of Freire's (1970) work on developing critical consciousness and dialogic exchange in which students learned the importance of "reading the word and the world" (Freire & Macedo, 1987). Educators and scholars have since expanded on these ideas in research and practice by focusing on *the dual centrality* of critical literacy development alongside asset pedagogies which emphasize the cultural and linguistic strengths, knowledge, and practices of historically marginalized and minoritized communities in everyday classroom practices (Ladson-Billings, 1995a; Moll, Amanti, Neff, & Gonzalez, 1992; Paris & Alim, 2017). The work of Paris and Alim (2014) was the most recent iteration to continue to push back against deficit-laden views of the languages, literacies, and perspectives of Youth of Color, while extending the conversation to include the critical repositioning the multiculturalism, multilingualism, and multiliteracies of minoritized youth as central to schooling in democratic societies. Scholars in this area work with educators as they seek to thoughtfully incorporate the cultural and linguistic pluralism of students into both the formal and informal curriculum, while also providing space for students to critically examine themselves, their communities, and society (Paris & Alim, 2014).

Studies looking at writing and critical literacy with multilingual and multicultural youth have looked at how learners engage with writing around important social and identity issues (Cummins et al., 2015; Ghiso, 2015; Franquiz, 2012). Research on educators who engage in critical literacy practices has found that students in these classrooms tend to show higher levels of engagement with the writing process and therefore often make important learning gains (Cummins et al., 2015; López, 2016). Teachers and researchers in these studies guided and collaboratively coached students as they made important choices about the content, perspectives, formatting, and language(s) used to communicate their own ideas and experiences (Cummins et al., 2015; Rogers, 2014). The work of Franquiz (2012) also found that students at times write multilingually and select topics that connect to their sense of belonging within their schools and communities. At the elementary level, a few scholars have also looked at how students in grades K-5 constructed arguments and creative writing pieces rooted in their own personal beliefs, experiences, and emotions (Cummins et al., 2015; Ghiso, 2015; Hermann-Wilmouth, 2017). Student writing topics in these studies addressed a variety of themes such as gun violence, immigrant experiences, the physical and natural environments of communities, health/wellness, and LGTBQ+ issues.

The current study seeks to add to this growing body of research on critical literacy development at the elementary level. The remainder of this chapter, therefore, explores the theoretical underpinnings, methodological decisions, and findings focused on how the focal students' writing artifacts spoke to the intersections of writing development, student identities, and improving the educational engagement and learning opportunities of EBLs in K-5 classroom settings during a politically charged year.

CONCEPTUAL FRAMING

Integrative models of identity acknowledge the myriad of ways in which "identities are both claimed subjectively and ascribed collectively" (Deaux & Martin, 2003, p. 416) as individuals negotiate the tensions between individual agency and the realities of structural constraints associated with diverse social contexts. Within this tension, intersectionality scholars emphasize the ways in which historically marginalized groups are at times pushed further into the margins by essentialized identity categories (Crenshaw, 1991; McCall, 2005). For this reason, understanding how social, institutional, and political structures impact patterns of inequality and opportunity across social contexts and categories is central to understanding the experiences of minoritized youth in educational spaces (Núñez, 2014).

For EBLs, the process of learning to use a new language is sensitive to issues of identity, in part, because "it is also a complex social practice in which the value and meaning ascribed to an utterance are determined in part by the value and meaning ascribed to the person who speaks" (Norton & Toohey, 2002, p. 416). Indeed, there is evidence of the connections between the value placed on the language use of EBLs and their identity development (Olsen, 1997; Suárez-Orozco & Suárez-Orozco, 2000). Scholars have thus conceptualized language and culture as central to how students come to view themselves through their literacy practices (Caraballo, 2017; Gee, 2001; McCarty, 1993).

To explore this complexity, I drew from *communities of practice* (Wenger, 1998) and *identity investment* (Cummins, 2016) perspectives to make sense of the multifaceted identity work transpiring through the students' writing. Wenger (1998) outlined a social theory of *learning as participation* in diverse communities of practice where the meanings, practices, and identities developed mediated learning as doing, experiencing, belonging, and becoming. The participants were, therefore, part of a "nexus of multimembership" in which "participation . . . refers not just to local events of engagement in certain activities with certain people, but to a more encompassing process of being active participants in the practices of social communities and constructing identities in relation to these communities" (p. 3). As students participate in communities of practice, they begin to "develop, negotiate, and share" in the construction of theories, assumptions, and worldviews that begin to guide their lives in personal and social ways (Wenger, 1998 p. 48). This framework provides a lens through which to make sense of the socially constructed (Erikson, 1994; Sarup, 1996), fluid (Anzaldúa, 1999), and recognized (Gee, 2001) identities of EBLs from diverse linguistic, racial, familial, and SES backgrounds in a shared classroom community.

As a part of what Wenger (1998) calls the process of identity formation and learning, three modes of belonging are outlined: *engagement, imagination, and alignment*. In the context of this study, *engagement* refers to the practices, interactions, learning histories, and relationships in which students participated on a daily basis. *Imagination*, on the other hand, relates to students' emerging worldviews and the ways in which they see themselves connected with broader communities and narratives. *Alignment* more broadly involves connections, coordination, and at times compliance questions that connect micro-level practices with broader discourses and structures that influence a community of practice. I will utilize these three constructs as a means to make sense of the student identity negotiation taking place through their writing in this study.

Finally, I also drew from Cummins's (2006) definition of *identity investment* in order to better explore the links between the students' identities and the writing artifacts they produced. Identity investment, in line with other asset pedagogies, asserts that students embedded in learning communities invested in both their academic and individual identities will achieve greater academic gains. More specifically, it "proposes that optimal academic development within the interpersonal space of the learning community occurs only when there is both maximum cognitive engagement and maximum identity investment" (Cummins, 2006, p. 60). Like other similar frameworks (i.e., funds of knowledge and culturally responsive teaching), it seeks to challenge the overemphasis on dominant language, culture, and norms by acknowledging the importance of students' linguistic and cultural capital as an explicit part of the curriculum. In line with this theoretical positioning, the research question guiding this study was: In what ways did the opinion-argumentative, identity-text writing sessions create space for both academic engagement and identity investment simultaneously for the focal EBLs?

PARTICIPANTS, METHODS, AND DATA ANALYSIS

Alma Elementary School was an upper elementary campus with approximately 450 students in the fourth through sixth grade in a large urban Arizona setting. Demographically, the students at Alma Elementary were approximately Latinx (65%), White (12%), Native American (9%), Black

(9%), Asian (2%), and mixed-race (3%), of which about 80% were on free or reduced lunch and 15% were classified as ELLs.

At the start of the spring of 2017 semester, I purposively selected one fifth-grade dual language bilingual education (DLBE) classroom and the fifth-grade SEI classroom from which to select focal participants. The two focal students (Jeff and Danny) discussed in this chapter were selected in close consultation with their teachers. While in different classrooms (DLBE vs. SEI), both students were classified as ELLs (referred to throughout this chapter as EBLs), spoke Spanish as a home language, and identified as Mexican Americans. The DLBE classroom participant, Danny, received 50% of his coursework in English and 50% in Spanish from two teachers throughout the day. The SEI classroom participant, Jeff, received all instruction in English-only from one teacher each day. The data collected from students included one initial interview, weekly classroom observations, and three to four writing sessions with each student throughout the spring semester. During the initial interview session, we discussed each student's backgrounds, families, languages, in-school and out-of-school interests, and a memoir piece they wrote during the fall semester that year. These student details are provided in the findings section to follow.

Despite the state-mandated SEI curricular policies, both classrooms followed similar curriculum and content sequences (see Baca (2021) for a description of the administrative resistance to strict SEI curricular programming at this school site). Therefore, the main difference between the two classrooms was the language of instruction used to teach academic content and individual teaching styles. It is also important to note that the DLBE classroom teachers followed a strict separation of languages philosophy wherein the students engaged in English and Spanish separately each day. The SEI classroom, according to the teacher, was required to adhere to the state law requiring that instruction for students in her classroom be in English. Both the DLBE and the SEI teachers positioned writing well in English (over Spanish) as an essential learning goal for their students. They admitted that this was, in part, due to the fact that state testing was in English-only (see Menken (2008) for analyses on the effects of English-only testing on DLBE programs). For these reasons, all student writing produced as a part of this project was, unfortunately, limited to English.

At the start of data collection, opinion-argumentative writing was the focus in both classrooms. The fifth-grade teachers organized their class's daily 30 to 40 minute writing period around different literacy genres, using a writer's workshop approach (Atwell, 1998; Calkins, 1994). While each teacher's style was unique, in class the teachers collectively took a process writing approach in which they centered the students' ideas and interests (Graves, 1983) and took the students through various stages of prewriting, drafting, revising, editing, and publishing their work. Along the way, they provided modeling, genre-specific wall displays, and conducted whole class and small group mini-lessons. For the writing sessions I conduced with the students, the teachers requested I work with the focal students one-on-one or in small groups to develop an additional opinion-augmentative writing artifact that would complement the piece they were working on with the students in class (which was about if schools should allow sugary beverages in school cafeterias).

In my sessions with Danny and Jeff, the teachers and I collectively decided on having the students write letters to the president (or another individual of their choosing) about a social or political issue that was important to them. I then engaged in identity-text writing sessions with each focal student on the topic they selected. The writing sessions primarily took place during the students' writing block three to four times throughout the semester and each session lasted between 20 and 40 minutes. After my initial interview with the students, I invited the students to brainstorm and share their own opinions on the topic(s) verbally. For students who were uncertain about what to choose, I provided a list of ideas. More specifically, I gave students a prompt with a list of topics related to health, education, environmental, social, and political issues. During session two, I carefully selected and scaffolded authentic texts based on the students' initial ideas and opinions. Given the nature of the writing project, I purposively selected articles that affirmed their identities, opinions, and ideas. As we read through the articles, we jotted down notes about the types of evidence they thought they could use to support their ideas in their letters. We also referenced example letters to public officials and reviewed the model texts provided by their teachers in class. The remaining sessions varied with each student, but involved re-reading, brainstorming, and writing an initial draft of their one-page opinion letters to President Trump.

The writing sessions produced student opinion/argumentative identity-text artifacts, researcher-student interactional/interview data, and fieldnotes. For the initial interviews, I transcribed each session verbatim and I engaged in a multiphase coding process. In the first cycle, I used a combination of In Vivo and Values Coding (Saldaña, 2016). In Vivo coding uses participants' own words to "prioritize and honor the participants voice" (Saldaña, 2016, p. 106) and Values Coding aims to portray participants' worldviews, attitudes, beliefs, values, or ideologies (Saldaña, 2016). During the second phase, I coded inductively moving from specific codes to more general categorizations until I reached a point of saturation in which larger themes, interpretations, and analyses emerged (Roulston, 2010; Corbin & Strauss, 2008). In the findings, I sought to preserve student voice through the portrayal of their opinions, arguments, and values as reflected in their writing (Saldaña, 2016).

As a participant observer during the students' writing time (Spradley, 2016), I relied on "jottings" while I was in the classroom. I then wrote more extensive fieldnotes immediately following my observations (Emerson et al., 2011). Over the course of the semester, this resulted in approximately 45 fieldnote entries, documenting 35 to 40 hours of classroom activity. Analysis of fieldnotes was ongoing and those deemed relevant to the research question were coded both thematically and via process coding (Saldaña, 2016). Process coding emphasized the actions observed in the classroom often using gerunds (-ing words) to code observed happenings (e.g., reading/writing interactively with the teacher, discussing ideas with peers, and so on). While the observations were part of a larger ethnographic study, for the purposes of this chapter, I focused only on observations that pertained to the two focal students.

FINDINGS AND ANALYSIS

To make sense of the data, I relied on the constructs of engagement, imagination, and alignment from within Wenger's (1998) conceptualization of identity within distinct communities of practice. In what follows, I organized the findings by focal student. I first provide an overview of each student individually followed by an analysis of their identity-text artifact in light of my observations, interviews, and writing sessions with each student.

Danny

In the classroom, Danny was quiet and easy-going. He sat at the back table near one of the classroom doors with a group of four peers from a combination of Spanish-dominant, bilingual, and English-dominant homes. He was an engaged but seemingly introverted learner. As one of only a few new students to the dual language program that year, I did not frequently see Danny volunteering to speak up during whole class instruction (in Spanish or English). This may have been due to a number of individual and social factors, including the frequency with which I witnessed his table peers volunteer on behalf of their table. He often seemed to prefer working on his own as well. For example, during the writing hour of the day, I noticed he often wrote in his composition notebook under his desk, looking up at times in seemingly pensive thought. During their creative writing and culture unit at the end of the year, I stopped to ask him what he was writing. He informed me that he was writing a goofy song about his mom's tacos, called *The Shape of Tacos*. When I asked if I could take a closer look, I read a witty song thoughtfully dedicated to "my people," his love of his family, and of course tacos.

At home, Danny lived with his mom, two sisters, and his older brother. He informed me that his first language was Spanish but he preferred to speak in English. With his family, he explained that he spoke in both Spanish and English. However, he said he really only spoke in all Spanish when he was speaking to his grandparents, whereas with his mother he spoke in a mixture of both languages. With everyone else (i.e., siblings, friends, neighbors, and others), he recalled almost always using English.

It was Danny's second year at Alma and his first year in the dual language program. When I asked him about the move from the SEI classroom to the DLBE classroom, he said he liked his new classroom and then explained how his mom really wanted him to be in the dual language classroom and "she always wanted." He added that he enjoyed being in the dual language program because "it's fun," "I made even more friends," and "my mom is happy." He also shared that he found it more challenging because "English it's easier, because I know a lot more English, but in Spanish it's a little bit harder because I don't know that much Spanish." He again expressed that he enjoyed the Spanish portion of the day because he was pleasing his mother by being able "to talk to her in Spanish" and because he believed that learning in two languages was good because "you get smarter and understand people more." He explained that he used more Spanish at home now, especially "if she [mom] doesn't understand, then I say it in Spanish." He also emphasized that in reality he still speaks to his mom in a mixture of Spanish and English, because "she understands English too."

Identity-Text Sessions

I met with Danny four times over the course of the spring semester for 20–40 minutes at a time as he developed his opinion-argumentation letter. As we discussed the possibility of writing a letter to President Trump, Danny shared with me that he "watched the election" and he felt "kind of scared." He added that no one is his family wanted the president to win because "everyone says that he's racist. He, he's gonna build a wall and um, he said he might even remove Mexicans. . . . And my families, they are Mexicans." I listened and told him to think about if he wanted that to be the topic of his letter. During the following session, he informed me that he wanted to write a letter to the president about the border wall and combating racism. Ultimately, he decided to focus primarily on the border wall. He was against the idea of expanding the border wall, therefore, we spent the remaining sessions reading authentic news articles that took an anti-wall position (which I selected and scaffolded) and drafted the letter in his composition notebook.

Identity-Text Content

At the start of the letter, Danny penned the date and "Dear Mr. President" in the top left corner of his paper. He immediately followed with a brief introduction of himself and a statement introducing his central argument. Specifically, he wrote, "My name is Danny. I am a student at Alma and I am writing today to share my thoughts about the Wall. I say you should not build the Wall because it's going to cause a lot of trouble." He followed with a brief body paragraph giving examples of the "trouble" it would cause, most of which he pulled from the articles we read. Specifically, he wrote:

> For example, if you build the Wall the animals that live near the border will go extinct. Also if you do build Wall it will cost tens of billions of dollar to build the Wall. Additionally, it will threaten national parks, national monuments and national forests and numerous areas. As well if you do build a wall you will not be nice because you're going to disrespect people with the Wall.

He ended with a "thank you" and a closing sentence urging attention to the matter.

Synthesis

Danny was a dedicated student who frequently expressed his love for sports, food, and his family. During class, he was soft-spoken and often brief, but to the point. Although classified as an ELL officially, he saw himself as more of a Spanish-learner, than an English-learner and he made his preference for English clear. His interactions in class and his composition notebook both confirmed that he used English more often than Spanish, although his notebook also had short examples of his Spanish-only writing. Within school he identified as a "good" student who saw his place in the dual language program as tied to his mother's desires more than his own. However, he also viewed his place in the dual language program as linked to extended peer social circles, fun, and his belief about his own intelligence as a multilingual user. In this way, Danny's sense of belonging in the dual language program was connected with what Wenger (1998) refers to as *ownership of meaning*. In other words, Danny was in the process of negotiating what his first language meant to him as he simultaneously negotiated the process of becoming and imagining himself as a multilingual speaker through the dual language program.

In analyzing his identity-text, it was clear that Danny closely *aligned* his perspective with that of his family and linked it to broader discourses about Mexicans in the United States. Although, he did not elaborate on his personal fears in his letter, Danny's prewriting commentary about feeling fearful after the election was linked to both his choice of topic and his conscious decision to downplay his personal connection to the issue due to what Danny saw as the threatening nature of the target-audience (i.e., President Trump). At the same time, the letter writing exercise gave Danny the opportunity to raise his voice and claim power in the face of the vulnerability of his family and the broader affront on his extended Latinx community. Likewise, Danny sought to incorporate his understanding of racism, which he incorporated via the final sentence of his body paragraph where he called out the "disrespect" that building the wall engendered. His emerging worldview was visible in his willingness to openly criticize the pro-wall position and the institutional racism it represented to him. On the other hand, his inclusion of arguments related to the environment and excessive cost were more closely tied to broader discourses he came across in articles he read prior to beginning his writing.

Jeff

Jeff was the first student I met in the SEI classroom. The teacher introduced me to him as a student who she knew would be happy to show me around the classroom. He struck me as outgoing, thoughtful, and very talkative during our first meeting. I arrived during "guided reading" time, therefore he showed me the two different reading programs he worked in weekly. He gave detailed instructions, explaining the nuances of the games, and then explained that it was for kids who "weren't from here," but quickly clarified that he was "from here."

During class, Jeff was typically eager to learn and participate. At times I saw him raising his hand urgently to signal that he wanted to be called on by his teacher. He enjoyed having his desk right next to the teacher's and I noticed he often engaged with adults more than his peers when possible. His teacher informed me that they were monitoring him closely and planned to have him tested for dyslexia and other reading-related difficulties. They felt he needed to be evaluated because his speaking and listening were very high on the proficiency scale, whereas, when not assisted, he was testing at the preemergent level in reading and writing.

At the time of data collection, Jeff was in his second year at Alma and he shared that it was his first time being at a school for more than one year when he said, "every year we used to move to a different school" but he "liked this one the best," explaining how he feels "at home when I'm here . . . because I'm always having fun here." Despite the difficulties and concerns reported by his teachers, Jeff positioned himself as a strong student academically. He shared that he had some small behavioral issues last year, but said he was doing "better," having received gold star achievement and character awards at school this year.

In his interview, Jeff informed that he considered himself half-Mexican on his mom's side and shared that he had family in both Mexico and the United States. At home, he lived with his mom and dad, but clarified that dad was not his birth father and was recently released from prison. He reported speaking with his grandparents and some relatives only in Spanish but said at home he spoke with his parents in both Spanish and English equally. On the other hand, with his friends, cousins, and brother he always spoke in English. Like Danny, he felt his English was stronger than his Spanish, but also expressed that he enjoyed speaking both languages. He added that English was especially "good for your parents."

Identity-Text Sessions

Jeff's writing sessions lasted between 20 and 40 minutes and included another student (not highlighted in this chapter) in three of the four sessions. At the start of the first session, Jeff explained that if he were to write to the president he would write about either combating racism or the border wall. He put it this way, "I don't like the way he acts with Mexicans. He's racist. He's rude . . . except for the people that like him, he thinks that he's better than everybody else, but he's not, he's not better than everybody." However, upon hearing that his peer's topic choice was combating homelessness, he asked if he could write two letters. I let him know that we he would have to pick one given our timeframe, but that he was more than welcome to write additional letters on issues he felt were important at a later date. Ultimately, he decided on writing against the border wall and chose to use a fake name, which is the pseudonym I used for him throughout this study. In the following sessions, Jeff read through the same news articles I read with Danny and outlined the key points he wanted to make. From there he began drafting his letter, the details of which are presented below.

Identity-Text Content

Jeff's letter started with the date and "Dear Mister President." From there he introduced himself by stating, "My name is Jeff and I am a student at Alma Elementary. I am writing to shere my thought about the wall with you." His body paragraph followed and said:

> My opinion is you should not billd the wall. First, it will make people mad because they disagree with you. Second, it will indanger more animls than they are endangered. Third, it will cost aforchin for everybody and we can spend it on houses for homeless or for our schools like food for schools.

He ended with a strong plea, writing:

> So will you listen to the people of the United States? I ask will you build the wall? Yes or No? Listen to your citizens. I beg you to not bulid the wall. Thank you for your time. . . . Sincerely, Jeff.

Synthesis

Jeff had a strong sense of curiosity and interest in school. He embodied a naturally optimistic outlook on life and showed a clear desire for one-on-one and small group work with teachers. Yet, the vision Jeff articulated of himself as a top student, at times contrasted with his teachers' views of him as a struggling reader in need of additional learning support.

In looking more closely at his letter, it was clear that his choice of topic was intimately linked to his identity as a Mexican American. As his prewriting comments indicated, he was both offended by and fearful of the degree of racism propagated by the sitting president. He initially wanted to incorporate more about anti-racism as well but instead felt it was more important to address ways he thought the funds to build a wall could be better spent on combating hunger insecurity and homelessness instead. At the same time, his inclusion of food for schools and homes for the homeless clearly connected with his knowledge of and concern for the struggles experienced in his immediate community.

From within Wenger's (1998) framework, his letter demonstrated a sense of belonging to his family and also allowed Jeff to define a writing trajectory that connected his personal identity with the experiences of others within his local and extended communities. The experience of brainstorming for and writing the letter allowed Jeff to imagine a scenario in which he could express his personal disapproval of a border wall and his criticism of the way funding would be allocated away from other important issues. Additionally, like Danny, his conscious decision to carefully avoid disclosure of his personal connections with the issue as well as his use of a false name, indicated a strong desire to protect himself (and his family) from racial hostility.

DISCUSSION AND CONCLUSIONS

The students' opinion-argumentation letters on an issue of importance to them served as "identity-texts" which allowed the students to reflect positively on themselves through the process of critiquing power structures at the intersections of immigration, ethnicity, and social class issues. Likewise, the activity allowed the focal students to engage with critical literacy through their writing by creating a space for students to express their emerging worldviews as aligned with broader discourses and perspectives on their selected issue. The student writing artifacts and prewriting commentary point to the importance of recognizing the process by which social identities are situated within specific communities of practice and simultaneously connected to broader sociocultural-historical and political contexts (Nuñez, 2014).

By focusing on opposing the border wall, the students provided a small glimpse into their individual identities through their writing and also attested to their interest in grappling with issues directly connected with their families and communities. Danny's and Jeff's voices, therefore, emphasize the place of critical inquiry and the possibilities of positioning youth as scholars, researchers, and activists who learn alongside their instructors as they examine important issues of social justice, race, class, power, and identity (Nieto & Bode, 2018). Providing students with opportunities to make connections with their families, passions, and community can thus contribute to what it means to make space in the curriculum for engaging students' sense of purpose, knowledge, and belonging (Moll et al., 1992). The writing sessions described in this chapter allowed for an examination of students' fluid, social, and recognized identities because it provided a space for students to create, critique, and merge their academic and home lives.

López (2016) outlined the teaching practices associated with culturally responsive pedagogies and found that first language use (Spanish), critical awareness, and funds of knowledge were associated with an increase in student reading outcomes. Likewise, Paris and Alim (2017) define the role of schools in pluralistic societies as fostering spaces for pedagogies that "perpetuate and foster—to sustain—linguistic, literate, and cultural pluralism as part of schooling for positive social transformation" (p. 1). Central to their argument is recognizing the fluid and dynamic ways that youth engage with culture, language, and literacy through their race, ethnicity, and other identity markers in diverse educational contexts.

The current study adds to this literature by showing some ways linguistically diverse elementary-age students can engage in critical literacy, consciousness raising, and building their own agency to become advocates within their local and the global communities. At the same time, it provides a glimpse into what it might look like to deepen youth engagement with writing as they develop their knowledge of diverse literacy genres—in this case writing an opinion-argumentative letter.

NOTE

1. García (2009) coined the term *emergent bilinguals* to better capture the strengths of bilingualism found in students who are still in the process of acquiring English. She argued this term was more appropriate than English learners or limited English proficient because it puts the importance of bilingualism at the center of teaching,

learning, and policymaking for bilingual students who are developing proficiency in both English and their home language simultaneously.

REFERENCES

Acuña, R.F. (2015). *Occupied America: A History of Chicanos* (8th ed.). Upper Saddle River, NJ: Pearson.

Anzaldúa, G. (1999). *Borderlands/La frontera: The new mestiza* (2nd ed.). San Francisco: Aunt Lute.

Arias, M.B., & Faltis, C. (2012) *Implementing Educational Language Policy in Arizona: Legal, Historical and Current Practices in SEI*. Clevedon, GB: Channel View Publications.

Atwell, N. (1998). *In the Middle: New Understandings About Writing, Reading, and Learning*. Portsmouth, NH: Boynton Cook Publishers, Inc.

Baca, E. C. (2021). From compliance to resistance: administrator perspectives on implementing structured English immersion and dual language bilingual education programs. *International Journal of Bilingual Education and Bilingualism*, 1–14.

Calkins, L. M. (1986). *The Art of Teaching Writing*. Portsmouth, NH: Heinemann.

Caraballo, L. (2017). Students' critical meta-awareness in a figured world of achievement: Toward a culturally sustaining stance in curriculum, pedagogy, and research. *Urban Education*, 52(5), 585–609.

Corbin, J. S., & Strauss, A. A. (2008). *Basics of Qualitative Research: Techniques and Procedures for Developing Grounded Theory*. Thousand Oakes, CA: SAGE Publications.

Costello, M. B. (2016). *The Trump Effect: The Impact of the Presidential Campaign on our Nations' Schools.* Montgomery, AL: Southern Poverty Law Center.

Crenshaw, K. (1991). "Mapping the margins: Intersectionality, identity politics, and violence against women of color." *Stanford Law Review*, 43(6), 1241–1299.

Cummins, J. (2006). Identity texts: The imaginative construction of self through multiliteracies pedagogy. In O. García, T. Skutnabb-Kangas, & M.E. Torres-Guzman (Eds.), *Linguistic Diversity & Language Rights: Imagining Multilingual Schools-- Languages in Education and Globalization* (pp. 51–68). Clevedon, GB: Multilingual Matters.

Deaux, K., & Martin, D. (2003). Interpersonal networks and social categories: Specifying levels of context in identity processes. *Social Psychology Quarterly*, 66(2), 101.

Emerson, R. M., Fretz, R. I., & Shaw, L. L. (2011). *Writing Ethnographic Fieldnotes*. Chicago, IL: University of Chicago Press.

Erikson, F. (1994). *Identity and the Life Cycle*. New York, NY: W.W. Norton.

Flores, R. D., & Schachter, A. (2019). Examining Americans' stereotypes about immigrant illegality. *Contexts*, 18(2), 36–41.

Fránquiz, M. E. (2012). Key concepts in bilingual education: Identity texts, cultural citizenship and humanizing pedagogy. *New England Reading Association Journal*, 48(1), 32–42.

Freire, P. (1970). *Pedagogy of the Oppressed.* New York, NY: Bloomsbury Publishing.

Freire, P., & Macedo, D. (2005). *Literacy: Reading the Word and the World*. London, UK: Routledge.

Gándara, P., & Orfield, G. (2012). Segregating Arizona's English Learners: A Return to the "Mexican Room"?. *Teachers College Record, 114*(9), 1–27.

García, O. (2009). Emergent bilinguals and TESOL: What's in a name? *TESOL Quarterly, 43*(2), 322–326.

Gee, J.P. (2001). Identity as an analytic lens for research in education. In W. Secada (Ed.), *Review of Research in Education, 25* (pp. 99–125). Washington DC: American.

Ghiso, M. P. (2015). Arguing from experience: Young children's embodied knowledge and writing as inquiry. *Journal of Literacy Research, 47*(2), 186–215.

Graves, H.H. (1983). *Writing: Teachers and Children at Work*. Portsmouth, NH: Heinemann.

H.B. 2064, English Language Learners, Arizona Legislature (2006). https://www.azleg.gov/legtext/47leg/2r/summary/h.hb2064_02-27-06_astransmittedtogovernor.doc.htm.

Hermann-Wilmarth, J. M., Lannen, R., & Ryan, C. L. (2017). Critical literacy and transgender topics in an upper elementary classroom: A portrait of possibility. *Journal of Language and Literacy Education, 13*(1), 15–27.

Krashen, S., MacSwan, J., & Rolstad, K. (2012). Review of "Research summary and bibliography for structured English immersion programs" of the Arizona English language learners task force. In B. Arias & C. Faltis (Eds.) *Implementing Educational Language Policy in Arizona* (pp. 107–118). Bristol, UK: Multilingual Matters.

Ladson-Billings, G. (1995a). Toward a theory of culturally relevant pedagogy. *American Educational Research Journal, 32*(3), 465–491.

Ladson-Billings, G. (2013). Lack of achievement of loss of opportunity? In P.L. Carter, & K.G. Welner (Eds.), *Closing the Opportunity Gap: What America Must Do To Give Every Child An Even Chance* (pp. 11–24). Oxford University Press.

López, F.A. (2016). Culturally responsive pedagogies in Arizona and Latino students' achievement. *Teachers College Record, 118*(5), 1–42.

Luke, A. (2012). Critical literacy: Foundational notes. *Theory into Practice, 51*(1), 4–11.

Lutz, E (2019). *Trump vows to begin deportation of "millions" next week*. Retrieved from: https://www.vanityfair.com/news/2019/06/trump-vows-to-begin-mass-deportation-of-millions-next-week.

Mahoney, K., MacSwan, J., Haladyna, T., & García, D. (2010). Castañeda's third prong: Evaluating the achievement of Arizona's English learners under restrictive language policy. In P. Gándara & M. Hopkins (Eds.). *Forbidden Language: English Learners and Restrictive Language Policies* (pp. 50–64). New York, NY: Teachers College Press.

McCall, L. (2005). The complexity of intersectionality. *Journal of Women in Culture and Society, 30*(3), 1771–1800.

McCarty, T.L. (1993). Language, literacy, and the image of the child in American Indian classrooms. *Language Arts, 70,* 182–192.

Menken, K. (2008). *English Learners Left Behind: Standardized Testing as Language Policy*. Buffalo, NY: Multilingual Matters.

Moll, L.C., Amanti, C., Neff, D., & Gonzalez, N. (1992) Funds of knowledge for teaching: Using a qualitative approach to connect homes and classrooms. *Theory into Practice, 31*(2), 132–141.

Nieto, S., & Bode, P. (2018). *Affirming Diversity: The Sociopolitical Context of Multicultural Education.* White Plains, NY: Pearson.

Norton, B., & Toohey, K. (2011). Identity, language learning, and social change. *Language Teaching, 44*(4), 412–446.

Núñez, A. M. (2014). Employing multilevel intersectionality in educational research: Latino identities, contexts, and college access. *Educational Researcher, 43*(2), 85–92.

Olsen, L. (1997). *Made in America: Immigrant Students in Our Public Schools.* New York, NY: The New Press.

Ortmeier-Hooper, C. (2017). *Writing across culture and language: Inclusive strategies for working with ELL writers in the ELA classroom.* Urbana, IL: National Council of Teachers of English.

Osorio, S. L. (2018). No room for silence: The impact of the 2016 presidential race on a second-grade dual-language (Spanish-English) classroom. *Occasional Paper Series, 2018*(39), 4.

Paris, D., & Alim, S.H. (2017) *Culturally Sustaining Pedagogies: Teaching and Learning for Justice in a Changing World.* New York, NY: Teachers College Press.

Powers, J. M., & Williams, T. R. (2012). State of outrage: Immigrant-related legislation and education in Arizona. *Association of Mexican American Educators Journal, 6*(2).

Rolstad, K., Mahoney, K. S., & Glass, G. V. (2005). The big picture: A metaanalysis of program effectiveness research on English language learners. *Educational Policy, 19*(4), 572–594.

Roulston, K. (2010). *Reflective interviewing: A guide to theory and practice.* Thousand Oaks, CA: SAGE Publications.

Saldaña, J. (2016). *The Coding Manual for Qualitative Researchers.* Thousand Oaks, CA: SAGE Publications.

Sarup, M. (1996). *Identity, Culture, and the Postmodern World.* Athens, GA: University of Georgia Press.

Spradley, J. P. (2016). *Participant Observation.* Long Grove, IL: Waveland Press.

Suárez-Orozco, M., & Suárez-Orozco, C. (2000). Some conceptual considerations in the interdisciplinary study of immigrant children. In E.T. Trueba & L.I. Bartolome (Eds.), *Immigrant Voices: In search of Educational Equity* (pp. 17–36). Lanham, MD: Rowman & Littlefield.

U.S. Census Bureau (2019). Quick facts: United States. Retrieved from https://www.census.gov/quickfacts/fact/table/US/PST045219.

Vasquez, V. (2007). Using the everyday to engage in critical literacy with young children. *New England Reading Association Journal 43*(2), 6–11.

Vygotsky, L.S. (1978). *Mind in Society: The Development of Higher Psychological Processes* (M. Cole, V. John-Steiner, S. Scribner, & E. Souberman, Eds. & Trans.). Cambridge, MA: Harvard University Press.

Wenger, E. (1998). *Communities of Practice: Learning, Meaning, and Identity.* New York, NY: Cambridge University Press.

Chapter 2

"What Do You Mean, You *Feel* Latina?"

Use of Pan-Ethnic Identity Labels among Middle School Bilingual Youth

Jenny E. Jacobs

INTRODUCTION

Trump-era politics took public rhetoric to new heights, with anti-immigrant sentiment characterized by xenophobia and racism often describing the foreign born and their offspring as competition for working-class jobs and as criminals (Valencia, 2017). Nevertheless, such rhetoric is not new (Ngai, 2004). Long before the recent hyped-up context in which we find ourselves, there has been a tradition of divisive political rhetoric drawing clear lines between the "worthy" and "unworthy" among immigrants (Campbell, 2016; Olsen, 1997).

Identity politics for Spanish speakers in the United States encompasses not only race, culture, ethnicity, and ancestral national origin but also language proficiency and legal immigration status. These play out in public discourse today as Latinx students struggle to make their voices heard on college campuses and unafraid "daca-mented" youth come out of the shadows to challenge their marginalization in U.S. society (DeGuzman, 2017; Seif, 2016). To publicly claim a social identity associated with immigrants in the United States is a political act that opens the speaker up to painful and discriminatory attacks or more subtle forms of symbolic othering and being made invisible (Perea, 1997; Valencia, 2017).

All of these aspects of identity politics play out in one way or another in the lived experiences of U.S.-born Latinx youth at school. Educators and social scientists have long pointed out that schools are microcosms of society with the potential to both reproduce and disrupt dominant assumptions about how the world works (Anyon, 1981; Morrell, 2007). Young people develop "raced epistemologies" partly through their interactions in schools, where they often encounter primarily Eurocentric systems and ways of being as the norm (Delgado Bernal, 2002).

Anti-immigration sentiments have also fueled anti-bilingualism movements embodied in English-only education policies (Bartolomé & Leistyna, 2007; García, 2009). The result is schools that promote English-only spaces or the occasional use of home languages only in the service of acquiring English (Bale, 2012). Not only do such policies run counter to established best practices of tapping into students' prior knowledge and experiences to promote further learning, but they simultaneously contribute to widespread intergenerational language loss, resulting in monolingualism (Wong Fillmore, 1991). In this way, the predominance of English-only and suppression of bilingualism reproduces dominant assumptions about a diverse population of people, "immigrants," by denying the linguistic and cultural resources they bring to classrooms.

In stark contrast, dual language bilingual education is a model that promotes linguistic and cultural equality. In dual language education, the curriculum is taught via immersion in two languages, and children from each language background are enrolled and given opportunities to serve as language and cultural models for one another (Howard et al., 2018). In addition to providing high-quality academic education in two languages, leading to bilingualism and biliteracy across all content areas, dual language programs aim to promote cross-cultural competence and positive ethnic identity development (Feinauer & Howard, 2014). Dual language schools also represent what Pratt (1991) called "zones of contact," unique spaces in our society where young people from diverse sociocultural and ethno-linguistic backgrounds have opportunities to negotiate, deconstruct, and reconstruct social identities in daily interaction with one another. Research has shown that such schools can be spaces where dominant assumptions are disrupted and minoritized languages and their speakers are repositioned as agents of change and equal partners in learning (Freeman, 1998; Palmer, 2008). Nevertheless, identity politics and ethno-linguistic status still play out even in policies and systems within these educational micro-spaces (Mackinney, 2017; Stolte, 2017). The participation of white/European students in these schools can result in the subtle reproduction of institutional systems of privilege and asymmetries of status and power within dual language schools and classrooms (Palmer, 2009; Valdés, 1997).

This chapter offers a close look at a small group of 12-year-old middle school students attending a predominantly Latino/a dual language school. Using interviews and group discussion data, I analyze how students construct the ethnic identity labels Hispanic and Latino/a.[1] At a critical age in their identity development, participants in this unique educational setting provide a window into the potential ways dual language schools offer alternative spaces for ethnic identity formation. Implications include recommendations for inclusion of ethnic studies and other student-centered curriculum, as well as explicit opportunities for discussions of ethnic identities, and the role of language, culture, and immigration status in the lives of students.

CONCEPTUAL FRAMEWORK

This chapter is grounded in both LatCrit theory and Critical Discourse Analysis. LatCrit is field of study within critical race theory (CRT); while both LatCrit and CRT are concerned with how race and racism function to uphold systems of subordination in society, LatCrit is more specifically interested in illuminating the particular experiences of Latinx groups (Delgado Bernal, 2002). LatCrit promotes a shared pan-ethnic identity among people of Spanish-language heritage in the United States (Perea, 1997). The terms "Latinx" and "Hispanic" are considered pan-ethnic identity labels because they refer to a variety of ethnic groups which are socially identified in the U.S. context by a single label derived from shared colonial ties to Spain. National surveys by the PEW Research Center have shown that people of Hispanic heritage tend to prefer national-origin labels such as Salvadoran and Venezuelan (Taylor, Lopez, Martínez, & Velasco, 2012). However, LatCrit scholars argue that the continued use of these national-origin terms serves to uphold and reproduce divisions among U.S.-born Latinxs and downplay shared experiences of discrimination in this country (Perea, 1997).

Critical discourse analysis (CDA) is both a methodology and theory concerned with illuminating the ways that language in use (discourse) functions to maintain societal systems of dominance (Rogers, 2011). Speakers in interaction with one another reveal their assumptions about the social world and their positions within that world through their language use. Rather than treating language as a tool for describing things or communicating, language is seen as reflecting and influencing the way we understand the world, as well as our actions and reactions to one another. Shared ways of using language, which reflect ways of seeing and being in the world, are referred to as discourses (Gee, 2004). By exploring how language "both reflects and constructs the social world" (Rogers, 2004, p. 5) CDA also provides tools for seeing how educators can create opportunities for disrupting such systems. These research tools include cultural models, situated identities, and positioning.

Cultural models refer to a group's shared stories about the way the world works (Gee, 2004). Certain discourses associated with our cultural models become ingrained in how a community talks as they develop shared ways of seeing and being in the world (Gee, 2004). Young people are socialized into functional aspects of language use in such settings as school, church, or the baseball field. They might learn, for example, that greeting an adult by first name is acceptable at church but not at school. Such patterns of greeting repeated over time reinforce how they view the world and what they think of as natural or normal, including relationships and authority within these settings. Sociocultural information about cultural models can be communicated through the use of languages (i.e., Spanish, English, Spanglish) or other aspects of language such as interactional patterns (e.g., turn-taking, talking over someone), word choice (e.g., "usted" or "tú"), or grammar (Fought, 2006; Ochs, 1986).

Situated identities are the socially recognized identities we enact in a given context during interaction with others (e.g., good student, boss, illegal person) (Gee, 2004). In contrast to the notion of identity as fixed and unchanging, situated identities are dynamic, change over time, and are constantly re-negotiated through interaction. Individuals have multiple identities, which can conflict in a given situation (Norton & Toohey, 2011). For example, when a young person who has always been a good student begins to associate with a group of friends for whom academics is not a desirable endeavor, she may experience her good student identity in conflict with her identity as a member of this group of friends. Positioning refers to the ways speakers signal their assumptions about the situated identities being enacted, and how they view themselves or people they interact with as insiders or outsiders to particular groups (Davies & Harre, 1990). For example, the friend may adopt language about how "we" would rather hang out with friends than study, positioning herself as part of the circle of friends and no longer part of the good student group.

These theoretical tools made visible the ways youth participants defined and positioned one another with relation to pan-ethnic and other social identities, and the shared and unique discourses they used to construct and situate these identities within their cultural models.

METHODS

Research Context

This chapter is based on an ethnographic study conducted while I co-taught with the middle school Spanish-language arts teacher. The larger study looked broadly at language ideologies circulating among youth in this setting. In addition to researching as a participant observer in the school, I had an existing professional relationship with this school, having taught at another school in the same district. At the time of data collection, my daughter was also enrolled in Kindergarten at the school. I lived and was raising my bilingual, bi-ethnic children (I am U.S.-born, of white/northern European heritage, my partner is an immigrant of white/Andalusian Spanish background) in the same neighborhood as four of the youth participants, near the school, and frequently interacted with families and school personnel in my capacity as colleague, neighbor, and parent. This privileged insider perspective in the school community allowed me natural bridges for building relationships in the school, but these had to be carefully managed to protect information shared in confidence (Lawrence-Lightfoot & Davis, 1997).

A Caribbean School in the Northeast United States

The Espada[2] School is a small dual language bilingual public school of about 400 students in grades pre-K through eighth. Located within a large urban district in the northeast United States, the student body at the time of this study was about 90% Hispanic, 6% white, and 3% African American, as reported by the district. About 75% of students were from low-income families, and 67% had a first language other than English. A majority of the teaching population was classified as Hispanic, with a third white and two African Americans, and most teachers were fluent bilinguals. Known for its strong academic performance, the school followed a mostly "50/50" model of language immersion in which all subjects were taught in English and Spanish.

The Espada school provides a unique type of dual language learning experience. Dual language programs are often referred to as "two-way" bilingual or immersion schools because historically they enroll about half of students from English-speaking and half from Spanish-speaking homes. This enrollment strategy was designed to create an additive bilingual experience for two groups of linguistically and culturally distinct groups of students (often an "Anglo" group and a "Hispanic" group). However, demographic shifts in the United States have led to an increase in predominantly Hispanic dual language programs; as the number of U.S.-born children of Hispanic heritage increases, enrollment strategies have been adapted in dual language programs like the Espada and a growing number of the English-dominant population are actually Hispanic heritage language students with some familiarity with the Spanish language (Cervantes-Soon, 2014). The school's Hispanic population is predominantly U.S.-born, second- and third-generation students. Just under half of the Hispanic population is classified as "English dominant" upon enrollment, with the rest classified as "English learner" (EL). Families have dynamic and complex language practices at home and Hispanic students come with varying degrees of proficiency in both languages.

Furthermore, the Hispanic population at Espada is predominantly Dominican and Puerto Rican. Non-Caribbean students constitute the minority at the Espada, and include families of either Central/South American or European descent. By contrast with other dual language bilingual schools which emphasize membership in a global Spanish-speaking community and a multicultural curriculum, Espada is a place marked by its tie to Caribbean language and cultural practices, which are characterized by parents as a warm, caring community with a traditional, sometimes strict, approach to discipline. Such a setting constitutes a language and cultural immersion experience of a particular type, providing Caribbean youth with an institutional enclave-like setting where Caribbean linguistic and cultural practices remain vibrant and serve as funds of knowledge for learning. Graduates from the school often return to describe the jarring sense of confusion and culture shock they experience upon moving on to high school, where their cultural and linguistic reference points are no longer a given.

Participants

Participant selection was made with an effort to reflect the predominantly Hispanic/ Caribbean, second-generation school population, while also including a mix of voices from diverse ethno-linguistic backgrounds. All students from the sixth grade were initially invited to complete a photography project and personal interview with the researcher. A small group was needed to collect and analyze extended, rich group discussion, so six students were later asked to join an after-school discussion group, which met for six weeks in May and June. Participants knew one another well, having been at the Espada school together in a small cohort of about 50 students from pre-kindergarten through the end of sixth grade.

Johnny, Yanelis, and Luis were children of Dominican immigrant parents. Since cultural and ethnic identity among Latinx families are often associated with Spanish-language use (Lopez, Gonzalez-Barrera & Lopez, 2017), I include this background information here. Luis's and Yanelis's families had slowly shifted from using Spanish only to using some English at home. Johnny's father still spoke with him mostly in Spanish, but his mother, with whom he lived, used mostly English with him. Perla was the daughter of a Mexican immigrant father and a U.S.-born mother of mixed Bolivian and French Canadian descent. They used only Spanish when she was younger, but used both languages interchangeably with her by the time she was in middle school. Annie was from an English-only home with Irish and Jewish heritage. Nora was identified by her teachers as an "American" student (meaning of European/white background) because she is being raised in an English-only home with two parents of European heritage. However, during the time of

Table 2.1 Summary of Participants

	Annie	Johnny	Luis	Nora	Perla	Yanelis
Age	12	12	12	12	12	12
Sex	F	M	M	F	F	F
Primary language(s) used at home	English	English	Spanish	English	English and Spanish	Spanish
Self-described social identity markers introduced by participants	Caucasian Jewish	Dominican 50/50	Dominican Hispanic	Latina Puerto Rican From (Northeast city)	Mexican Bolivian French Canadian Hispanic Latina	Dominican Latina

this study she began to identify as Latina because a biological parent, who she was in touch with but lived in another state and was not part of her upbringing, was Puerto Rican. Teachers and peers continued to express surprise at her self-identification during the course of the study. All six were U.S.-born and described using mostly English or only English with siblings, cousins, nieces, or nephews.

Data Collection and Analysis

Data presented here come from one-on-one interviews and a group discussion toward the end of our after-school meetings. I carefully designed interviews to let them introduce social identity labels into the conversation, beginning with photos they had taken of people and places where they use Spanish and English. As they described themselves and family members, I took note of the terms they used and reintroduced them in my questions later. The group discussion consisted of an activity familiar from their humanities classes where participants were asked to take a position on a continuum between two signs, "agree" or "disagree," in response to a series of statements. In the segment analyzed, the prompts were: "I would call myself Latino/a" and "I would call myself American." Half of our group discussions were conducted in Spanish and half in English; the data reported here were collected on an English day.

After line-by-line thematic analysis of all interviews and group activities (Braun & Clarke, 2013), segments were selected for CDA; by identifying what Rogers (2002) calls "critical incidents": moments when there seemed to be a shift or disruption in how participants constructed social identities.

The research question driving this project is: *How do middle school students construct pan-ethnic identity labels in two contexts: during one-on-one interviews with me and during group discussion with their ethno-linguistically diverse peers?*

FINDINGS

Varied Familiarity with Pan-Ethnic Identity Labels

Participants' use of and identification with pan-ethnic identity labels varied during initial interviews. All three participants with some European background introduced the term Latino/a in talking with me. Annie used the term several times to refer to people in different places in her life, as in "I go to school with mostly Latinos," or "sometimes at the store like all the clerk people are like Latino," or "everybody there (at friend's barbecue) is Latino." Nora similarly introduced the term Latina in her interview, using it several times to describe groups of people in different places in her world. For example, she described "seven Latina girls on the team" in softball and "most of us are Latina or Latino" in hip-hop dance class. She also mentioned the relative lack of diversity at summer camp, saying "I might be the only Latina girl."

Perla also used the term "Latino" when I asked her what terms her family members might use to talk about themselves. Later, she stated "I'm Hispanic and also I'm like Canadian I guess." Later, I asked her if she could explain what she meant by Latino and Hispanic. Her response indicated that she saw the terms as related to her mixed ancestry: "To me, it (Latino) means Hispanic I guess, but it doesn't only have to be Hispanic. It means like Hispanic and another background, I guess." Perla spoke with authority, using an emphatic and confident tone. Her use of "I guess" did not come off as hedging or self-doubt, but in a sort of deference to me as an adult and a researcher. Her tone seemed to position her as an expert on the topic and this interview as an opportunity to educate me.

Annie, Nora, and Perla all used pan-ethnic labels with apparent comfort and ease, as if they were familiar terms they had heard. In Annie's and Nora's cases, this apparent comfort with the label might be explained by their situation as minority students at Espada from monolingual English-speaking homes with white parents of European ancestry; we can imagine the label being used as a shorthand at home to talk about Spanish-speaking families as a group. In Perla's case, as a child of a multiethnic background, she seemed familiar with discussions of cultural background and difference.

By contrast, Johnny and Yanelis used the term "Dominican" or "Spanish" to describe themselves or family members, rather than pan-ethnic labels. Johnny did not use pan-ethnic labels at all in our interviews or other group discussions prior to the final group activity when we discussed the terms as a group. Instead, he provided extended examples of his feelings of straddling two worlds, which he labeled as "here" or using the name of his neighborhood, and Dominican, for example when he told me, "I would say I was born here but my parents are Dominican." This is not to say that pan-ethnic terms were not familiar to him, but that these labels were not key for describing himself and his life to me.

Yanelis similarly tended to use the national-origin term "Dominican" to describe herself and her family. There was a single incident when Yanelis did use the term Latino. She was telling me about her recent tour of the citywide public exam school, which she was considering attending the following year. I asked why she said she felt nervous.

Cause it's such a big school, with like different people. I'm so used to the same thing every year, and I'm probably not expecting the same languages either. Like, in this [Espada] school, there's . . . mostly like Puerto Ricans and like Dominicans and stuff, like, Guatemalans and Mexicans, and like Lat—Latinos I guess you could say? [pause] kind of? And like over there [at the new school], I'm expecting there could be like, everything, like all races, like Asians, white people, black people, like Puerto Ricans, yeah.

(Yanelis, personal interview)

It was evident how Yanelis stumbled over the word Latino, hedging as she spoke it out loud, her intonation rising twice, as if posing a question. These cues signaled that this pan-ethnic label is new for her. The middle school Spanish teacher, a veteran at Espada, reported that it was not uncommon for graduates moving on to more diverse schools to comment on their surprise at being lumped together under a single label with others from different national-origin backgrounds. This seemed evident in Yanelis's retelling of her high school tour; it was as if moving beyond the small Espada community surfaced an awareness of a label others use for her.

In contrast to the relative absence of pan-ethnic labels in Johnny's and Yanelis's interviews, Luis seamlessly introduced the word Hispanic multiple times in his interview. For example, when he described his baseball team coaches as "Hispanic," I asked him to tell me more about what the word meant to him. He replied:

When I hear Hispanic, I don't think automatically of the race, I kind of understand, and I'm not trying to say that anybody who speaks Spanish is Hispanic, that's not true, but I automatically think that they have, not automatically but sometimes I think they would have a connection in some way or they didn't have any connection at all and just wanted to learn, and spend a lot of time doing that. So I kind of have a good connection with those people, that um, have studied and tried.

(Luis, personal interview)

Here, we see how Luis grappled with complex ideas about the interplay between language, race, ethnicity, and interpersonal attitudes and relationships as he explored the meaning of the term Hispanic. He began with two disclaimers; when he says "I don't automatically think of race" and "I'm not trying to say that anybody who speaks Spanish is Hispanic," Luis is acknowledging assumptions he is aware exist among those around him. Disclaimers are an important discourse marker often used to signal shared cultural knowledge; Luis would not feel the need to make such statements if he did not take for granted that such shared ideas about the label are commonly held assumptions. His use of disclaimers here showed his understanding that this identity label is commonly associated with race and language. Luis attempted to push back on these assumptions and re-define the label in his own, more positive, terms. Luis went on later to describe his disgust with the use of the term Hispanic as an insult and people's tendencies to group people by race. He also later introduced the label Caucasian, juxtaposing it with Latino, saying "they [Caucasians] get paid more than most Latinos." Luis was unique in naming whiteness during the interview with me. Luis's use of these ethnic and race labels indicated a familiarity and comfort with using them not just as a way of grouping people, but also for talking about social inequalities. I got the sense that Luis's awareness of social injustice came from conversations with his father about workplace and other life experiences, which he mentioned several times during the interview.

Looking across these interview excerpts, it is clear that these 12-year-olds had a wide range of experiences with and levels of comfort using the pan-ethnic identity labels Hispanic and Latino/a. Johnny did not use them with me; Yanelis seemed to have an emerging awareness that others will use "Latina" to describe her; Annie, Nora, and Perla used the terms in matter-of-fact ways that accepted them as ways of grouping people; and Luis was both familiar with and critical of their use and associations with social inequalities.

Latino/a as Positive Identity

In general, identifying with Latino/a culture seemed to be positive and desirable among participants, especially those with European and ethnically mixed backgrounds. In response to my question of whether she considered herself bicultural, Annie stated,

> I mean you could say I'm part of Latino culture because I know the language and but I'm, I'm not from there? but it kind of feels like I am because I go to a school with mostly Latinos so, I think that's it, so yeah, I could consider myself bicultural.

(Annie, personal interview)

Elsewhere in her interview, Annie shared multiple stories about her efforts to fit in at her friends' houses and her love of "their culture," pointing to things such as birthday parties, laughter, and listening to loud music. She clearly had multiple positive associations with people she referred to as Latino.

As mentioned above, Nora was being raised by European, monolingual English-speaking parents and had recently begun to identify as Latina. When I asked Nora when she started calling herself Latina, she described how this shift took place and contrasted the normalcy of being Latino at school as compared with the unique positive status this identity had in her neighborhood:

> This year because I was doing so much more around [my neighborhood] where you can find almost anybody [of different backgrounds], and so I think this year. Because [before] I didn't have that recognition that that's more what I am. I used to think of myself as from [this city], that's it. While, this year, at hip-hop here [at the Espada school], it's kind of like, oh you're Puerto Rican, Ok. [even/deadpan tone] While there [at the neighborhood dance studio] it's like *oh, you're Puerto Rican, really? That's cool.* [enthusiastic tone] and more questions. While here [at the Espada school] it's just like everybody . . . is Latina, so.
>
> (Nora, personal interview 2)

Here Nora indicated a growing awareness of the meaning that this label had beyond the walls of her school. The social capital this label had afforded in her dance studio classes in the city neighborhood—"that's cool"—was also part of her experience on a citywide softball team and at a suburban summer camp, where she had recently discovered that identifying as Latina opened doors to starting conversations with new people. Nora also shared that she imagined possibly living in Puerto Rico in the future.

"I know my roots": Setting Parameters for Being and (not) Feeling Latino/a

During group discussion of the prompt "I would call myself Latino/a," all but Annie positioned themselves under the "Agree" sign. Luis began the conversation with,

> I think, I agree with this statement because I know my roots, I know where my parents are from, and they have proof because I went over to their house in the DR, so that's how I know that I am Latino.

Here, he set the basis for the group's discussion of social identity labels with a focus on family roots and providing proof of one's insider or outsider status. This roots discourse was pervasive throughout the group conversation, and was one all speakers kept coming back to. In the first several turns, Luis, Perla, Yanelis, and Johnny all contributed to setting the acceptable parameters of what roots meant in defining a Latino identity. It included family background and history, national origin, blood, and ancestors.

By contrast, they established what did not count as proof of being Latino, as shown in the following interaction:

Group Excerpt 1

1. Perla—I ***strongly*** agree that I'm Latina because I have a Latina background and I *feel* Latina and I'm ***proud*** of it.
2. Luis—(to Perla) I have a question for you. How do you, what do you mean by you feel Latina?
3. Yanelis—(smiles, nods at Luis) I know, how's it like to *feel* Latina?
4. Johnny—(talking over Y, makes comical movement) I *feel* Latina.
5. Yanelis—(face turns serious) She has the blood flowing through her.
6. Perla—(smaller voice) I don't know, I just, there's this feeling?

By questioning Perla's use of the word "feel," Luis problematizes the idea that feelings are relevant for constructing ethnic identity. Note that her focus on "pride" is also completely ignored here. Yanelis and Johnny build on Luis's push-back by using humor tones to imitate Perla's claim. The teasing tone may function here to diffuse the group tension while also sending a clear message that the idea of "feeling" Latina does not fit into the roots-based discourse already established by the group. Yanelis brings this home redefining "feeling" as related to the physical: "blood flowing through her." This serves to rein in Perla's idea of feeling pride and clearly mark the boundary of this pan-ethnic identity label as primarily defined by family background, blood, and roots.

Discourses are shared ways of seeing and being in the world (Gee, 2004). Here, we can see clearly how the roots discourse emerges as dominant in this micro moment of group discussion, shutting down for the moment the possibility that "feelings" are related to "being" Latino. It is important to note that such moments are fleeting; I do not argue that this moment determines how Perla defines herself. Rather, it is the accumulation over time of such peer interactions which contributes to a longer process of identity formation throughout her time at the Espada school. Perla appeared to accept their redirecting of her contribution and backed down with a small voice. This moment had power for Perla within this group context; throughout the remaining 20 minutes of this discussion, she never reintroduced the notion of cultural or ethnic pride into the discussion, though she had brought it up at other times in previous weeks.

The roots discourse allowed all but Annie to position themselves as Latino/a. Interestingly, in the next few moments of this group discussion, Luis created space for Annie to participate more fully in the discussion.

Group Excerpt 2

1. Researcher—Annie, tell us how you're feeling right now, what are you thinking?
2. Annie—I'm thinking that I disagree with that statement
3. Researcher—Yeah?
4. Annie—cause I'm not Latina (Pronounces "Latina" in an anglicized way with final "a" deemphasized)
5. Nora—AH, LatinAH, that's the . . . (Latinized pronunciation; emphasizes the final "a")
6. Luis—Don't you **kind of** feel . . . ? Because you've been here for a while and
7. Yanelis—(cuts Luis off) Yeah, I know. (pause) That's why I said she was Latina because (pauses as Nora grabs her arm and pulls her closer to herself and the "agree" sign) . . . that's why I said everyone was Latina or Latino because you've been here for like forever so I can say you're Latina even though you're not.
8. Annie—(moves toward the middle of the room, partway between "Agree" and "Disagree" signs) I took a step over here.
9. Researcher—You took a step, why did you take a step?
10. Annie—Cause I've been with these people for eight years and (pause) with a Latino (pronounced slowly, drawn out "Lat TEE no"), uh, community (voices drops very low, almost imperceptible)
11. Researcher—So you've been here for eight years in a Latino community and that makes you feel kind of, like there's a part of you that's Latina?
12. Annie—Sort of, yeah, I would say
13. Researcher—And did somebody say that they consider Annie partly Latina?
14. (All raise their hands or nod heads in agreement.)
15. Perla—I consider her partly Latina
16. Yanelis—Even though you know she doesn't, her parents aren't Latino or anything, I consider her Latina because she's been here, like, I don't know being around, just being around so much like me being a Latina and being around her so much, like, I guess. everyone's a Latino, so like her being around makes you feel like she's also a Latina, like it's so long, yeah. (As she speaks, Luis waves his hands in the air, using a signal commonly used in the school classrooms to show agreement with the speaker.)

Luis's use of "feel" in line 6 was notable as it contrasted with his previous questioning of Perla's use of "feel Latina." As the group negotiated a new meaning of this ethnic identity label as it applied to Annie, they created a new discourse, shifting their emphasis from roots to history and participation in this community. This use of a history discourse allowed the group to overcome an uncomfortable social moment where one of their own was in an obvious position of difference. Emphasizing a common history and social connections allowed them to diffuse this discomfort and signal their connection with Annie.

Significantly, this history discourse also allowed Annie—but not Perla—to *feel* Latina. Note Yanelis's caveat "even though you're not" in line 7, which emphasized Annie's difference. Yanelis later expanded with "even though her parents aren't Latino or anything, I consider her Latina because she's been here." Yanelis's words "I can say she's Latina" and "I consider her Latina" served to highlight her own authority as an insider. It is from her position as true insider (based on her roots) that she had the authority to position Annie as semi-insider (based on Annie's participation in this community). Both Luis and Yanelis focused on Annie's history in the Espada community. However, Luis emphasized Annie's feelings based on her participation, whereas Yanelis focused on her own choice to accept Annie's presence after an extended time together. Yanelis's focus positioned herself as a gatekeeper, giving Annie permission to cross the room. Through these interactions, thus, participants constructed a new discourse for Latino which allowed Annie to shift her position from outsider to semi-insider by virtue of her extended participation in the dual language bilingual school community.

Nora's participation in the above interaction was subtle but significant as well. In line 5, she quietly corrected Annie's pronunciation of the word "Latina," asserting her knowledge of Spanish pronunciation and, by extension, her insider status and right to be on the "agree" side of the room right in that moment. Nora's move in line 7 indicated another subtle bid to more firmly establish herself as an insider. She even reached out to establish physical connection with Yanelis, emphasizing her similarity with the most vocal participant in this discussion. As Nora took steps to establish her public identity as Latina, these micro-moments were small and less verbal, but significant.

Again, these moments have power within this group context. This interaction is a clear example of how participants' cultural models about what it meant to be Latino/a were both shaped by and gave shape to the moment-to-moment process of ethnic identity formation. As students engaged in these discussions, they created micro-spaces for imagining and taking up situated identities, as well as defining them. For Annie, the embodied experience of moving across the room toward her peers as she was (conditionally) invited into a Latino world had another outcome: she also seemed to interpret this invitation as authorizing her to participate in defining that world. After the above interaction, Annie and Nora participated more vocally in subsequent discussion about these identity terms. This contrasts with Perla's experience of having her claim of feeling ethnic pride truncated. The restraining of Perla in juxtaposition with the active invitation to Annie is a powerful reminder of what these micro-spaces for identity exploration can do to open or close doors.

DISCUSSION

Initially, Latinx youth and their mixed heritage and European American peers showed mixed degrees of awareness and comfort with pan-ethnic labels. Some introduced the terms Latino/a and Hispanic and used them confidently; others seemed more hesitant. Pan-ethnic labels were generally constructed as positive social identities across interviews and group discussions.

During group discussions, I found two discourses that seemed to circulate easily among the group when they talked about ethnic identities: a *roots* discourse of being Latino as based on family ties, and a *history* discourse of being Latino as based on participation in a community. A third discourse of *feeling* Latino as based on connection and pride was also introduced and seemed to disrupt the accepted ideas among the group. Each discourse created was taken up in unique ways by the group. The *roots* discourse allowed certain speakers to emphasize their authenticity as insiders of the pan-ethnic majority group at the school. The *history* discourse allowed these insiders to position Annie as partly Latina despite her family heritage; this also served to emphasize a unifying social identity as Espada school insiders for all. The group's questioning of Perla's introduction of a *feeling* discourse served to shut down the possibility of exploring a sense of connection and pride in her identity.

Benjamin Bailey (2002) has described how, for Dominican Americans, race, ethnicity, culture, and national origin tend to be equated. He has pointed out that U.S. notions of black/white racial identities are based on phenotype, whereas for Dominicans, family history and language are more salient in defining social identities. This chapter supports his findings; Johnny, Yanelis, and Luis all had an emerging sense of belonging to a larger social group within the United States that might be called Latinx or Hispanic, but tended to use the term Dominican when talking about themselves and their families. Their definition of all of these labels drew primarily on a roots discourse, which emphasized heritage, ancestry, and the national origin of their family.

Latinx students attending dual language schools find themselves in unique "zones of contact" (Pratt, 1991) since these schools are designed with systems meant to integrate students across ethno-linguistic lines of difference and emphasize linguistic and cultural equality (Howard et al., 2018). In such settings, young people learn to navigate differences in particular ways. During group discussions, my participants found ways to emphasize their social connections and sense of community within their dual language school, even as they engaged in potentially polarizing conversation about ethnic identity labels. Such a display of solidarity and connection points to a strong school community. Indeed, students in dual language programs benefit from an educational setting which honors multiple cultures and language resources and provides opportunities to develop positive ethnic identification. Nevertheless, such an environment might also shelter them from the realities of discrimination and inequality that youth in English-only programs face on a regular basis. Lack of experience with such societal inequalities could leave them underprepared to face such inequalities when they move on to secondary schools or other settings where they may need to navigate such realities. The fact that only Luis made explicit connections between ethnic identity labels and racial discrimination during the interview is likely related to the protected school environment they have been a part of. Furthermore, my participants' lack of precise language around topics of culture, ethnicity, and race is evidence that they had little prior guidance or opportunities to explore these topics.

Reyes and Vallone (2007) have pointed out that dual language schools need to create spaces for critical identity development, especially among older Latinx students. Within this dual language school community, Latinx youth and their peers had claimed the "Latino/a" label as a positive identity. This stands in striking contrast to dominant anti-immigrant rhetoric which tends to associate this label with criminality, laziness, and other negative behaviors (Valencia, 2017). It was from a positive position of authentic insider that Latinx youth were able to create a discourse of historical participation in a Latinx school community and authorize a self-identified non-Latinx white peer to publicly identify as feeling Latinx. That this identity was coveted is clear in the way that Annie eagerly repositioned herself and took up the label rather than rejecting or belittling the invitation. The positive status of identifying as Latinx and aligning oneself with an identity label associated with immigration in the United States is no small matter; this constitutes a disruption of pejorative discourses of Latinx people which circulate in dominant social spaces in the United States. As a predominantly Hispanic dual language school, the Espada has created a unique space for Latinx students for positive ethnic identification.

Despite a national trend toward dual language education, with many states introducing statewide initiatives in expanding this program model (U.S. Dept. of Education, 2015), it is not clear that traditionally marginalized students such as ethno-linguisic minorities and ELs have equal access to these programs (García Mathewson, 2017; Scanlan & Palmer, 2009; Valdés, 1997; Williams, 2017). Future research will need to monitor this question carefully.

In the meantime, schools like the Espada, which serve mostly low-income and minority students and successfully create positive academic and cultural environments for this population, should be seen as models which offer alternatives to the deficit view of immigrant and bilingual families that dominate identity politics in this country.

CONCLUSION

As anti-immigrant public rhetoric became increasingly inflammatory and xenophobic during the political regime under Trump, identity politics continue to be a real part of the daily experiences of Latinx people living in the United States (Peralta, 2016). There is an increased sense of fear and uncertainty about the future and the role of Hispanics in this country (PEW Research Center, 2017). This social reality is also relevant for adolescent Latinx youth and their peers, and schools must create systems that support positive ethnic identity formation.

While the Espada provides unique educational micro-spaces for forming "raced epistemologies" that diverge from the dominant Eurocentric approach circulating in most U.S. schools (Delgado Bernal, 2002), this research has implications beyond dual language. More work must be done to expand the pedagogy and curriculum of these schools and beyond (Reyes & Vallone, 2007). For some Latinxs who lived through the Trump era, historical knowledge about the sociopolitical circumstances of persons of Latinx heritage in the United States provided a tool to counter derogatory language used by Trump and other public figures (Peralta, 2016). For example, when Trump lauded the virtues of the Eisenhower administration's approach to mass deportation, descendants of Mexican Americans in the United States may have found it useful to counter such broad generalizations with specific facts about the human rights abuses which actually took place. The ethnic studies movement, which has its roots in the 1960s Civil Rights Movement but gained renewed momentum with the recent struggle to maintain a Mexican American studies program in Tucson Unified School District, can provide students with this kind of historical knowledge (Cuauhtin, Zavala, Sleeter, Au, 2019).

Youth participatory action research and similar youth-centered curricula offer another promising avenue for dual language programs (Cammarota & Fine, 2008; Roxas & Gabriel, 2016). The curricula at the Espada school, like many such schools, included opportunities to learn about positive Latinx role models and experience authentic Latin American and Spanish literature. However, these units were often removed from the experiences of young people. For example, the middle school teachers I worked with at the Espada struggled to make relevant units of study about the labor rights movement and Dolores Huerta's life. Students rejected such history as removed from their own realities, at least partly because as children of Dominican and Puerto Rican migrants to the urban northeast, they did not identify with Mexican Americans or the rural migrant labor movement. Classroom discussions of social injustice were more effective and real to students when they started with personal accounts of inequality. In my discussions with Luis, it was clear that his father had shared his own stories of discrimination in the workplace and his struggle to establish himself as a knowledgeable computer technician in a world where having an accent relegated him to the sidelines. Teachers working with young people like Luis could benefit from professional development and curriculum that helps them listen carefully to students' experiences and grow a relevant curriculum from those stories, bridging the unique experiences of young people in front of them with larger themes of social justice and anti-racism.

Through our complex discussions, my participants showed a nuanced understanding of social identities as both fluid and situated, as well as an ability to discuss differences while creating a sense of unity. This engagement and openness emerged from a participatory research methodology that began with their photos and stories, building on topics that were inherently engaging activity for them. Listening to one another's perspectives and ideas sparked interest and deepened our dialogue. It is important to center curricula and pedagogy about social identities around students' own experiences, as I did here beginning with the photovoice project.

NOTES

1. Latinx was not in common use in this community at the time of data collection. Participants used the term Latino or Latina and I followed their lead. Thus I use these terms in my reporting of findings and discussion of participants' interactions with one another. I use the term Latinx in my own writing, from my current position as researcher in acknowledgment of the term's importance in moving away from heteronormative and binary-centered language.

2. All names are pseudonyms.

REFERENCES

Anyon, J. (1981). Social class and school knowledge. *Curriculum Inquiry, 11*(1), 3–42.
Bailey, B. (2002). *Language, Race, and Negotiation of Identity: A Study of Dominican Americans.* New York: LFB Scholarly Publishing.

Bale, J. (2012). Linguistic justice at school. In J. Bale & S. Knopp (Eds.), *Education and capitalism: Struggles for learning and liberation*. Chicago: Haymarket Books.

Bartolomé, L. & Leistyna, P. (2007). Naming and interrogating our English-only legacy. *Radical Teacher, 75*, 2–9.

Block, N. (2011) The impact of two-way dual-immersion programs on initially English-dominant Latino students' attitudes. *Bilingual Research Journal, 34*(2), 125–14.

Braun, V. & Clarke, V. (2013). *Successful Qualitative Research: A Practical Guide for Beginners*. London: Sage.

Cammarota, J. & Fine, M. (2008). *Revolutionizing Education: Youth Participatory Action Research*. New York: Routledge.

Campbell, K. (2016). The "new Selma" and the old Selma: Arizona, Alabama, and the immigration civil rights movement in the twenty-first century. *Journal of American Ethnic History, 35*(3), 76–81.

Cervantes-Soon, C. G. (2014) A critical look at dual language immersion in the new latin@ diaspora. *Bilingual Research Journal*, 37:1, 64–82.

Cuauhtin,T., Zavala, M., Sleeter, C., & Au, W. (2019). *Rethinking Ethnic Studies*. Milwaukee, WI: Rethinking Schools Publications.

Davies, B., & Harre, R. (1990). Positioning: The discursive production of selves. *Journal for the Theory of Social Behavior, 20*(1), 43–63.

DeGuzman, M. (2017). Latinx: ¡Estamos aquí!, or being "Latinx" at UNC-Chapel Hill. *Cultural Dynamics, 29*(3), 214–230.

Delgado Bernal, D. (2002). Critical race theory, Latino critical theory, and critical raced-gendered epistemologies: Recognizing students of color as holders and creators of knowledge. *Qualitative Inquiry, 8*(1), 105–126.

Department of Education, Office of English Language Acquisition. (2015). *Dual Language Education. Programs: Current State Policies and Practices*, Washington, DC. Retrieved from http://www.air.org/sites/default/files/downloads/report/Dual-Language-Education-Programs-Current-State-Policies-April-2015.pdf.

D'Orio, W. (2017). Hamilton goes to high school. *Education Next*, Summer *17*(3). Retrieved from http://educationnext.org/hamilton-goes-high-school-how-students-learn-history-from-broadway-musical-lin-manuel-miranda/.

Feinauer, E., & Howard, E. (2014). Attending to the third goal: Cross-cultural competence and identity development in two-way immersion programs. *Journal of Immersion and Content-based Education, 2*(2), 257–272.

Fought, C. (2006). *Language and Ethnicity*. New York, NY: Cambridge University Press.

Freeman, R. D. (1998). *Bilingual Education and Social Change*. Philadelphia: Multilingual Matters.

García, O. (2009). *Bilingual education in the 21st century: A global perspective*. Malden, MA: Wiley–Blackwell.

García Mathewson, T. (2017). Rising popularity of dual-language education could leave Latinos behind. *The Hechinger Report*. Retrieved from http://hechingerreport.org/rising-popularity-dual-language-education-leave-latinos-behind/.

Gee, J. P. (2004). Discourse analysis: what makes it critical? In R. Rogers (Ed.), *An Introduction to Critical Discourse Analysis in Education* (19–50). Mahwah, NJ: Lawrence Erlbaum Associates.

Howard, E. R., Lindholm-Leary, K. J., Rogers, D., Olague, N., Medina, J., Kennedy, D., Sugarman, J., & Christian, D. (2018). *Guiding Principles for Dual Language Education* (3rd ed.). Washington, DC: Center for Applied Linguistics.

Lawrence-Lightfoot, S. & Davis, J. H. (1997). *The Art and Science of Portraiture*. San Francisco, CA: Jossey-Bass.

Lopez, M. H., Gonzalez-Barrera, A., & Lopez, G. (2017). *Hispanic Identity Fades Across Generations as Immigrant Connections Fall Away*. Washington, DC: Pew Research Center. https://www.pewresearch.org/hispanic/2017/12/20/hispanic-identity-fades-across-generations-as-immigrant-connections-fall-away/.

Mackinney, E. (2017) More than a name: Spanish-Speaking youth articulating bilingual identities. *Bilingual Research Journal, 40*(3), 274–288.

Morrell, E. (2007). *Critical literacy and urban youth: Pedagogies of access, dissent, and liberation*. New York: Routledge.

Ngai, M. (2004). *Impossible Subjects: Illegal Aliens and the Making of Modern America*. Princeton, NJ: Princeton University Press.

Norton, B., & Toohey, K. (2011). Identity, language learning and social change. *Language Teaching, 44*(4), 412–446.

Ochs, E. (1986). Introduction. In B. B. Schieffelin & E. Ochs (Eds.), *Language Socialization across Cultures* (1–13). New York: Cambridge University Press.

Olsen, L. (1997) *Made in America: Immigrant Students in Our Public Schools*. New York: New Press.

Palmer, D. (2008). Building and destroying students' 'academic identities': The power of discourse in a two-way immersion classroom. *International Journal of Qualitative Studies in Education, 21*(6), 647–667.

Palmer, D. (2009). Middle-class English speakers in a two-way immersion bilingual classroom: "Everybody should be listening to Jonathan right now . . ." *TESOL Quarterly, 43*(2), 177–202.

Peralta, E. (Author and Editor). (2016, June). Latinos and American identity in a time of Trump: A postcard from El Paso [Audio podcast episode]. In *Weekend Edition Sunday*. Washington, DC: National Public Radio.

Perea, J. (1997). 'Panel: Latina/o identity and pan-ethnicity: Toward lat crit subjectivities: Five axioms in search of equality'. *Harvard Latino Law Review, 231*, 231–237.

Pew Research Center. (2017). *Latinos and the New Trump Administration*. http://www.pewhispanic.org/2017/02/23/latinos-and-the-new-trump-administration/.

Pratt, M. L. (1991). Arts of the contact zone. *Profession* (*Modern Language Association*), *91*, 33–40.

Reyes, S., & Vallone, T. (2007). Toward an expanded understanding of two-way additive bilingual/bicultural pedagogy. *Multicultural Perspectives, 9*(3), 3–11.

Rogers, R. (2002). Between contexts: A critical analysis of family literacy, discursive practices, and literate subjectivities. *Reading Research Quarterly, 37*(3), 248–277.

Rogers, R. (2004). *An introduction to critical discourse analysis in education*. Mahwah, NJ: Lawrence Erlbaum Associates.

Rogers, R. (2011). Critical approaches to discourse analysis in educational research. In R. Rogers (Ed.), *An Introduction to Critical Discourse Analysis in Education* (2nd ed.). New York: Routledge.

Roxas, K., & Gabriel, M. L. (2016). Amplifying their voices. *Educational Leadership*, 78–81.

Scanlan, M., & Palmer, D. (2009). Race, power, and (in)equity within two-way immersion settings. *Urban Review: Issues and Ideas In Public Education, 41*(5), 391–415.

Seif, H. (2016), "We define ourselves": 1.5-Generation undocumented immigrant activist identities and insurgent discourse. *North American Dialogue, 19*, 23–35.

Stolte, L. (2017). Discussing difference: Color-blind collectivism and dynamic dissonance in two-way immersion contexts, *Bilingual Research Journal, 40*(2), 205–221.

Taylor, P., Lopez, M. H., Martínez, J., & Velasco, G. (2012, April 4). *When Labels Don't Fit: Hispanics and Their Views of Identity*. PEW Hispanic Center. http://www.pewhispanic.org/2012/04/04/when-labels-dont-fit-hispanics-and-their-views-of-identity/.

Valdés, G. (1997). Dual language immersion programs: A cautionary note concerning the education of language-minority students. *Harvard Educational Review, 67*(3), 391–429.

Valencia, Y. (2017). Lo que duele es que la gente lo cree: What hurts is that people believe it. *Journal of Latin American Geography, 16*(2), 183–196.

Williams, C. (2017, December). *The intrusion of white families into bilingual schools*. The Atlantic. https://www.theatlantic.com/education/archive/2017/12/the-middle-class-takeover-of-bilingual-schools/549278/.

Wong Fillmore, L. (1991). When learning a second language means losing the first. *Early Childhood Research Quarterly, 6*, 323–346.

Chapter 3

"Why Isn't Cinco de Mayo 365 Days a Year!"

Culturally Sustaining Practices in an Age of Distrust

Orlando Carreón

The ideas of this chapter stem from research conducted between 2016 and 2019 (Carreón, 2018). During his run for the presidency, the 45th president of the United States implemented a campaign of fear as he called into question an entire country and its people:

> When Mexico sends its people, they're not sending their best. . . . They're not sending you. They're sending people that have lots of problems, and they're bringing those problems with us. They're bringing drugs. They're bringing crime. They're rapists. (Phillips, 2017)

The racist rhetoric served as a discursive precursor to the actions taken by his administration. For example, after taking office, the Department of Homeland Security, including U.S. Immigration and Customs Enforcement Agency, used their power to detain families in cages for an unspecified amount of time while separating newborn children from their mothers (Aguilera, 2019).

To move forward with such heinous acts, public leaders bypassed accountability structures (e.g., journalism) and commonly accepted notions of truth (i.e., facts). Rather than appealing to the public's perception of rationality—a construct of modernity that favored science and facts over religion—the 45th president and his administration appealed to the public's emotion and fear (Strom & Martin, 2017), and I would add, their notions of white supremacy. In this environment, Latinx and undocumented Latinx communities became the target of outlandish lies and belligerent xenophobia, creating intense distrust between Latinx communities and public leaders. In essence, common understandings of truth and rationality are hijacked, creating the discourse of post-truth.

I argue that communities of color have always lived within a sphere of lies and mistrust that a post-truth environment is hardly new. For example, "white supremacy" is false, yet society has constructed an entire racial apparatus that embodies real material consequences for people constructed as racialized subjects in the United States. Indigenous peoples and historically oppressed communities experience a world where truth and facts are hijacked, resulting in a perpetual state of violence for the past 400 years (Acuña, 2000; Smith, 1999). Perhaps, a more accurate description of the post-truth environment is our society's most advanced stage of coloniality. The result is an extreme level of distrust between the community and its leaders, a symptom of a society in crisis.

Within education, a perpetual sense of distrust between educational leaders and Latinx students is nothing new. Perhaps the most demonstrative illustration of distrust comes from the students themselves. In 1968, in East Los Angeles, thousands of high school students walked out of their high schools to protest the poor educational conditions they were experiencing. Among the demands of student protesters were bilingual courses, Chicano/a Studies courses, bilingual teachers, and so on (Acuña, 2000; Montoya, 2016). The failure of educational leaders to learn from the lessons of history resurfaced on the national stage in 2010 when it was found that Latinx students who participated in the Mexican American Studies (MAS) program in Tucson, Arizona were outperforming their white counterparts in academic achievement measures (Cabrera et al.,2014). Rather than praise the MAS program, the state sent lawyers to pass legislation HB 2281, which created the legal rationale to terminate the program (Cabrera et al., 2014). What if educational leaders concerned with the education of Latinx learned from the mistakes made from their historical predecessors? What if instead of sending lawyers to dismantle the MAS program, public officials sent research teams and educational leaders to learn from the educational bright spots in Tucson, Arizona? What if educational leaders listened to the voices of young people?

The goal of this chapter is to highlight what can happen when educational leaders learn from the mistakes of the past and dedicate their resources to establishing trusting relationships with Latinx youth. I narrate my experiences at a North Bay Area High school after a cultural microaggression occurred on campus between administrators and students on Cinco de Mayo, 2016. Rather than modeling the reactionary and incendiary examples of today's public leaders, this chapter illustrates what is possible when resources are committed to rebuilding trust, listening to the wisdom of young people, and embracing the cultural gifts brought forth by Latinx student and their families.

I begin by discussing the theoretical frameworks that ground the culturally responsive and sustaining training conducted at Hope High School (HHS). I provide context of HHS, followed by an explanation of how one particular school attempted to heal from a traumatic microaggression. I document the transformation I observed between Cinco de Mayo 2016 (labeled year 1) and Cinco de Mayo 2017 (labeled year 2). I end the chapter with a discussion on the lesson learned.

THEORETICAL FRAMEWORK

Coloniality

In this chapter, I use the notion of coloniality to situate education in the United States as a postcolonial project. Coloniality refers to the long-standing patterns of power that survived conquest and imperialism. While conquest and imperialism defined the global project of European expansion, colonialism was the modus operandi that ensured control of the colonies and its inhabitants (Smith, 1999). According to Maldonado-Torres (2007), coloniality describes the manner in which control is established by defining:

> culture, labor, intersubjective relations, and knowledge production well beyond the strict limits of colonial administrations. Thus, coloniality survives colonialism. It is maintained alive in books, in the criteria for academic performance, in cultural patterns, in common sense, in the self-image of peoples, in aspirations of self, and so many other aspects of our modern experience. In a way, as modern subjects, we breathe coloniality all the time and every day. (p. 243)

Coloniality informs how U.S. society constructs students of color through its institutional apparatuses—and education is no exception. For example, standard educational terms such as "achievement gap," "English Language Learners," and "at-risk students" are racialized terms that construct student identities as "fixed" or "permanent"—and mark the ways in which administrative institutions interact with students labeled as such. At the curricular level, the impact of coloniality is understood by whose stories are told and worthy of academic consideration. When the stories of students of color are not considered, the effects can be deleterious and contribute to the despiritualization of Latinx youth and school failure (Arce, 2016; Pizarro, 1998; Villanueva, 2013).

The literature on the school-prison-pipeline serves as a prime example of how students of color, especially black and brown youth, are controlled and criminalized within educational institutions. For example, zero-tolerance policies that were initially used as a no-nonsense approach to the presence of firearms, gangs, and violence in schools, are being extended to common adolescent misbehavior, such as dress code violations and food fights to create what Railble and Irizarry (2010) describe as a "diminishing adult understanding of and patience for the mistakes and unwise choices made by the young" (p. 1199). The perpetual state of violence experienced by students of color is a characteristic of a colonial experience.

Culturally Responsive Pedagogies

To disrupt the oppressive conditions brought forth by the legacy of colonialism, "asset-based" pedagogies aim to re-center students' cultural repertoires to make use of the cultural gifts that students of color bring to the learning environment. For example, Tara Yosso's (2006) notions of Community Cultural Wealth ask educators to value and make use of the cultural capital that Latinx families bring to the classroom, such as their familial, linguistic, aspirational, social, navigational, and resistance capital. Angela Valenzuela's (1999) notion of authentic caring is central to understanding Latinx student's cultural understanding of what it means to be educated. Valenzuela's study reveals that for Latinx students to care about school, they must first feel cared for—as caring, trusting, and respectful interpersonal relationships is a prerequisite to becoming a well-educated person. Valenzuela's notion of authentic caring evokes Bartolome's (1994) notion of political clarity when she states that authentic caring relationships must include a "more profound and involved understanding of the socioeconomics, linguistic, sociocultural, and structural barriers that obstruct the mobility of Mexican youth needs to inform all caring relationships" (p. 109). Thus, authentic caring of Latinx youth, is a cultural and political undertaking requiring care, confianza (trust and solidarity), and consciousness to be communicated in culturally responsive ways.

Culturally Sustaining Pedagogies

The latest iteration of asset pedagogies asks the question, "What are we sustaining?" Culturally Sustaining Pedagogy (CSP) aims to support young people in sustaining the cultural and linguistic competence of their communities while simultaneously offering access to dominant cultural competence (Paris, 2012). CSP pushes schools and educators to sustain the multicultural and multilingual repertoires that young people need as part of the ever-changing pluralistic democratic project. Educators are encouraged to go beyond fixed notions of culture that often oversimplify culture in deterministic ways. CSP asks educators to create spaces where young people can express the dynamic ways they experience culture while simultaneously challenging regressive practices (Paris &Alim, 2017).

How do these frameworks help young people when new forms of coloniality challenge their humanity? In Tucson, Arizona, the MAS program used indigenous epistemologies such as the Mayan principle of In Lak Ech to guide their practice. In Lak Ech is a Mayan philosophy that embodies the ethos of "You are my other self" and reflects a philosophy of interconnectedness (Paredez, 1968, as cited by Rodriguez, 2012). CSP acknowledges that communities of color have always used ancestral ways of knowing to survive the onslaught of white supremacy (Caraballo, Martinez, Paris, & Alim, 2020). Rather than be led by fear and anger, In Lak Ech and other ancestral epistemologies offer educators and students with knowledge that is ethical and useful for the survival of the greater collective (Holmes & Gonzalez, 2017). According to MAS educator Curtis Acosta (2007), In Lak Ech provided young people with a foundation with which to interrogate the world that challenged their humanity. CSP challenges educators to sustain the values and practices that lead to a more humanizing educational experience for young people. The following section examines the context in which the study took place.

COMMUNITY CONTEXT AND RESEARCH

HHS is located in an agricultural/suburban community about an hour's drive from a major U.S. metropolitan city, in Northern California. During the 2015–2016 school year, when the data were collected, HHS reported a total of 1,845 enrolled students. Forty percent of the school populations reported receiving free and reduced lunch. Latinx students represented the largest student demographic, at 53%. Among teachers at HHS, 88% were reported as white, while the next closest subgroup of teachers was Latinx at 6% (CDE, 2018).

It is important to note that this research was focused on the Effective Teaching of Latinx Students, where the primary focus was on pedagogy and not specifically on understanding the racialized tensions between the two largest demographic groups in Hope Valley (i.e., white and Latino). However, during the time I collected data (2015–2016), a microaggression occurred between administrators and students during the 2016 Cinco de Mayo celebrations that swept me into a series of meetings where I witnessed the events discussed in this chapter. Although not related to the initial research focus, I continued to document through memos and fieldnotes; the experiences witnessed while on site.

As a researcher in the community where I grew up and currently live, I navigated multiple roles: a community member, researcher, and culturally responsive consultant. I grew up in Hope Valley, where I often experienced tensions as a Latinx student growing up in schools that did not value my cultural roots. I also attended HHS as a teenager, where I experienced racial microaggressions by classmates and teachers. Thus, I intimately understood how white supremacy manifested itself within this context. While collecting these data, I also served as an educational consultant for Acosta Educational Partnerships, hired by HVUSD to conduct culturally responsive training at HHS. The analyses of these data stemmed from the composite roles I enacted as a community member, researcher, and consultant.

Culturally Responsive Sustaining Humanizing Training (CRSH)

During the 2016–2017 academic school year, my consulting team provided professional development in what we call CRSH Pedagogies. We provided participants with a deep dive into the history of colonialism in education with the intent of cultivating political consciousness for how factors such as race and identity impact the chances of success for Latinx and other historically oppressed students. Our training comprised multiple two-day intensive institutes, two consecutive days in the Fall Semester, and two consecutive days in the Spring semester.

The CRSH trainings were in line with the frameworks discussed in the theory section of this paper, namely, Postcolonial Theory and Culturally Sustaining Pedagogies. For example, we used videos such as *Facundo the Great* to make the connection between mispronouncing a student's name and the erasure of someone's identity resulting in the potential loss of trust between a student and educator. We also created lab opportunities for teachers to develop CRSH practices. They modeled for one another how they used the Cultural Wealth Model and Authentic Caring Relationships in their classrooms. We brought in student speakers from the community to share their experiences. We asked questions such as: What is working for you at HHS? What is not working for you at HHS? Do you feel like your cultural background is (e.g., home language, ethnic background, gender, identity, etc.) is honored at your school? What advice do you have for teachers, administrators, and educators to ensure that the students that come after you succeed personally and academically? Our goal was to model the importance of centralizing young people's voices as young people have the extraordinary capacity to state what is not working form them as it relates to fairness, equity, and justice.

At the beginning of each training, participants recited the poem of In Lak Ech (translated as You are my other me), similar to how educator Dr. Curtis Acosta began his courses with his high school students in Tucson, Arizona. By infusing the values of In Lak Ech throughout our training, CRSH practices were taught not as a means to develop static lesson plans for a particular content unit; but rather; as a value-driven stance that guided all pedagogical undertakings.

HHS's principal at the time, was heavily involved in finding strategic ways to ensure that the effects of CRSH training reached as many teachers and students as possible. Most of the teachers who participated in CRSH training were from the English and Social Studies Department. Placing teachers in this manner was a strategic decision to ensure that CRSH practices reached as many students as possible as every ninth- and tenth-grade student was required to take English and Social Studies. Finally, curricular themes were developed around identity so that each grade level had a theme they would address in their content areas. The themes provided teachers and students with self-reflection opportunities to reflect on their identity in context to their community. In the following section, I document the events in year 1 (2016), followed by the transformation I observed in year 2 (2017).

YEAR 1: 2016

In May 2016, the local television news media falsely reported a "riot" involving Latinx students at HHS (although I was not present during the incident, I arrived minutes later and spent a great portion of the day with the students, administrators, teachers, and police officers who were involved in the incident). This was not the first time HHS experienced microaggressions related to Cinco de Mayo. In May 2010, the local newspaper reported the burning of a Mexican flag in protest of the Cinco de Mayo celebration. The 2016 incident involved Latinx youth and the school's administration, which prohibited students from bringing flags to school to celebrate Cinco de Mayo. A confrontation occurred between administrators and students, when an administrator grabbed a student's Mexican flag after being told to put it away, and the student resisted by saying "Why . . . this is me!" (Gabriel, Tenth-Grade Student, Fieldnotes). Soon after, two police cars arrived, a motorcycle unit, including a helicopter unit circling the quad area where students congregate to have their morning breakfast. The presence of police on the school campus is described in the literature as the hypercriminalization of black and brown youth (Gray, 2019; Rios, 2006).

The following narrative stems from my fieldnotes that begin with a text exchange with Sal (pseudonym) a colleague who taught predominately Latinx youth at HHS.

On the morning of 5 de Mayo at 10:31 am, Sal texted me and told me that an administrator was texting him to ask when he would arrive on campus because "there are about to be arrests with your kids wearing the flag." When I received this message, I decided to go early to support Sal. My plan was to help him out in the classroom, as I knew that Sal would be spending a large chunk of time in the office sorting things out. My presence on campus quickly drew me into a series of events, one of which included a discussion between students, HH administrators, and a high-ranking administrator from the district office who arrived on campus when he was informed of the incident. During this discussion my role quickly changed when I felt that the district administrator was using his power to try to find a culprit, "I am like the fireman, I want to know who lit the match," he stated. Quickly, my roles changed as I went from a colleague, to community supporter, consultant, restorative circle leader, and at one point I invoked my role as father. I include a portion of the previous memo to illustrate the various roles enacted.

Seeing that the district administrator was pushing his weight aggressively, I decided to step in, as I was upset that the district official was aiming for the students and my colleague's program. I stepped in and said, "I keep hearing from the students and from the administrators that you all felt 'disrespected' as both students and administrators have used that word multiple times. I have to admit that I also felt disrespected especially when I heard that someone was telling students that they were going to be arrested because if someone would have told my daughter that she was going to be arrested for wearing a flag, I would have flown in on a helicopter myself." I heard a few chuckles from the students and I perceived from Doug's (district officer) reaction that I made him uncomfortable; as I noticed his eyes get a little larger. My hunch was that he was expecting me to back him up on his charge against the students. But I didn't. I continued my mediation. "Can one of the students say why you felt disrespected? I would like the administrators in the room to listen because I am going to ask that you to respond in a manner that lets students know that they were heard." A few students spoke up and mentioned that they felt disrespected because they saw that others students on campus get to where their flags all the time and that when they wear their flags there is police and helicopters on campus.

Gabriel also mentioned that he didn't feel like the school supported their heritage. Gabriel said "There are no murals and there is nothing about us in our books . . . and the issue is not really the flags or Cinco de Mayo but why are we not celebrating our heritage 365 days a year?" I then asked Doug if he could let the students know that they were heard . . . I asked the students if Doug had understood them and they said, "Yes."

The fieldnotes above are an example of how the dialogue continued, a dialogue that lasted almost two hours. The discussions were intense and at various points in the dialogue, two administrators shed tears. The dialogue eventually evolved to students contributing a list of ideas of what could be done at HHS to make the school responsive to their needs. As students spoke, I wrote their ideas on the dry erase board. In parentheses, I add context to what was written on the dry erase board.

- Symbolic Presence of Diversity (This was a critique by students that their culture and history was not visible at HHS via murals or textbooks).
- Apology from admin and students for what happened (The students felt they were unjustly being singled out for the Cinco de Mayo incident when in reality there were many people involved).
- Teachers don't believe in students.
- Mexican Flag in whole School (This was students' critique and solution to the administrator's decision not to allow students to bring their flags to school. Students suggested that rather than tell the students to keep their flags home, admin should tell students, "you don't need to bring your flag, we will put it up for you."
- Being recognized 365 days a year as opposed to only on Cinco de Mayo.
- The importance of administrators to understand students first by "throwing down a ladder" before charging them with consequences. (Students stated that they did not feel like someone was watching out for their best interests in the front office where disciplinary consequences are mediated.)
- The importance of administrators "taking off the badge" before punishing students (This was a recommendation and critique for administrators.) Students used the metaphor of "taking off the badge" (i.e., police badge) when dealing with disciplinary issues with students, with the goal of first understanding where students were coming from.

It was clear that many of the items listed were a direct response to students not feeling like their ethnic culture was valued, including the items related to disciplinary issues. I was impressed, but not surprised by students' political clarity. What is surprising is that young people continue to be the most underutilized resource in education's quest for equity. Young people do not carry the constraints of institutional norms and jargon that often obfuscate issues of equity and justice. Rather than make use of students' contributions, the district administrator dismissed their contributions by saying "this is all good and great that we are talking about all of this, but at some point I need to hear some agreements from the students because just talking about our feelings I am not okay with." The administrator's response was dismissive of the brilliance that the students had previously shared. His inability to listen corresponded with his rush to find short-term solutions to a problem that had existed in this community for decades. Unfortunately, on this day he did not show up to listen, he showed up to discipline.

The following day I was invited to a meeting to debrief with the principal's administrative team and a few teachers. Below is a narrative of my field notes of this meeting:

The meeting the next day was attended by the Principal, three Assistant Principals, a Math teacher, Sal, and myself. The purpose of the meeting was to check-in to ask how everyone was feeling and to collectively think about where they could they go from here. Some assistant administrators reported that they felt severely unprepared for that moment. That it was intense and they felt like they did not know what to do and that it wasn't a good feeling. Everyone went around to check in how they felt. I waited until the end to respond. I told the group that I was disturbed by how the district officer handled the conversation the day before. . . . I told the group "I am less concerned with who threw the match; but rather, why the grass is dry." I told them that these issues will continue to happen at HHS unless these bigger issues are addressed.

The energy in the room was one of fatigue. One teacher was concerned that they didn't think the student's voices were still being heard. It was suggested that they form a committee that addressed these issues. . . . The assistant principal

Figure 3.1 Tweet 1: August, 2016: *Staff Discussing Facundo the Great and Humanizing a Person's Name.* [The principal snapped this picture of the assistant principals teaching and watching *Facundo the Great* with his entire staff in the school library.]

Figure 3.2 Tweet 2: August 17, 2016. *Students in Mrs. L's English Class Learning How to Spell and Pronounce Each Other's Name.* [The picture shows a teacher at the front of the classroom leading an assignment where students spent time learning the importance of pronouncing each other's name correctly. This lesson was taught on the first day of school—an action that connotes value and importance.]

> volunteered and the Math teacher also said that he would be part of it. I suggested that the students needed to be a part of the very first meeting. Finally, I said that HHS was in a really great position, and that they were lucky to have students who are willing to sacrifice themselves for what they believe in. I reminded the team that this type of leadership needed to be harnessed, coached, and developed.

The meetings continued throughout the day, weeks, months, and the following school year.

YEAR 2: 2016–2017

The following academic school year I noticed a remarkable shift in the principal's tweets. Rather than the typical tweets that boasted proudly the accomplishments of its sports teams, the principal's tweets included pictures of teachers and students embracing the concepts discussed in their culturally responsive trainings. Below is a composite of the principal's tweets:

Figure 3.3 Tweet 3: March 30, 2017: *Santi, Mari, Jose, Kathy, Christina Sharing with English Department Community Responsiveness.* [Here the principal tweets a picture of a student panel conducted at one of our CRSH trainings. The principal mentions "community responsiveness," a nod to the discourse of our trainings that emphasized the importance of teachers becoming ethnographers of their communities.]

Figure 3.4 Tweet 4: April 5, 2017: *Teacher's Working on Their Identity Crest as Part of Plaza CRSH Week.* [The principal's tweets a picture of the staff filling out their identity crest as part of plaza CRSH week. Plaza CRSH week refers to a week-long activity where students and faculty express their identity through various themes and forms. Each day of the week corresponding to a unique identity theme. CRSH plaza week was created and led by a student ambassador team created after the previous Cinco de Mayo event. In this tweet I also noticed that "CRSH" had entered the common school discourse and was being used to name their traditions (i.e., CRSH week). Finally, this activity was not designated for a particular content team; rather, all teachers (and students) were responsible for the activity.]

Why Isn't Cinco de Mayo 365 Days a Year! 59

Figure 3.5 Tweet 5: April 5, 2017—*A Rainbow of Colors Celebrating the Cultural Wealth #crushedit.* [The picture is of approximately 80 teachers and students (mostly students) standing proudly and looking up at the camera. The teachers and students stood in clusters most visibly distinguished by the color of their t-shirt. From left to right, the clusters of t-shirts were represented by the colors purple, blue, green, yellow, red, in that order. Each color represented an aspect of the teacher/student's identity. Here I notice the discourse of CRSH morphed into a verb and picked up a social media signifier as represented by the hashtag #crushedit.]

DISCUSSION

The narrative weaved through the tweets and pictures taken by the principal are not meant to suggest that the school had undergone a radical decolonial transformation. Neither am I suggesting that the school had healed from decades of microaggressions experienced by its students and teachers or that this school has gone far enough. I am also not suggesting that having a few cultural celebrations is the answer. None of this is true. What I do want to illustrate is that in one year, HHS school begun to markedly transform the way students experienced Cinco de Mayo, a holiday stained with racial trauma for decades, including when I was there as a student. In one year, HHS school made a hard pivot to valuing the cultural wealth that students brought to the learning environment. Below are some of the key lessons learned on the journey toward equity.

Lesson Learned

1. Trust: Any attempt to make a progressive change within education must begin with gaining student trust. For HHS, trust began by learning how to say each other's names (as evidenced by Tweets 1 and 2). The attempt

Figure 3.6 Picture Taken Using my iPhone Video Camera: Cinco de Mayo 2017. [The picture illustrates brown and white students dancing to a popular Mexican song that is fast-paced and intended to be danced in uniform. In the distant background is the umbrella of a street vendor selling various fruits in a plastic cup with lime and red chili powder. Across the sky, the bright colors of "papel picado" blow gently across the campus, connected by a single string.]

to pronounce students' names correctly is centered on humility, honesty, and trust. Humility to say, for me to know you, I have to begin with a shift in myself. A shift in the way I perceive you. A shift in the way I care about you. Language has an ideological element that is embedded within the politics of pronunciation that is best revealed by activist poet Warsan Shire when she states "Give your daughters difficult names. Give your daughters names that command the full use of tongue. My name makes you want to tell me the truth. My name doesn't allow me to trust anyone that cannot pronounce it right" (Shire, 2020). Within Shire's powerful statement, we feel the weight of the colonial experience.

2. All Hands-on Deck: The second lesson learned was that to create any type of systemic change toward equity, it takes an "all hands-on deck" approach (as evidenced by Tweets 1, 4, and 5). What I find in my work as a consultant is that equity is typically examined by a small group of people examining a narrow set of test results. There are several problems with this approach. One problem is that equity is narrowly defined by a set of data that is based solely on academic measures. A typical response may look like this: Latinx youth are not doing well on standardized tests. Thus, let's have them take more English support classes. The result is often a misunderstood notion of the problem, and ultimately, a plan is constructed that is

unsupported by teachers, families, and students. By making CRSH activities the responsibility of all stakeholders on campus, HHS experienced a shot in the arm where CRSH principles were injected into the bloodstream of the entire school. The all hands-on deck approach initiated by HHS is in line with CSP as the approach attempts to address the sustainability principle by institutionalizing what it values (e.g., student identity).
3. Student Voice: The third lesson learned is that equity begins with the voices of students themselves (as evidenced by Tweet 3). I have found that young people are able to describe the problems that affect them without the bureaucratic language educators often hide behind. In my work as a consultant, I have conducted multiple youth panels. The first two questions that I ask students are: What is working for you at X School? What is not working for you? The answers to these questions are usually a treasure of equity leads that are often not on the radar of the equity data found within institutional reports. Furthermore, I have also found that when students speak, adults often miss (or dismiss) their claims, similar to how the district administrator dismissed student's ideas. Students may not always be right, but if we do not listen to them, we may never understand what right is. Learning to listen to the needs of young people is in line with CSP, as it helps educators learn about the dynamic and shifting ways that young people experience culture. Students have the opportunity to talk back to the discourses of coloniality that places dehumanizing labels on them, such as "at-risk" and "English Language Learners" that were historically formulated from a white gaze. (Paris and Alim, 2017)
4. Ethnic studies for all: Why isn't Cinco de Mayo 365 days a year? Gabriel's question is a piercing critique that takes us back to why students from East LA walked out of their schools in 1968. The students' resistance is a response to the denial of the truth and a denial of their humanity. Rather than dismiss Gabriel's critique, educational leaders have an obligation to expand his vision so that Latinx and other students of color can self-actualize with a decolonial notion of the truth. Ethnic Studies frameworks based on CSP principles are essential for all students whose journey for liberation is interconnected—as described in the ethos of In Lak Ech. Nothing short of Ethnic Studies for all students can be accepted if we are to create a culturally sustaining future.

CONCLUSION

What are we sustaining? Paris's (2012) question asks us to listen to the lessons of the past in order to walk into the future. Rather than follow the punitive playbook, a move that is all too common in the way schools have historically attended to the needs of Latinx and other youth of color, administrators and teachers chose to dedicate resources to regaining students' trust and harnessing their cultural wealth. Instead of asking retributive questions such as "Who lit the match?" a more honest question is "How do we re-build trust with our sacred youth?" The lessons learned from this study—beginning with regaining student trust, using an all hands-on deck approach, incorporating student voice, and moving toward ethnic studies for all—are central to any legitimate effort rebuilding decades of dehumanizing schooling practices for both students and educators brought forth by the legacy of colonialism. In short, we cannot have a humanizing relationship with students of color if we do not understand the dehumanizing legacy of colonialism.

My goal with this chapter was to provide evidence of a moment in time when our community responded by listening to young people with humility. The efforts of HHS are but a "moment" in the decolonial struggle. After all, during the writing of this chapter, HUSD closed its only ethnic studies program, a project initiated at HHS. For a moment in time, the school's decision to listen to students' words and actions was a step in the right direction to arriving at a fuller notion of the decolonial truth. The road toward reconciliation will require energy, humility, resources, youth voice, regaining trust, and a concerted effort to implement ethnic studies for all youth, as Gabriel wisely suggested. The cost in resources will be substantial, as it should be; the cost of not moving in this direction is infinite. How do you measure the harm created by punitive actions (associated with the criminal justice system) of black and brown youth? What is the psychological cost of not being culturally seen or heard? How do you quantify the racial battle scars associated with surviving what scholars are calling the "educational survival complex" (Love, 2019). The cost of not moving toward a decolonial effort is moral, cultural, and spiritual bankruptcy.

This chapter is an opportunity to illustrate how one school chose to lean into discomfort and listen to the voices of young people. It is crucial to capture moments in time when our educational leaders do not respond based on fear, lies, and punitive course of actions even though this is modeled for them in society at large. We must remember moments in time when school leaders chose to double down on our community's most precious resource, our youth. My hope is that these moments can be a source of strength for our communities and serve as "precious community memory" (Yosso and Burciaga, 2016). In fact, our future depends on it.

REFERENCES

Acosta, C. (2007). Developing critical consciousness: Resistance literature in a Chicano literature class. *English Journal, 97*(2) 36–42.

Acuña, R. (2000). *Occupied America: a History of Chicanos* (4th ed.). New York: Longman.
Aguilera, J. (2019, October 25). Here's What to Know About the Status of Family Separation at the U.S. Border, Which Isn't Nearly Over. *Time*. Retrieved from https://time.com.
Arce, M. S. (2016). *Xicana/o indigenous epistemologies: Towards a decolonizing and liberatory education for Xicana/o youth.* Whitewashing American Education: The New Culture Wars in Ethnic Studies, *1*, 11–41.
Bartolome, L. (1994). Beyond the methods fetish: Toward a humanizing pedagogy. *Harvard Educational Review, 64*(2), 173–195.
Cabrera, N. L., Milem, J. F., Jaquette, O., & Marx, R. W. (2014). Missing the (student achievement) forest for all the (political) trees: Empiricism and the Mexican American studies controversy in Tucson. *American Educational Research Journal, 51*(6), 1084–1118.
California Department of Education. (2018). *Cohort Outcome Data for Class of 2015-2016.* Retrieved from https://www.cde.ca.gov.
Caraballo, L., Martinez, D. C., Paris, D., & Alim, H. S. (2020). Culturally sustaining pedagogies in the current moment: A conversation with Django Paris and H. Samy Alim. *Journal of Adolescent & Adult Literacy, 63*(6), 697–701.
Carreón, O. (2018). *Effective Teaching of Chican@/Latin@ students: A Community Responsive Approach.* Davis: University of California.
Domonoske, C., & Gonzalez, R. (2018, June 19). What We Know: Family Separation And 'Zero Tolerance' At The Border. *NPR*. Retrieved from https://www.npr.org.
Gray, M. (2019). Blocking the bathroom: Latino students and the spatial arrangements of student discipline. *Critical Education, 10*(2), 1–15.
Holmes, A., & González, N. (2017). Finding sustenance: An indigenous relational pedagogy. In D. Paris & H. S. Alim (Eds.), *Culturally Sustaining Pedagogies: Teaching and Learning for Justice in a Changing World* (pp. 207–224). New York: Teachers College Press.
Love, B. L. (2019). *We Want To Do More Than Survive: Abolitionist Teaching and the Pursuit of Educational Freedom.* Boston: Beacon Press.
Maldonado-Torres, N. (2007). On the coloniality of being. *Cultural Studies, 21*(2), 240–270. doi:10.1080/09502380601162548.
Montoya, M. (2016). *Chicano Movement for Beginners.* Danbury: For Beginners.
Paris, D. (2012). Culturally sustaining pedagogy: A needed change in stance, terminology, and practice. *Educational Researcher, 41*(3), 93–97.
Phillips, A. (2017, June 16). 'They're rapists.' President Trump's campaign launch speech two years later, annotated. *The Washington Post*. Retrieved from https://www.washingtonpost.com.
Pizarro, M. (1998). Contesting dehumanization: Chicana/o spiritualization, revolutionary possibility, and the curriculum. *Aztlán: A Journal of Chicano Studies, 23*(1), 55–76.
Raible, J., & Irizarry, J. G. (2010). Redirecting the teacher's gaze: Teacher education, youth surveillance and the school-to-prison pipeline. *Teaching and Teacher Education, 26*(5), 1196–1203.

Rios, V. M. (2006). The hyper-criminalization of Black and Latino male youth in the era of mass incarceration. *Souls: A Critical Journal of Black Politics, Culture, and Society, 8*, 40–54.

Rodríguez, R. (2012). Tucson's maiz-based curriculum: MAS-TUSD profundo. *Nakum Journal, 2*(1), 72–98.

Shire, W. (2020). "Poem of the Day 'Give Your Daughters Difficult Names.'" *English Department,* english.duke.edu/news/poem-day-give-your-daughters-difficult-names.

Smith, L. T. (1999). *Decolonizing methodologies: Research and Indigenous peoples.* London; Dunedin, New Zealand: Zed Books; University of Otago Press.

Strom, K. J., & Martin, A. D. (2017). Thinking with theory in an era of Trump. *Issues in Teacher Education, 26*(3), 3–22.

Valenzuela, A. (1999). *Subtractive schooling: US-Mexican youth and the politics of caring.* Albany: Suny Press.

Villanueva, S. T. (2013). Teaching as a healing craft: Decolonizing the classroom and creating spaces of hopeful resistance through Chicano-Indigenous pedagogical praxis. *The Urban Review, 45*(1), 23–40.

Yosso, T. J. (2006). *Critical Race Counterstories Along the Chicana/Chicano Educational Pipeline.* New York: Routledge.

Yosso, T. J., & Burciaga, R. (2016). Reclaiming our histories, recovering community cultural wealth. *Center for Critical Race Studies at UCLA Research Brief, 5*.

Section II

VOICES OF TEACHERS

Introduction
The Making of a Radical Educator
Melody Esqueda

At the time of the 2016 presidential election, I was volunteering at a middle school in the South LA area. Roughly 90% of the student population was Latinx and all qualified for free or reduced lunch. The day after Trump was elected, it was nearly impossible for our curriculum to move forward as planned. As one of my Harvard professors once said, "A good teacher knows when to pause instruction to deal with real-life news that impacts your kids." We had many students take absences, and the few that did show up did with blood-shot eyes and matted hair. Some of the younger students asked if the president was going to deport their mothers. Overall, there was a feeling of despair in the air, and some of my students questioned what the point of school was anyway when so many of the issues that affected them directly seemed so far away and out of their hands. It is in times like these that radical steps need to be taken to help remind adolescents that they do have the power to be heard and make real change. Rather than school being seen as something distant and cut off from reality, it was necessary to help them understand that when powered by their community, teachers, and mentors, they can take active roles in advocating for their marginalized groups. Especially in today's political climate where students are seeing and hearing messages that they are not enough, it is necessary for radical educators to remind students of the fact that you see them, that their voice matters, and that they are worthy of both self-love and community love.

As an undergraduate at the University of Southern California, I had the unique experience of pursuing higher education right in the heart of the neighborhood I grew up in. As a first-generation college student, I entered very confused about what to study and what options there were. By my sophomore year, I decided to pursue Narrative Studies because I was fascinated by the power personal narratives and storytelling have to make change, strengthen community, and build empathy. Although I had grown up just a 20-minute drive from the university, it became evident during my time as a student that many of the research opportunities and resources made available by the university remained guarded behind its red brick walls.

In my junior year, I distinctly remember being in an air-conditioned lecture hall one Wednesday afternoon, with the latest technology and accommodations. One hour later I moved off campus to a small room across the street that housed a tutoring center for high school youth in the area. The room had very little ventilation, not nearly enough chairs, and one laptop for roughly every four students. We were working on college applications for the rising seniors, and I remember watching so many of the students idly waiting around for their turn to use one of the tutors' laptops. Some of them never even got around to their turn. But even in the 90° Los Angeles heat in a crowded basement with no windows, the students I was set to tutor were nothing short of excited to find out I was working with them. One of the young women of color I was working with told me I was the first Latina college student she had come across and that she would have been more inclined to look into the college process had she had more mentors and teachers of color. Some of the students in the program who lived in South Central LA had never even stepped on campus. One of my students told me, "USC is in our hood but it doesn't feel like it." Some of the greatest changes to systems come from within, but it is difficult to access these ideas if we do not provide spaces to validate and highlight the resiliency that exists in our underrepresented populations. So I work with youth to help access knowledge, ideas, and new ways of thinking that are already present in our communities.

Although my mind was set on the path of an educator, it was met with some resistance from my Latinx community. As the oldest of four siblings and the first in my family to graduate with a college degree, I understand my role as a caretaker and mentor. But while I understand the financial risks, I wish to be a teacher of color that can serve as a mentor for students that just need a little push to achieve their goals. It's not uncommon for people to ask why I'd want to "come back to the hood when [I] had a free ticket out with a college degree." But I've always viewed education as a tool to be used to access the networks, resources, and wisdom necessary to come back and make change through education.

As a student myself, I almost didn't even apply to the Harvard Graduate School of Education because I couldn't afford the application fee, and I doubted my potential to get accepted. When my welcome to Harvard letter did arrive, I cried from excitement but was also feeling apprehensive. Coming to Harvard directly from undergrad as a first-generation Latina from the West Coast, I was met with my first real experience of imposter syndrome and culture shock (until I began networking with students from similar backgrounds).

I signed up right away for a "First Generation College Student Workshop" spearheaded by Anthony Abraham Jack who would later release his book "The Privileged Poor: How Elite Colleges Are Failing Disadvantaged Students" that same year. With his friendly candor and heartwarming smile, he spoke to the very few people who showed up and explained that this was the first-year Harvard even had a first-generation workshop for graduate students. Between not knowing what office hours were but being expected to go, and having the additional responsibility of having to support his family while in college, Jack knew that first-generation college students need extra supports. He explained that the university had first-generation programs and workshops for undergraduate students but that at the graduate level they were nowhere to be found because "the research showed most first-gens didn't make it all the way to graduate school."

As a first-generation college student himself, though, he knew this wasn't true and wanted to support the few of us that were there. I was left feeling more inspired to make sure my students knew that it was possible to take up space in institutions historically not meant for people like them. At every step, there was someone who may have doubted our speaker's potential, and every other person in the room. But here we were at Harvard as low-income, black and brown, first-gens committed to social change through education. Helping students realize that they too can have a voice in elite spaces, is a radical act. I also make sure my students know that elite universities are lucky to have them in the first place and that they are coming onto campus with a great amount of cultural wealth.

As a student-teacher working in a very different community context than my own, I realized during my year of student-teaching that it was going to be key to partner with stakeholders in the community. I wanted to make a conscious effort to be intentional and thoughtful about ways I learned about and joined the city I was teaching in but felt cut off because of how far I was from the city. At the time of my student-teaching, I was taking three buses every day, and it took me roughly two hours to make it to my school site because I lived so far from the closest T-station or subway stations. With transportation getting increasingly difficult, I reached out to see if anyone could help temporarily house me.

Luckily, I was offered a room in the home of two activists (and recent empty nesters) in the community who were deeply tied to the city. Their daughter had recently graduated from the same high school I was doing my student-teaching in, and both took up active roles in local politics and non-profits in the area. The husband was an elected official on the City Council and the wife led co-counseling circles for youth in the area as a safe space for their feelings to be expressed. Their daughter also happened to be affiliated with an eco-justice nonprofit in the city that one of my students was working for during the school year. It was through affiliation with this lovely family and the individuals I met through them that I was able to learn about things such as the recent gentrification of the city and local politics. Engaging with key community stakeholders like the local politicians, artists, nonprofit managers, and activists in the city after my move, greatly improved how I navigated my student-teaching (especially as someone new to the area).

I refer to myself as a "radical" educator because I grew impatient about waiting around for the change I wanted to see. Rather, I understood that if anyone should have a voice when it comes to community change, it should be individuals from those very communities. As a beginning teacher, I intentionally work lessons into my teaching that focus on voice, power, public advocacy, and radical self-love. This is an empowering process through which students come to understand their own power, that they are indeed worthy of a great education, and that their unique intersectionalities and cultural wealth are a source of beauty and not shame. I ask my students to think about whose voices are typically heard by the public and why their voices—either because of their age, social class, gender expression, or ethnicity—tend to take a back seat in these discussions. That being said, I try to help them understand the power they have in their voices, and things they can do to advocate for themselves and their communities as the powerful youth they are. In class, my students hold many academic discussions. One example of this was when we read a few vignettes from *The House On Mango Street* and engaged in a fish bowl–style discussion around gender norms in minority households, both as reflected in the book and from our own homes.

No matter our context, it only takes a few crucial steps to network with community members, hear the voices of students, and partner with parents in authentic ways. Without these steps, my teaching feels cut off from the needs of the community. Our students are powerful and beautiful. It is through schools that teachers can remind the youth of their true power and challenge political climates that seek to rewrite this narrative. While I don't think every community-centered teacher needs to be *from* the communities they teach in, I *do* believe it takes intention, patience, and a willingness to go out of the way to create authentic relationships that allow teachers to critically engage in practices that highlight and value the communities in which they serve. And in the challenging sociopolitical times, these practices are increasingly necessary so that schools, parents, students, and community members can be in nourishing partnerships that stimulate growth, value and build on cultural wealth, and cultivate radical self-love.

Chapter 4

Rising Up to Lead in the Post-Truth Era

A Teacher's Path from the Classroom to City Hall

Laura Gomez and Ruth Luevanos

In September 2017, almost a year after the 45th president of the United States was elected, the state of California passed Senate Bill 54 that declared California to be a sanctuary state by preventing local and state agencies from using resources to "investigate, interrogate, detain, detect or arrest individuals" for immigration purposes (Ulloa, 2017). SB54 was approved as a counterreaction to a growing political rhetoric and policies passed targeting marginalized populations. Furthermore, SB54 was also approved with the intent to protect immigrants without legal residency as a result of the deportation orders under the Trump administration (Ulloa, 2017). Subsequently, on March 2018 former general attorney Jeff Sessions announced that his Department of Justice was suing California for "obstructing justice" (Lind, 2018). This disagreement between the federal government and the state of California's role of local and state law enforcement in enforcing immigration laws triggered a bigger conversation that led to actions between groups of Californians that were actively supporting California's measure to become a sanctuary state and those groups that were not.

   This political division expanded to all forms of private and public sectors in California's societal systems leading to anti-Mexican, anti-immigrant, xenophobic, hate rhetoric present in this post-truth era where facts are viewed as irrelevant in comparison to personal opinions and beliefs. This hate rhetoric has been met with a resistance against intolerance and exclusion of historically marginalized groups such as immigrants. The current political rhetoric of division and the criminalization of marginalized communities has given rise to a broader resistance through teacher leadership in order to effectuate broader change.

Through the use of testimonios as a methodological tool (Delgado, 2013; Aleman, 2010; Delgado and Stefancic, 2001; Burciaga, 1993), this chapter reflects a collaboration between the two authors and explores the second author's (Ruth) personal journey as a teacher from the classroom to city hall. The authors explore the social, political, cultural, and educational context that shaped her experiences as a teacher from underrepresented communities in the greater Los Angeles area and as a result, led her to serve as a council woman in city hall. Ruth's testimonio reveals personal and political fights for educational equity and social justice as a leader teacher and advocate for the inclusion of historically marginalized groups. As a Latina first-generation college student and K-12 educator in predominantly Latinx low-working-class communities, Ruth's testimonio "bears witness" to the current political rhetoric of division and the criminalization of marginalized communities which has given rise to a broader resistance through involvement in leadership to enact broader change. This form of resistance is enacted through leadership in order to change structural inequalities present within our societal systems. Through Ruth's testimonio, we also illuminate the hope, resiliency, and resistance residing within this same narrative analyzed through a LatCrit theoretical framework which examines the ways Latinx experience race, class, gender, as well the Latinx experience issues of nationality, language, immigration status, ethnicity, and culture (Bernal, 2002; Pérez Huber, 2010; Solorzano & Delgado Bernal, 2001).

WHO ARE TEACHER LEADERS?

Defining the meaning of what is or who is a teacher leader can be identified as subjective. However, it is clear that those teachers that advocate for students and the teaching profession itself is a good indicator of a teacher leader (Jacques, Weber, Bosso, Olson & Bassett, 2016). According to the National Network of State Teachers of the Year (NNSTOY, 2015) teacher leadership is:

> The process by which highly effective educators take on roles at the classroom, school, district, state, or national levels in order to advance the profession, improve educator effectiveness, and/or increase access to great teaching and learning for all students.

Furthermore, teacher leaders take on roles outside the classroom that will impact students and teacher peers in the classroom and as a result, they advocate and support the professional learning of peers, they influence policy and/or decision making which ultimately has an impact on student learning (Wenner & Campbell, 2017). The theory behind the support of teacher leadership can best be explained as a micro- to macro-influence approach. This micro to macro approach is the idea that accomplished teachers' influence will transcend from the classroom to school and fellow district teachers, to school administrators, to policymakers and beyond (Illinois State; College of Education, 2016). Advocates for teacher leadership support and development argue that leadership opportunities for teachers can be an investment in the teaching profession because they will have the opportunity to improve teaching and learning throughout their schools, districts, and states. These improvements can be represented by the teachers' expertise in the classroom that can then serve as a bridge to link policy with best teaching practices based on teacher informed decisions about instruction and curriculum which will ultimately impact student success (Illinois State; College of Education, 2016).

On the other hand, there is growing scholarship that has identified teacher leaders in terms of a way of thinking and being, as a way of taking a stance, and not as a set of behaviors and characteristics that can be identified and reproduced (Carver, 2016; Poekert et al., 2016; Smulyan, 2016). Nonetheless, it is important to provide stories outside of the status quo–dominant culture in order to disrupt normative myths about the Latinx experience as well as to reinforce collective resistance, cultural survival, and solidarity (Brabeck, 2003). For this reason, the counter-story presented in this chapter is utilized to highlight the narrative of Ruth as a Latina teacher leader navigating education as well as political and societal systems in a post-truth era. Ruth's activism and, therefore, her social justice consciousness have risen to enact change in the classroom and beyond.

Moreover, teachers' backgrounds and identities such as race, gender, and socioeconomic status can be amplified through teacher leadership and can also impact underrepresented communities. It is important to have teacher leaders from underrepresented communities who are navigating societal systems as they continue to be underrepresented in education leadership roles because of identified time requirements and restrictions, lack of district and administration support, as well as racial barriers (Durias, 2010).

THEORETICAL FRAMEWORK

The authors utilize LatCrit in order to examine the effects of a post-truth era in the field of education and specifically, with Latinx teacher leaders and their students whose communities have been singled out, attacked, and criminalized through the political rhetoric present in this post-truth era. Building on Critical Race Theory (CRT), Latino/a Critical Race Theory (LatCrit) seeks to expand the exploration of civil rights analysis beyond race which is at the center of CRT (Aoki and Johnson, 2008). This expansion by LatCrit to go beyond race challenges the dominant discourse by highlighting the Latinx lived experiences (Bernal, 2002; Pérez Huber 2010; Solorzano & Delgado Bernal, 2001). LatCrit is concerned with a progressive sense and consensus in the Latinx shared experiences specifically with ethnicity (Valdes, 1996), and seeks to better articulate the experiences of the Latinx community through a more focused examination of their unique, but shared experiences (Pérez Huber, 2010; Solorzano & Delgado Bernal, 2001). LatCrit is utilized to expose the ways Latinx individuals experience race, class, gender, and sexuality, as well as acknowledging the ways Latinx experience issues of nationality, language, immigration status, ethnicity, and culture (Bernal, 2002; Pérez Huber, 2010; Solorzano & Delgado Bernal, 2001). Furthermore, LatCrit challenges the immigration discourse set in the dominant concepts about the topic that have distorted and erased the experiences of naturalized and undocumented Latinas/os.

As a result, LatCrit is based and ascends as a political movement rather than a racial movement (Iglesias & Valdez 1998), and attempts to link scholarship with teaching, theory with practice and the academy with the community (LatCrit Primer, 1999). Moreover, LatCrit examines other tenets that highly influence the Latino experience such as nationality, language, and immigration status, which CRT does not. As a result, we utilize LatCrit in order to examine the effects of a post-truth era in the field of education and specifically with Latinx teacher leaders and their students whose communities have been singled out, attacked, and criminalized through the political rhetoric present in this post-truth era.

METHODS

Counter-storytelling are counter-narratives that provide stories outside of the status quo–dominant culture (Yosso, 2009; Aleman, 2010). They provide stories and experiences from historically disenfranchised groups such as African American, Native American, and Latinx people (Aleman, 2010; Burciaga, 1993; Crow Dog, 1991). Furthermore, counter-stories are oral histories or testimonios utilized by disenfranchised groups to disrupt mainstream ideas of knowledge, of truth, and of normative knowledge production and acceptance that reproduce the status quo of the dominant culture (Delgado, 2013; Delgado & Stephancic, 2001). In the same way, testimonios are utilized by

Latinx communities to disrupt normative myths about the Latinx experience as well as to reinforce collective resistance, cultural survival, and solidarity (Brabeck, 2003). Furthermore, testimonios acknowledge and conserve cultural community knowledge that has existed in a generational collective memory and utilized as a resource against racism, classism, nativism, and other forms of oppression that have affected communities of color (Pérez Huber, 2009, Yosso, 2009). Testimonios include the narratives of an individual who is moved to tell their "true testimonio" pushed by an experience that merits the urgency in telling their oral histories usually associated with stories of injustices and the effects of those injustices on the individual(s) and communities (Brabeck, 2003; Yudice, 1991) that simple interviews might overlook. Ultimately, testimonios are utilized as a tool to dismantle racial and social injustice by revealing the oppression that pushes communities of color toward the margins of society in an attempt to end the same oppressive conditions and move toward social justice (Pérez Huber, 2009). As a result, our use of testimonios as a methodology follows these scholars who have previously utilized this form of interview to explore and highlight the oral histories of populations whose stories do not integrate within the acceptable norms of the status quo. Specifically, we will utilize testimonios in education through a Latino CRT lens in order to challenge the dominant discourse by highlighting the Latinx lived experiences which go beyond race relations (Bernal 2002; Pérez Huber 2010; Solorzano & Delgado Bernal 2001) in examining the effects of a post-truth era with teacher leaders.

Ruth enjoys a unique dual role as a full-time teacher and an elected official whose identity origins are attached to Mexican, working, immigrant communities. She has taught English learners as well as gifted and special needs students in Title I low-income K-12 public schools in the country's second largest school district for 20 years. She was elected councilwoman in the city in which she resides. As a longtime teacher leader and recently elected local official, Ruth feels empowered to effectuate policy that impacts the residents in the city. She is able to advocate for funding and policy changes on state and federal levels by bringing her real-world classroom experience and those of her students and their families to forums where these policies are being shaped. She had met with state and federal representatives to address and advocate for education funding, gun violence issues, addressing domestic abuse, and immigration policies which directly impact her at-risk students and their families. In turn, policy makers have sought Ruth's expertise as a union teacher leader, as a National Board Certified teacher and as a Latina to reach out to the Latinx community, help at-risk students, and deal with collective bargaining issues.

The first author facilitated Ruth's testimonio using 17 semi-structured open-ended questions (Brenner, 2006; Kvale, 1996). The interviews tapped four main areas of interest: (1) General Demographic Information; (2) Education; (3) Teaching Experiences; and (4) Current and Future Plans.

Data Analysis

The testimonio was analyzed using descriptive coding (Miles, Huberman, & Sandaña, 2014; Sandelowski, 2000. We utilized Miles, Huberman, and Saldaña's (2014) descriptive method approach to qualitative data, in which symbolic meaning is attached to the information that was gathered through Ruth's testimonio. The authors read through the transcripts, creating codes for the testimonio data. They identified topics within the four themes that highlighted the experiences of Ruth as a teacher leader, as a Latina raised by immigrant working-class parents, and as an advocate for social justice. These contexts may have influenced her career choices in education, her activism, and her path to become the first Latinx council woman in her urban community city council.

RESULTS

Shaping a Teacher Leader

One policy that Ruth remembers shaping her experience as a young student was being bussed from her working-class Latinx community school to a different community school as part of the desegregation movement:

> We are all part of the outcome of the desegregation movement. And so again since our last name was a Mexican/Spanish surname, we were chosen to desegregate the white schools in Northridge so we were bussed from San Fernando to Dearborn Elementary. And we were you know, the poor bussed Mexican kids. You know, we had special lunch tickets. People knew that we were poor because of the special colored lunch tickets and because we had to work in the cafeteria.

This clear separation of students had an impact on Ruth, who was aware that she belonged in the group of students who worked in the cafeteria and as a result, it was clear to her that they were treated differently. This experience speaks to the potential for policies having negative long-standing effects on historically marginalized communities, even if the policies were intended to help those same communities:

> I did not think about it at the time but it was just something you had to do. Like another chore but you know now it's like why did we have to work in the cafeteria? You know hindsight is 20/20 right?

Ruth recognized that policies usually have positive and negative aspects and it is always important to allow different voices and experiences in the development and implementation of policies. Ruth identified the negatives and positives of being bussed as a policy that had a large impact on her education:

> We had a lot of opportunities that I think we wouldn't have had at the local school. We did miss out on the cultural life. We didn't have Cinco de Mayo. We didn't celebrate you know Spanish music but we went on field trips. We were part of the gifted program. There were a lot of opportunities we had at that school that we wouldn't have had at the local school. We went on at least two field trips every year. I got to learn Shakespeare and Robert Frost and Emily Dickenson, and I can say we had a kiln, so we got to do clay, we got to raise chickens we got to do a lot of hands on stuff. I mean there was a lot of stuff that we got to do at that school that didn't happen at the local elementary. So we were appreciative of a lot of our opportunities and I think that really helped prepare us.

Ruth also identified her parent's expectations and influence in her and her siblings' education choices and her experiences navigating the education system as a first-generation college student:

> So both my parents having been the oldest siblings in their families, they had this philosophy of you know you have to get this done. And my oldest sister, I think always felt that pressure because she's the oldest. You know she got the worst, I think my dad said she was the train, everyone else are the caboose so the way you go, is the way everyone else will go. So she definitely felt more pressure.

Her educational path was definitely tied to familial expectations either by accepting those expectations or pushing them away:

> You know, in my senior year, I said I want to do community service. So I ended up being a peer educator. I had to justify to my dad why I was not going to play softball that year. He couldn't understand why I would want to do community service like "Why are you going to work for free?" And I'm like because I want to help people. And then I went away to college. I was the only one. All of my siblings went to college in Irvine so they were very close by. I was the only one to go away to college. I went to George Washington University in Washington D.C. because I wanted to be an FBI agent. That was like I was determined to go into law enforcement. That was my destiny was to be you know the Latina version of Clarice Starling.

As part of the Latinx familial experience, family expectations and responsibilities included being active members of the family and helping out economically or otherwise. This is true of many Latinx families, especially for the children of immigrant parents. These expectations can shape the higher education experience of Latinx students and their career choices in order to meet family expectations.

> After college, I decided I needed to be home. My grandfather had passed away. My sister was having my nephews and I felt like I needed to be home. So I came back to L.A. for law school which was quite a transition.

Her desire for teaching was awoken when, after graduating from Loyola Law School, she took the bar exam and while waiting for the results, was encouraged by a friend to apply for a substitute teacher position. So she did apply and she got hired, and as a result never left teaching. Since then, all of her training and certifications has been geared toward teaching and has been paired with her past degrees. She is National Board Certified in Early Adolescent Social Studies. She has a Multiple Subject credential and a Single Subject credential in social studies from California, a bachelor's degree in Criminal Justice from George Washington University, a law degree from Loyola Law School, and a Masters in Instructional Leadership. Furthermore, although she loves teaching and has no intention of leaving the classroom anytime soon, she has learned that her pathway lies in policy because she feels she can be effectuating change at a larger scale through policy.

> When I got the opportunity to run for city council I said it's not educational policy per se. But, it is a leadership position where I could work with the youth council. I can have some influence. I can be a good influence in my community as a Latina, as the first Latina for city council. And that did definitely matter to me. We have only had one Latino city council member for the past 20 years. The same person for 20 years.

Ruth stated that she never planned on being a teacher but that she always knew she would work with people. She worked for social justice causes in high school, college, and law school, whether it was advocating for the homeless, working for public interest immigration law firms, or being a bilingual juvenile probation officer. When she was hired as a teacher for the country's second largest school district, she thought of it as a temporary position that would help her transition to public interest law once she got her bar exam results. However, the more time she spent in the classroom, the more she realized that her prior experiences made her a good fit for teaching in that she would be able to provide the support that her students and their families so sorely needed. In her 20 years teaching at Title I schools, she stated that everything in her educational background and work experiences has helped her be a better teacher. For example, she says that she has used her background in the law to help advocate for and connect resources to her immigrant students and their families which, in turn, has motivated her immigrant students to do better in school and be more motivated to graduate and go to college. Her educational background, bilingual skills, and rapport with students and their families spurred many of her colleagues at school to invite her to participate in student intervention programs, professional development, and teacher leadership opportunities, such as grant writing.

> So we wrote a Pac Bell grant for $50,000 dollars and we got a computer lab for the parents and taught the parents computer classes and we had a great grant writing committee. So every Friday we would get together and the kids would go play with the T.As. And we would write grants and it was just a wonderful atmosphere in terms of collegiality and learning from each other and growing. We had a program called Tame C's for at risk kids. We started a soccer league and we taught the kids how to play soccer. We went on field trips. We had mentor youths from CSUN who came and mentored the kids and we taught them conflict mediation.

Justice and Teaching

Ruth's 20 years teaching at Title I schools with at-risk youth and their families as well as her background in criminology helps her understand and advocate for the importance and implementation of wrap around services:

> Every aspect of the wrap around services that I had gotten to do as a juvenile probation officer in Arlington, Virginia, I was doing it now by providing support at school and I think when you reflect on it now like I think that's what the appeal was to me. And so I wanted to bring that work everywhere that I went because those kids so desperately needed that support and the parents and the community needed a beacon of light and hope. You know I think I felt drawn to that.

As a result, she advocated for justice through wrap around services:

> Restorative justice only works when you have the wrap around support services and that is why the only place where it worked was in the Bay Area where they provided the wraparound support service. So I have seen restorative justice

work but you have to have all the components. So it is like saying you're going to make a sandwich and all you have is baloney. When all you have is baloney you don't have bread or mayonnaise or cheese then it is not a sandwich. It is just baloney. And so restorative justice doesn't work unless you have the wrap around support services.

Her experience working with low-income Latinx students has also helped her identify how policies can have negative effects on the students who are already at the margins of society. She shared how the policy restricting any kind of physical contact between teachers and students impacted her own relationship with students:

There's been too many lawsuits. Don't give the kids a high five if they do a good job and don't get too close. And honestly there's been times when that kid just needed a hug because they had such a horrible day and they are dealing with so much at home or you wanted to congratulate them for graduating. You know it's just a human component to console someone when they are going through a difficult time in their lives. It's just humanity. And it's gone because we are so worried about lawsuits. Sometimes just a pat on the back just say hey everything's going to be OK but we can't even do that anymore. That, I think definitely took the human component out of teaching, which is sad. Because it was detrimental to the kids more than anyone else.

Ruth identified budget deficits as one of the most negative policies affecting her classroom in more ways than one:

I talked to an assembly member the other day and she said I don't understand why you guys aren't getting raises. What's going on? Because we've increased funding to the schools by 30 percent in California, and I said, well it hasn't come to me. I've worked in classrooms and this has impacted me personally, and a number of teachers. I've worked in classrooms with mold, asbestos, no air conditioning, water full of lead, 42 to 45 kids crammed in a classroom. I mean having no desks, or chairs. And textbooks from 1999.

The lack of funding has also affected the ability of schools to allocate funding for mental health counselors. This is particularly detrimental to Latinx students, whose families do not always choose to access the community resources for mental health because there is still so much cultural stigma attached to these issues.

I think if there was one thing that I would require of all schools in order to reduce shootings it's not a security guard, it would be mental health and trauma counseling, to give every school a mental health counselor instead of more security guards.

The issues affecting Ruth's classroom have been further affected by Trump-era rhetoric. After all, schools are micro-representations of our broader society and therefore our values and beliefs as a society are reflected within our educational institutions. For this reason, the prevalence of anti-Mexican, anti-immigrant, anti-diversity rhetoric can be reflected in our school institutions, which can inform Ruth's experience expressed below:

> I was at a school right down the street here in Northridge the day Trump got elected. And the very next day, I went to that middle school where I was teaching and kids were chanting, and this was like a 78 percent Latino school, and the rest were you know a mix of mostly white. And some of the white kids were in the hallways so emboldened to say "Build a wall, build a wall! You stay over there on the Mexican side!" in the school hallways. I had to tell several students to knock it off. I was very upset because the administration refused to even acknowledge that it was an issue.

As a result of the unacknowledged forms of aggression in and outside of the school, Ruth took it into her own hands to help those students who were affected by the aggressions.

> So I had to create a sanctuary in my classroom. I think that's what I pride myself on the most is that I've always created a classroom that's a place of safety, whether it's for reading or discussing controversial topics or whatever. They just feel like they can come and talk to me about pretty much anything. And I created that environment in my classroom so that they felt safe knowing what was coming down the pipeline with Trump. You know we were all shocked, I think, when he was elected. But I put on my door, someone had posted online and I copied it and put it on my door and it said "Dear black students, in this classroom your life matters, you are loved. Dear Muslim students, we know you aren't terrorists, you are loved. Dear Mexican students, we know you are not rapists or drug dealers, you are loved. Dear LGBTQ, you are perfect just the way you are, do not change, you are loved."

Ruth's quote above serves as an example of how this hate is also creating an opportunity for building stronger communities.

> In November after the election I had 60 to 70 kids crammed in my classroom every day during break and lunchtime because it was a safe place for them. It

was a place where they felt like they weren't going to get bullied because they were in one of those categories.

Ruth also shared how as part of creating safe spaces, it is imperative to teach students how to build community, support each other, have allies, and learn to be critical consumers of information.

> We have very much been pitted against each other. I think Trevor Noah said it best in his book. I love Trevor Noah so I'm going to quote him. He said you know "apartheid was really apart hate." Which is that you get the groups within a region or an area to fight against each other then they don't realize that you're robbing them blind. You know pretty much that's what we have right now. We have so much hate and division and fear amongst each other that we don't see the bigger picture of what's really happening in the world. People are so caught up in their own bubble world that they don't see what's outside of that. And so I think we need to go back and teach history and not just civic engagement. There's been a lot of talk about civic engagement and I'm not against civic engagement as a matter of fact I'm very pro civic engagement. I've done mock elections and mock trials in my classroom for the last 20 years. Matter of fact I'm starting another one tomorrow but civic engagement is only effective if you understand the history behind it. And ALL the history needs to be taught not just selective history that's in textbooks that we were given but actually going back to teaching the content standards. We have excellent content standards in the state of California. I'm very proud of the people I know who have helped collaborate to write them. But we have too many teachers that teach to the textbook. You have too many school districts that you know that insist that teachers teach in the textbook instead of teaching to the content standards which is what we are really required to teach as educators.

Implications for Curriculum

Ruth identified how she uses curriculum to teach students about being critical consumers of information. This includes teaching students about nativism and nationalism prevalent in political rhetoric. She explained why social studies is a perfect vehicle to deliver such a curriculum:

> We have to go back to teaching social studies. Social studies is everything that is why I love Social Studies. It is math, it's statistics, and data, and numbers, and timelines and it's spatial skills like timelines, and it's geography and it is reading and writing and speaking and arguing and writing persuasive essays or argumentative writing, narratives and reading narratives and it's science because you're looking at scientific discoveries and explorations and it's

English obviously. I mean it's every subject area that's why I'm so passionate about social sciences because it's every subject area. I get to teach every subject area when I teach social studies. And I think you need to go back to the Social Studies which has been diminished so much from the curriculum.

Furthermore, she uses her personal experiences as well as those of other minority candidates running for office as a way to show her students there is a way to overcome and fight back.

So my kids are excited to see me running for political office. Even though it's you know, it's somewhere else because they've never met a Latina from immigrant parents who is as educated as I am and dared to go back and wants to teach at a school like the school at which I teach and loves it. And that is now running for political office in their eyes it is some sort of power or ability to effectuate change and shift. And I think it inspires them. You know, whether I win or not, I think it's inspired them to say hey I had a teacher once that ran for city council maybe I'll do that one day maybe I'll be like that, you know. I just told them about the governor. This woman was running for governor in Texas. She's the first LGBTQ Latina and my students were going nuts.

In a social and political context full of division, uncertainty, and hateful rhetoric, Ruth refuses to only see the negative in all of it. She explained that although this new era is causing growing pains, at the end of the day, it can serve as an opportunity for growth, change, and community building:

So it's just a scary time. But at the same time there's a lot of room for inspiration and hope and change and activism. And we're getting united and motivated in ways that we haven't since the civil rights era. So it is scary what we're up against and what we're fighting but it's also an opportunity that we haven't had in a long time to do right, to inspire, to make effective change.

IMPLICATIONS

What lasting impact do teacher leaders like Ruth have on their students, in their schools, and in their communities? Is this impact more profound given the social, political, and economic challenges that her students, their families, and their communities are facing? While she was running for office many of Ruth's students as well as their family members became directly involved in promoting civic participation and voting. Over 33 students registered to vote, nine students were trained to work as poll workers on election day, and dozens of students created posters to promote voting at their local community polling places.

Having teacher leaders who serve as bridges, advocates, and role models for their students and communities is critical. Because teachers serve as important models for civic engagement, it is imperative that we allow and support teacher endeavors to teach and connect students' experiences to civic life through social studies. This support may elevate the role of teachers by including them in reforming the sociopolitical context of our society and therefore, the classroom.

CONCLUSION

Moving forward, how can we cultivate more teacher leaders to take leadership roles in their Latinx communities? It is critically important to have Latinx teachers who come from similar backgrounds as their students and who advocate for them in and out of the classroom (Brabeck, 2003). Student may become more engaged when they see the sacrifices that their own teachers are making to achieve social change in their communities and in a larger societal role. Seeing teacher leaders who are active in local government also strengthens the connection and understanding of local issues which most directly impact students and their families. Most social studies curricula focus on federal and state government, but leave students with little to no understanding of local laws and government which have a much more direct impact on students' lives and their communities.

Political divisions in the United States have led to anti-Mexican, anti-immigrant, hateful rhetoric. This has been met with a resistance against intolerance and exclusion of historically marginalized groups. Ruth's testimonio delineates a path to leadership as a form of resistance to the current divisive rhetoric. We can support more teacher leaders by encouraging them to share their stories and identifying pathways to leadership through professional development. We should encourage interested teachers to get involved with community advocates who could help them seek local elected positions. All means of supporting teacher leaders will lead to better outcomes for marginalized students and provide role models for them to be inspired to advocate for themselves, both in their schools and communities.

REFERENCES

Alemán, Jr, E., & Alemaán, S. M. (2010). "Do Latin@ interests always have to 'converge' with White interest?": (Re)claiming racial realism and interest

convergence in critical race theory praxis. *Race Ethnicity and Education, 13*(1), 1–21.
Aoki, K., & Johnson, K. R. (2008). An assessment of Latcrit Theory ten years after. *Indiana Law Journal, 83*, 1151–1195.
Bernal, D. D. (2002). Critical race theory, Latino critical theory, and critical raced gendered epistemologies: Recognizing students of color as holders and creators of knowledge. *Qualitative Inquiry, 8*(1), 105–126. https://doi.org/10.1177/107780 040200800107.
Brabeck, K. (2003). Testimonio: A strategy for collective resistance, cultural survival and building solidarity. *Feminism Psychology, 13*(2), 252–258.
Brenner, M. E. (2006). Interviewing in educational research. In J. L. Green, G. Camili, & P. B. Elmore (Eds.), *Handbook of complementary methods in education research* (pp. 357–370). Washington, DC: Routledge.
Burciaga, J. A. (1993). *Drink ucltura: Chicanismo*. Santa Barbra, CA: Capra Press.
Carver, C. L. (2016). Transforming identities: The transition from teacher to leader during Teacher leader preparation. *Journal of Research on Leadership Education, 11*(2), 158–180.
Crow Dog, M. (1991). *Lakota woman*. New York: Harper perennial.
Delgado, R., & J. Stefancic. (2001). *Critical Race Theory: An Introduction*. New York: New York University Press.
Delgado, R. (2013). Storytelling for oppositionists and others. In R. Delgado & J. Stefancic (Eds.) *Critical Race Theory: The Cutting Edge* (3rd ed.). Philadelphia, PA: Temple University Press.
Durias, R. F. (2010). Teacher leaders of color: The impact of professional development on their leadership Available from ERIC. (964173261: ED524279). Retrieved from https://search.proquest.com/docview/964173261?accountid =14505.
Education Week (2018). Over 170 Teachers Ran for State Office in 2018. Here's What We Know About Them. https://www.edweek.org/ew/section/multimedia/teachers-runnng-for-state-office.html.
Huber, L. P. (2009). Disrupting apartheid of knowledge: "Testimonio" as methodology in Latina/o critical race research in education. *International Journal of Qualitative Studies in Education (QSE), 22*(6), 639–654.
Iglesias, E. M., & Valdes, F. (1998). Afterword: Religion, gender, sexuality, race and class in coalitional theory: A critical and self-critical analysis of Latcrit social justice agendas. *Chicano-Latino Law Review, 19*(503), 562–588.
Illinois State; College of Education. (2016). *Teacher Leadership Report. P-20 Teacher and Leadership Effectiveness Committee*.https://education.illinoisstate .edu/downloads/csep/Wallace%20TL%20Report%20Layout%20FINAL.pdf.
Jacques, C., Weber, G., Bosso, D., Olson, D., & Bassett, K. (2016). Great to influential: Teacher leaders' roles in supporting instruction. *AmericanInstitute for Research*. https://search.proquest.com/docview/2009555321?accountid=14505.
LatCrit Primer. (1999, April 29–May 5). *Fact sheet: LatCrit*. Presented at the 4th annual LatCrit conference, Rotating Centers, Expanding Frontiers: LatCrit Theory and Marginal Intersection, Lake Tahoe, Nevada.

Lind, D. (March 8th, 2018). *Sanctuary cities explained. Vox.com* https://www.vox.com/policy-and-politics/2018/3/8/17091984/sanctuary-cities-city-state-illegal-immigration-sessions.

Love, B. J. (2004). Brown plus 500 counter-storytelling: A critical race theory analysis of the "majoritarian achievements gap" story. *Equity & Excellence in Education, 37,* 227–246.

Miles, M. B., Huberman, A. M., & Sandaña, J. (2014). *Qualitative data analysis: A methods sourcebook* (3rd ed.). Thousand Oaks: Sage Publications.

National Network of State Teachers of the Year. (2015). *Our Strategic Plan.* http://www.nnstoy.org/about-us/our-strategic-plan/.

Perez Huber, L. (2010). Using Latina/o critical race theory (LatCrit) and racist nativism to explore intersectionality in the educational experiences of undocumented chicana college students. *Educational Foundations, 24*(1–2), 77–96.

Poekert, P., Alexandrou, A., & Shannon, D. (2016). How teachers become leaders: An internationally validated theoretical model of teacher leadership development. *Research in Post-Compulsory Education, 21*(4), 307–329.

Sandelowski, M. (2000). Focus on research methods: Whatever happened to qualitative description? *Research in Nursing and Health, 23*(4), 334–340.

Solórzano, D. G., & Delgado Bernal, D. (2001). Examining transformational resistance through a critical race and LatCrit theory framework: Chicana and Chicano students in an urban context. *Urban Education, 36*(3), 308–342.

Ulloa, J. (2017). Legislature declares California will be a Sanctuary State. Los-Angeles Times. https//www.latimas.com/politics/essential/la-pol-ca-essential-politics-updates-california-lawmakers-take-final-action-1505534909-htmlstory.html.

Valdes, F. (1996). Foreword: Latina/o ethnicities, critical race theory and post-identity politics in postmodern legal culture: From practices to possibilities. *La Raza Law Journal, 9,* 1–31.

Wenner, J. A., & Campbell, T. (2017). The theoretical and empirical basis of teacher leadership: A review of the literature. *Review of Educational Research, 87*(1), 134–171. http://dx.doi.org/10.3102/0034654316653478.

Yosso, T. J., Smith, W. A., Ceja, M., & Solórzano, D. G. (2009). Critical race theory. Racial microaggressions, and campus racial climate for Latina/o undergraduates. *Harvard Educational Review, 79*(4), 659–690.

Yudice, G. (1991). Testimonio and postmodernism. *Latin American Perspectives, 18*(3), 15–30.

Chapter 5

Unshifting Practices and Perspectives

Disrupting the Cycle through Anti-Racist Pedagogy

Christine Montecillo Leider,
Molly Ross, and Megan Schantz

INTRODUCTION

The single most defining moment of my first year of teaching was the morning of November 9, 2016. I woke up to the news of the presidential election in utter disbelief and fear. I will never forget that morning. I didn't know what to do, what to say, how to possibly make it through and be strong for my students, their families, etc. I could not move. I could not walk into a building of 1500 students, the majority of which would be deeply affected. I had my 28 SLIFE students, all undocumented, sitting in an advisory circle. We talked about our fears and questions, cried together, and eventually picked each other back up.—Megan

The day after Trump won the election was emotional for me. I had campaigned for Clinton and I was crushed when I woke to the news that our country elected Trump. But, like everyone else upset by the results, I pulled myself together and went off to work. I was truly not expecting the scene that I walked into. As the eighth-grade students filed onto the floor and headed to their lockers to get themselves ready for the day I started to hear the chants. A group of boys walked down the hall screaming, "We won! We won!" They were jumping up and down and egging each other on. Quickly things turned for the worse. They started telling the immigrant students to go home. The teachers were shocked by this behavior because while there had always been obvious tensions

> between students we had never witnessed something this out right. Most of the school had students that spoke another language at home and we had never experienced this type of language around immigrants before. Immediately the chants were stopped and the students filed into their homerooms to stop escalation. The eighth-grade teachers were forced to quickly hold a makeshift assembly to deal with the anger and hurt students were feeling. I know these tensions are not anything new and have been boiling below the surface. The election of Trump has given a voice and a power to that voice for people who want to blame immigrants. What happens in schools is exactly a mirror of what is happening outside of our schools.—Molly

The above excerpts are journal reflections from an early career teacher and a veteran teacher, respectively; the day after Trump won the election the two teachers were English as a Second Language (ESL) Teachers at public schools which predominantly served Latinx students. The nexus of our chapter stems from the line in Molly's journal *I know these tensions are not anything new and have been boiling below the surface. The election of Trump has given a voice and a power to that voice for people who want to blame immigrants.* While November 9, 2016, was a difficult day for many, it was not as if the population of people living in the United States woke up in a new racist country, rather the election of Trump had confirmed that we already lived in a deeply racist and anti-immigrant society. In our chapter, we offer insight into how this plays out in schools, particularly for Latinx students. Drawing from narrative research (Gudmundsdottir, 2001) we reconstructed narrative descriptions of how we've observed racism toward Latinx students in our work as educators. Through a series of meetings where we discussed these narratives, we discovered that our observations seemed to be the product of a similar cycle. We call this a cycle of unshifting perspectives and practices, and in this chapter, we argue that without anti-racist practices and pedagogy this cycle cannot shift. It is this unshifting cycle that led to the election of Trump and the ongoing racist, inequitable practices that Latinx students experience in public schools.

LATINX POPULATION: A MIS-INFORMED NARRATIVE

In line with the U.S. Census Bureau, and for the purpose of this chapter, we use Hispanic and Latinx interchangeably to refer to individuals of Mexican, Puerto Rican, Cuban, Central and South American, Dominican, Spanish, and other Hispanic descent; we also expand our understanding to include those who identify as Brazilian, Afro-Caribbean, Afro-Latinx, and/or Black

Latinx. The Latinx population are often underrepresented in media (Sui & Paul, 2017) and when they are present, they are often portrayed as violent, criminals, or undocumented immigrants (Cisneros, 2008; Conway, Grabe, & Grieves, 2007; Dixon & Williams, 2015). While this negative rhetoric and racist stereotypes are not new, there has been heightened "offensive political discourse" (Nithyanand et al., 2017), particularly targeting members of the Latinx population, specifically when we consider the emergence of Trump onto the political scene (Martin, 2016). Declaring his candidacy on June 16, 2015, Trump declared,

When Mexico sends its people, they're not sending their best. They're not sending you. They're sending people that have lots of problems, and they're bringing those problems with us. They're bringing drugs. They're bringing crime. They're rapists. And some, I assume, are good people.

Since then, he was elected to president and is infamously known for his rhetoric around building a wall between Mexico and the United States. These sentiments not only negatively portray Mexicans and Mexican-Americans but also falsely conflate the Mexican and Mexican American population with the larger Latinx population. Indeed, Hispanics with Mexican heritage are the largest Latinx ethnic group, however the Latinx population is much more diverse with heritage from over 20 different countries (Zong & Batalova, 2018) and speakers of Spanish, Brazilian Portuguese, and a number of indigenous languages to Central and South American as well as the Caribbean. Further, while immigrants with Mexican heritage comprised 30% of the 2015 migrant population in the United States, Mexico is no longer the top country of origin among immigrants to the United States (American Community Survey, 2017); the Latinx population as a whole, however, has continued to increase making up half of the international migrant population in the United States (Brown & Stepler, 2016) and 17.6% of the overall U.S. population (U.S. Census Bureau, 2017).

While the Hispanic population writ large is overwhelmingly portrayed in a negative light across social media (Guo & Harlow, 2014), news media (Gil de Zuniga et al.,2012; Sui & Paul, 2017), broadcast media (Mastro et al.,2008), and entertainment media (Bender, 2003), many Latinx youth face a double bind while attending school. The Latinx student population makes up more than 25% of all students in U.S. public schools and comprise nearly 75% of all classified English Learners (U.S. Department of Education, n.d.) that is students who received specific English Language Development services due to their English language proficiency. This classified English Learner status often places Latinx students in a double bind as the classification itself is often stigmatized (Dabach, 2014; Valdes, 1998): classified English Learners are often associated with negative stereotypes such as being less academically able and unmotivated (Vollmer, 2000). At the classroom level these misconceptions translate into the practice of watering down content or lowering expectations (Dabach, 2014) and at the administration level misconceptions lead to classified (and reclassified) English Learners being tracked into less rigorous academic coursework (Kanno & Kangas, 2014), over- and underrepresentation in Special Education services (Umansky et al.,2017; Counts et al., 2018), and underrepresentation in gifted and talented programs (Grissom & Redding, 2015; Levy & Perdue, 2017). These practices have a large impact on Latinx students who are more likely to drop out of high school and are less likely to attend or complete post-secondary education (Krogstad, 2016) compared to their white peers; although it is worth mentioning that despite these structural challenges, among Latinx students the high school dropout rate has declined and post-secondary enrollment has increased over the past few years (Gramlich, 2017).

While presence of the Latinx population and classified English Learners is not new, these numbers have grown steadily and rapidly in the past decade (NCES, 2019). For example, while states such as California and Texas have historically served a large Latinx population, some states have experienced rapid growth in the Hispanic population; the Latinx population in South Dakota, Tennessee, and South Carolina nearly tripled from 2000 to 2014 and in more recent past, this population has doubled in North Dakota (Stepler & Lopez, 2016). Similarly, the classified English Learner population has been increasing across state school districts, including many districts that have historically been low-serving districts, that is districts with fewer than 5% classified English Learners (U.S. DOE, n.d.). This trend of more cultural, linguistic, and ethnic diversity growth is especially important to consider as the teaching force population has remained largely white, monolingual, and female (U.S. Census Bureau, 2013).

POSITIONALITY AND METHODOLOGY

While we all identify as women educators, the three of us have varied experiences. Thus, we each begin with a brief statement of positionality.

Chris: I was born to Filipino immigrants and raised on a semirural island in southeast Alaska where I was privileged to grow up in a middle-class home. I identify as a brown woman and Filipina American. While my parents instilled strong cultural values that are tied to Filipino heritage, they did not pass down their native languages of Bisaya and Tagalog as they prescribed strongly to the belief that Americanization, and subsequently the English language, were necessary priorities in achieving the "American Dream." I am the first in my immediate family to graduate from college in the United States and the first in my entire extended family to attend graduate school and earn a doctoral degree. I have taught both Spanish and English across all age and grade levels from kindergarten to adult education. I currently work as a teacher educator in a private, predominantly white institution.

Molly: I was born and raised in a white middle/upper-middle-class suburb of Boston to first-generation Irish American parents. I was privileged to have attended a high school where 85.5% of students planned to go to a four-year college the year I graduated (MA DESE, 2019). While I was the first in my extended family to earn a master's degree, I was surrounded by peers who also completed graduate school. My four grandparents emigrated from Ireland and so I was raised with stories of immigration and the "American Dream." None of my grandparents graduated from college, my mother and two uncles graduated from a four-year college, and all of my generation of cousins graduated from a four-year college. However, we never discussed the privilege that came with being European white immigrants whose first language was English. I have taught ESL to students in grades one to eight and am now working as an instructional coach supporting teachers working with classified English Learners in the mainstream classroom as well as teaching courses to teacher educators on the same subject.

Megan: I was born and raised in a town located on the Jersey Shore in New Jersey. I am white and attended school in a predominantly white school district. I am currently in a graduate program earning my master's degree in literacy education. I have taught in a high school SLIFE Newcomers Academy in my district's high school and now work as an ESL teacher at the middle school level.

Massachusetts: All three of us live and teach in Massachusetts, a state where the overall percentage of classified English Learners has grown in the past decade from 5.8% to 9.5%; of particular concern are suburban and semiurban districts which have doubled in their classified English Learner population since 2008 and also districts which have experienced exponential growth, such as one district which increased from 2.8% in 2008 to 16.1% in 2017 (MA DESE, 2019); in many of these districts the dominant languages spoken among classified English Learners are Spanish and Portuguese (U.S. DOE, 2017). Massachusetts is a particularly interesting state because while it ranks first in the United States on National Assessment of Educational Progress (NAEP), less than one in three Latino fourth graders are on grade level in reading and one in seven classified English Learners drop out of school entirely (Massachusetts Education Equity Partnership, 2018); classified English Learners are also more likely to be assigned to teachers with less experience and/or teachers who have received poor teacher evaluation ratings (Massachusetts Education Equity Partnership, 2018). Further, at $77,385 for the median household income, Massachusetts is one of the wealthier states in the country with a median household income $17,049 higher than the national average (Guzman, 2018). However, similar to the opportunity gap in education, Massachusetts also has the sixth biggest gap between its highest-paid residents and the rest of the population with the top 1% of the families earning 31 times more than the average of the bottom 99% (Sommeiller & Price, 2018).

METHOD

As stated previously, the nexus of our chapter stems from Molly's reflection, "I know these tensions are not anything new and have been boiling below the surface." Drawing from narrative research (Salkind, 2010), we used personal narratives to describe how these tensions are part of an unshifting cycle. In line with Torill Moen (2006), our narrative process was grounded in the following three principles: we believe that humans structure their world experiences into narratives; we believe that these narratives are informed by our past and present experiences and values as well as the audience that we are narrating to; and we recognize that these narratives are a collective voice shaped by the larger societal context. Our work is thus based on these three principles. First, we use personal narratives as the process of reflecting on experiences and making sense of teaching experiences is within itself a storytelling, or narrative, process (Casey, 1992). For the purpose of this chapter Molly and Megan reconstructed narrative vignettes based on a series of journal reflections that were guided by the following prompt: "What are defining moments that have stood in our experience as ESL teachers, specifically when working with classified and reclassified Latinx students?" Second, in recognizing that our personal experiences and beliefs impact our professional lives and practices we discussed why these particular experiences were salient and looked for themes across the stories. Relatedly, we reminded ourselves that our narratives were for the larger audience of contemporary educators who may or may not share our own values, beliefs, and experiences. This iterative process of constructing and reconstructing vignettes lead us to develop what we saw as a common pattern across our narratives, which we conceptualized into a cycle of unshifting perspectives and practices that we also believe can be disrupted though anti-racist practices and pedagogy. The remainder of our chapter shares these vignettes as well as discussion of the cycle we observed in our vignettes and how anti-racist practices and pedagogy can work in breaking this cycle.

VIGNETTES: DEFICIT PERSPECTIVES IN PRACTICE

"I See Math Students"

I was meeting with a team of teachers about my students when the conversation veered to a video sent by our principal about the different types of racism in schools for teams to watch and discuss. I have worked with this team of teachers for years and have experienced how much they love teaching and their students. So I have to admit that I was surprised when, rather than openly discuss the video and the impact of racism on our school, they talked among themselves about how they loved and respected all their students and they truly didn't understand why the principal would think they needed to watch a video on racism. Several of the teachers self-proclaimed how they themselves "certainly weren't racist" and had "chosen" to work in a diverse community. What struck me most was how one teacher stated, "I don't see skin color, I only see math students." *If a self-proclaimed "non-racist" believes they only see math students, how can they truly support students' emotional, academic, and/or linguistic well-being?*

"They have no background knowledge"

In a teacher meeting I started by asking my colleagues what challenges they are facing right now. Immediately they discussed how "new students" (i.e., immigrant students) had "no background knowledge." This reminded me of a previous writing classroom I had worked in when we were beginning a research unit where students would write about information they learned on a topic of their choice. On the first day of the unit I observed the writing teacher model a brainstorm on coming up with new ideas. She began by saying, "I'm thinking of researching and writing about a country but I'm having a hard time deciding which country I want to research, so to help me decide my country I'm going to do a little brainstorm where I think about and then list countries that I want to visit." She then proceeded to write down Italy, France, and Germany. I felt my heart sink. The students in her class hailed from Brazil, Haiti, and Guatemala. Why didn't she do this in a way that listed countries she knew her students had expertise in? *If a teacher has a particular perspective about what counts as background knowledge, then how can students demonstrate what they know?*

"The Real Students"

Shortly after I was hired to be an ESL teacher, a teacher told me that she knew [white] parents were upset that "so much money" was being used to hire teachers for "the immigrant students." She argued that the parents believed that in doing this, resources were being taken away from "the real students" from the town. It was clear that this teacher in relaying this information to me was in accordance with the parent perspective. *If a teacher doesn't believe resources should be used to support immigrant students, then how do you think she actually treats her students who come from immigrant backgrounds?*

"These Students"

Once I was teaching a course for practicing teachers that was focused on how to meet the needs of English Learners. Early in the course we were having a discussion on language acquisition considerations for teaching English Learners. During this discussion, one student raised his hand to point out that his "grandmother came from Italy and did just fine." He then proceeded to state that she wasn't ever labeled an English Learner, didn't have ESL classes, and didn't have teachers who were trained on how to work with students learning English and yet she "managed to work hard, learn English, and succeed in school," so why do "these students" need so much support, they just need to "work hard enough." *If a teacher prescribes to the **grit perspectives** that all it takes to be successful is hard work, then how can they see that the current system does not actually support English Learners?*

"He's so Low"

Lucas started school in the United States in the third grade after having missed a significant amount of school in El Salvador. He was placed into the newcomers third-grade classroom with other students who were learning English; in sixth grade he began mainstream classes. Since he was a classified English Learner, he also was in my ESL Literacy class. In this class we kept daily journals and two entries stand to me, "i'm actually smart too at math and ela. working hard and showing people that i will do it and that i'm not going to give up" and "i want to achieve math and science and not to stay back to stay in 7 and go to 8," these entries were from sixth and seventh grade, respectively. Throughout these grades Lucas cycled between putting forth effort, getting poor grades while not seeing academic gains, giving up and facing consequences for disciplinary issues, and subsequently being convinced to put more effort into his schoolwork. While it was clear in his journal entries that he wanted to succeed I can't even begin to explain the amount of negative comments I'd heard about Lucas. Variations of "He's lazy," "He doesn't care about his school work," and "He's so low" were often the way the sixth- and seventh-grade teams would describe him. *If a teacher can't recognize a student's hard work and effort, then why would the student continue to engage in school?*

"Because She Is an English Learner"

Sara is one of the best students I have ever had in every way possible. She was mature, kind, and supportive of the other students in the class. She always tried her best on every assignment and often went above and beyond with her work. Her teachers also loved her and I know because they would often tell me what a wonderful student she was. However, when I was reviewing courses for the following year I noticed that Sara was not recommended for any advanced coursework, even though her teachers had praised her level of work consistently throughout the year. I wondered, did they have different expectations for Sara because she was an immigrant student? I took the initiative to meet with her English language arts teacher and asked her why Sara had not been recommended for the honors class; her response was pragmatic: "I do think she could do honors coursework, but I didn't think to recommend her for honors because she is an English Learner." *If a teacher doesn't believe a student is eligible for advanced coursework simply because she is an English Learner, then how can students gain access to more challenging and engaging course material?*

"They're So Loud"

"Molly, your classroom is so loud! They're all speaking in so many different languages. What are they even talking about?" one teacher commented as she entered my classroom. Students were discussing a painting of a family from the Renaissance and they were first sharing their thoughts with their peers. Teachers have always pointed out how loud my students were, especially if they were speaking in a language other than English even though I never thought they were any louder than the other middle school students around them. *If a teacher hears another language as too loud, then how can students be comfortable using the languages they are most comfortable with to access the curriculum?*

Unpacking Our Narratives

In discussing these narratives, the three of us were able to see that across all our narratives we observed a similar pattern where our colleagues would share racist and/or inaccurate perspectives regarding Latinx and/or English Learner educational abilities, and in each instance the underlying perspective or belief attributes a negative or deficit view of Latinx English Learner students. Which, in turn, set Latinx students, especially those classified as English Learners, up for failure. It is important to note that we acknowledge that these beliefs are based on prior life experiences and implicit biases stemming from those experiences that cannot be changed. That said, we do believe that reactions to these beliefs, for example, the fact that Sara's English teacher did not recommend her for the honors class, can be changed by having teachers address their own deficit perspectives. Not surprisingly, our narratives and discussion, aligned with the larger narratives in the education literature regarding students of color broadly (e.g., Berliner & Biddle, 1995; Jackson, 2002) and Hispanic and Latinx students specifically (Fuligni et al., 1999; Matute-Bianchi, 1991) has documented deficit perspectives among teachers. Further, empirical research has also demonstrated a relationship between deficit perspectives and the opportunity gap in terms of classroom practices (e.g., Lee & Hawkins, 2015; Lowenhaupt, 2015; Martinez, 2011). As we discussed the recurring patterns that Molly and Megan observed in their work as teachers as well as the documented deficit perspectives in the research literature, we began to recognize a cycle of unshifting perspectives and practices that all stemmed from initial inaccurate beliefs and perspectives that are consistently confirmed.

A Cycle of Unshifting Perspectives and Practices

An underlying assumption in education is that how teachers think affects their behavior (Shavelson & Stern, 1981; Stern & Shavelson, 1983), specifically with regard to working with bilingual students of color, such as the Hispanic student population, teachers' beliefs[2] about language and their students' experiences can affect their practice (e.g., Brousseau, Book, & Byers, 1988; Costa, Mcphail, Smith, & Brisk; 2005; Meskill, 2005). For example, research has suggested that teachers hold deficit perspectives regarding English Learners ability to meet academic goals (Sugimoto, Carter, & Stoehr, 2017) and also hold a number of inaccurate beliefs regarding language development (Liams, Shafer, Walker, & 2004; Reeves, 2006) and language instruction (Karabenick & Noda, 2004; Reeves, 2004). These deficit perspectives and misinformation are coupled with negative portrayal of the Latinx population in media which can play a further role in influencing opinions (Arias & Hellmueller, 2016) and racial attitudes (Wheeler, Jarvis, & Petty, 2001). These racist and linguist beliefs can be particularly strong in areas where population demographics have experienced dramatic shifts in a relatively short period of time, and research has suggested that community-wide misperception of cultural and ethnic groups work their ways into educator beliefs (Valdes, 2001). Further, Liams, Shafer, and Walker (2004) have found that drastic demographic shifts in communities that have been historically homogenous can translate into broader community misunderstanding.

We suggest that this pattern is a lockstep process that contributes to the documented differences between Latinx students and their white, monolingual peers on academic outcomes (U.S. DOE, 2017). Further, we argue that when teachers observe lower academic performance among Latinx students, this falsely confirms their initial deficit perspectives. This process, which we refer to as *a cycle of unshifting perspectives and practices*, is summarized in Figure 5.1.

For the purpose of this chapter, *teacher perspectives* refers broadly to teacher beliefs and perspectives about Latinx students and classified and reclassified English Learners. In the example of one our narratives, Sara's English teacher expressed a belief that she didn't think English Learners should be in advanced coursework. The *opportunity gap* refers to school-level and classroom-level practices that may result in an opportunity gap, that is a lack of access to rigorous or quality education. Again, returning to Sara's story, her not being referred for advanced coursework paved a path of less access to more rigorous learning; in the story of Lucas this opportunity gap translated into missed class time due to disciplinary action due to teacher's misinterpretation of his engagement in learning.[1]

Both Sara's and Lucas's experiences are consistent with research patterns on academic tracking (Kanno & Kangas, 2014) and higher rates of disciplinary action toward Latinx students (Wallace et al.,2005). Finally, *lower academic achievement* can refer to the documented differences between Latinx and English Learner students and their white, monolingual peers with regard to performance on academic tests, graduation rates, and post-secondary enrollment (U.S. DOE, 2017). While we've observed this cycle, we do

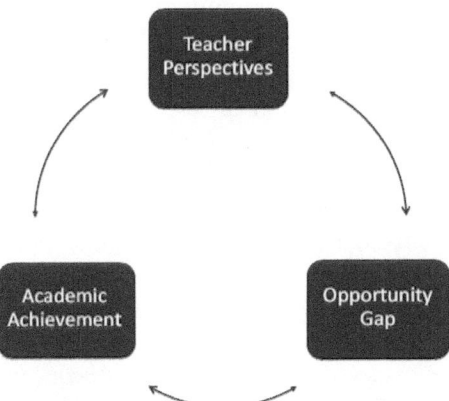

Figure 5.1 A Cycle of Unshifting Perspectives and Practices.

believe this cycle can be broken, as Molly started to describe in her journal reflection, we believe anti-racist pedagogy is a step forward in disrupting the cycle.

Disrupting the Cycle: Supporting Latinx Students through Anti-Racist Pedagogy

The deficit perspectives present in the narratives we shared have been present since before the election of Trump and in some ways the election of Trump, or at least his racist rhetoric, has confirmed that these perspectives are justified. Teachers' beliefs, however, are not necessarily stagnant and if they experience a shift, then this can impact their practices (Palmer & Martinez, 2013). In fact, research has demonstrated that professional development can disrupt negative attitudes and perspectives for working with multilingual learners (Fitts & Gross, 2012; Nieto, 2017).

As our schools have become increasingly diverse (NCES, 2019), methods for supporting a more culturally and linguistically diverse classrooms have evolved. From the early work of Gloria Ladson-Billings (1994) on culturally relevant pedagogy to the more recent use of culturally sustaining pedagogy (Paris, 2012), as well as asset-based perspectives such as funds of knowledge (Moll et al.,1992) and Yosso's (2005) community cultural wealth model, these critical perspectives have shaped the modern multicultural education movement. While there is no argument against the benefits of multicultural education, simply modifying the curriculum does not address deeply rooted issues of oppression. Drawing from Blakeney (2005), we are driven by the idea that issues of equity and access in education cannot be addressed by multicultural education alone, but must also include anti-racist pedagogy. We prescribe to the belief that anti-racist practices and pedagogy must include us reflecting on and then taking action on the following questions, as proposed by William Ayers (2004, p.11), "What am I teaching for? And what am I teaching against?" In line with this idea, we see anti-racist practices and pedagogy as needing to be at the center of this teacher perspectives-opportunity gap-academic achievement cycle, which we illustrate in Figure 5.2.

To unpack how we view anti-racist practices and pedagogy as a disruption, take the case of the teacher who claimed they "only see math students" as an example. In this instance a discussion on the false narrative of colorblindness and white fragility would be a good first step in working against this belief which, while unintentional, is dangerous and harmful. Working against beliefs, however, is not enough. Anti-racist work should also happen at the opportunity gap stage of the cycle. For example, if the teacher who only "sees math students" enacts this belief in practice then their classroom will not include culturally and linguistically supportive practices for the Latinx students in

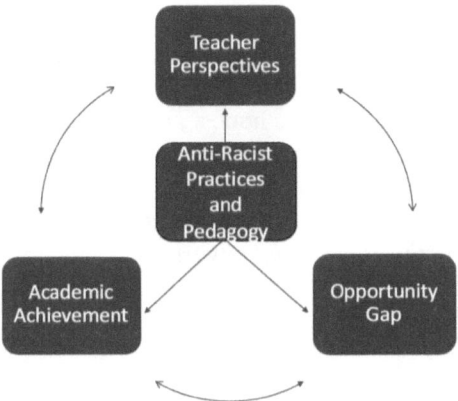

Figure 5.2 Anti-Racist Practices and Pedagogy as a Disruption.

their classroom. Thus, an anti-racist approach to this would be challenging this teacher to re-consider how their teaching practices, while well-intentioned, are actually harmful to the learning of their students. Finally, the conversation around academic performance is often at the student level, returning to the story of Lucas, teachers viewed him as "low" and therefore attributed his lower academic performance to him, himself being a poor student. In reality, Lucas spent his initial time in middle school working hard, however teachers consistently could not, whether intentional or unintentional, view him as engaged and invested in his own learning. An anti-racist practice in the discussion of academic achievement would push teachers to consider how academic success, or lack thereof, is a symptom of the system which inherently sets English Learners and Latinx students up for failure and to look for ways to shift school-level or classroom-level practices to support all students. Similarly, we believe that these anti-racist practices should be present in our pedagogical practices as we must support our Latinx and English Learners as well as work against the ingrained false perspectives and deficit beliefs that their white, monolingual peers may also hold. While we started our chapter with vignettes, we find hope in the fact that not all our stories are negative. In this next section, we share a new series of vignettes where we've engaged in anti-racist practices and pedagogy in our own schools with our students and colleagues.

VIGNETTES: ANTI-RACIST PEDAGOGY IN PRACTICE

Working on My Own Beliefs

I was privileged to be included in a district wide team of administrators, principals, and students who came together to start anti-racist work. I experienced firsthand the benefits of having a space to learn about and reflect on racism in schools while having open and honest discussions about how our implicit biases can impact our teaching practices. This experience changed me as a teacher. I am now able to be more honest and critical of my own beliefs and teaching practices. This is an ongoing process but being given this initial time and space has given me the tools to do this work. *If teachers are given time and tools to engage in anti-racists practices and pedagogy, will they become more critical of how they teach students from diverse backgrounds?*

Providing Space for Reflection

I began starting each class with time for students to write in their "do now journal." Students spent anywhere from 3 to 10 minutes just writing about whatever came to their minds and mattered to them in that moment. I then gave some time for students to share if they wanted to. I found that this gave students time to be themselves and express their own thoughts and feelings about their day instead of always trying to fit in to what was expected of them. I even allowed students to write in their home language if they wanted to and many did. This was also a great way for me to gain insight into what students were thinking and what they cared about. *If students are given more space for reflection will they feel they are allowed to be themselves, and will teachers be able to better support students' emotional, academic, and/or linguistic well-being?*

Using Students Background Knowledge

In teaching persuasive writing, an ELA teacher I worked with was purposeful about the topics she chooses for her students to work on. For example, students wrote about their opinions on school uniforms since many of our students had attended schools in their home countries that require uniforms. This gave these students an opportunity to be the experts. With my students, we always did research and wrote about topics around immigration and she allowed a lot of space for students to share their own expertise and experiences and discuss how that influenced their opinions. *If teachers choose topics that students have background knowledge in, will students be more successful at showing what they know?*

Helping Parents Find Their Voice

One year the ELL class sizes were growing rapidly; what started as around 10 students per class rose to rosters of over 35 students halfway through the school year. This seemed inequitable as it was difficult to ensure the needs of our students when they were so many students, not to mention all coming with various socioemotional needs and academic experiences. The Family and Community Engagement Specialist and I decided to work with the families of English Learners on a Saturday morning to discuss the benefits of small class sizes and a process for voicing this and other concerns. Subsequently, this particular group of immigrant parents coauthored a letter to the District's School Committee demanding comparable roster sizes to other classes. *If parents are included in decision making, will schools be able to meet all students' needs by rethinking policy and practices that are biased?*

Helping Students Find Their Voice

I always found that by giving students space to make choices about their work allowed them to find their voice and feel connected with the school work. We were still writing, building our academic language, and using the Massachusetts state standards. Yet, students were engaged because it was about something they not only cared about but also have background knowledge on. I did one unit from NPR's "This I Believe" podcast where students wrote about a belief they hold and then wrote a narrative to explain why this is something important to them. I was purposeful in choosing the model podcasts from NPR's vast collection, including topics my students would relate to from writers students could connect with. I was even able to find some examples of podcasts that included pieces in languages other than English. Students wrote about learning to cook from their mom, learning about how cooperation in school is important, the challenges they faced moving to the United States, and about losing a family member. Most importantly, my students were able to actually choose a topic that mattered to them and not a topic that mattered to me. *If teachers give more space for student choice, will students take ownership of their own learning and be more engaged in school?*

Meaningful Curriculum

Shortly after the election of Trump, a number of my students expressed interest in rights and protests. Since I had the flexibility to modify my curriculum, we dove into English Language Development units that centered on the Universal Declaration of Human Rights, the American Civil Rights movement, as well as more contemporary movements such as Black Lives Matter. *If teachers include topics based on social justice, will students be more willing to work hard and feel supported in their learning?*

Inviting Colleagues to See Our Students

Whenever I had the chance, I would invite colleagues in to see my students' work. When we finished the "This I Believe" podcast assignment, I invited my students' teachers to come and listen to the podcasts with us. One eighth-grade English language arts teacher took me up on my offer and when hearing a quiet student share his podcast commented that she had never heard that student speak in her class. We had a really productive conversation about how she was able to see him in a different light and she started to question why he wasn't able to speak up within her classroom. *If teachers are invited to see each student and their own unique abilities, will teachers be better suited to offer students more challenging and engaging opportunities?*

Encouraging students to use their home language. A teacher told me about how he had some former students of mine in his seventh-grade science class and how he loved having them. He described how they would work together on the engineering projects and that he never knew what they were talking about because they were speaking in their home language but that they would always come up with interesting ways of tackling the challenge. *If students feel encouraged and welcome to use their home language, will they have more success in accessing the curriculum?*

LIMITATIONS AND CLOSING REFLECTION

Similar to many of the teachers we discuss in our vignettes, I am a white woman who grew up in a middle class suburb of Boston. I can not change my experiences as they are in the past. I cannot change the language that I was taught to use when discussing minorities or lower socio-economic communities. However, I know that I can acknowledge these implicit biases and recognize them when they pop up because they do pop up, that is not something I can go back and change. When I am able to recognize these thoughts I am then able to challenge them and in doing that I am able to challenge my own behaviors. Being self-aware is really the first step in practicing anti-racist pedagogy because without this way of thinking and challenging myself I will never be able to question by own practice and choices as a teacher working with students of color and immigrant students.—Molly

The above excerpt is a journal reflection that Molly had after one of our initial meetings unpacking the narrative vignettes. As we mentioned at the start of our chapter, the nexus of our work stems from Molly's initial journal entry, *I know these tensions are not anything new and have been boiling below the surface. The election of Trump has given a voice and a power to that voice for people who want to blame immigrants.* In our chapter we've shared examples of how deficit perspectives not just play out, but are consistently reinforced in our racist and anti- immigrant society as well as examples of how we engage in anti-racist practices and pedagogy as a means to disrupt a cycle of inequity and also support Latinx and English Learner students. We do not view ourselves as experts in anti-racist work, but rather we strive to consistently center anti-racist practices and pedagogy in our work as educators. *If educators don't center anti-racism in their teaching practices, will Latinx students truly be supported or seen in schools?*

NOTE

1. For the purpose of this chapter, we use beliefs and perspectives interchangeably.

REFERENCES

Arias, S., & Hellmueller, L. (2016). Hispanics-and-Latinos and the US media: New issues for future research. *Communication Research Trends, 35*(2), 4–21.

Ayers, W. (2004). *Teaching toward freedom.* Boston: Beacon Press.

Bender, S. (2003). *Greasers and gringos: Latinos, law, and the American imagination.* New York, NY: NYU Press.

Berliner, D., & Biddle. (1995). *The manufactured crisis. Myths, fraud and the attack on America's public schools.* New York, NY: Basic Books.

Blakeney, A. M. (2005). Antiracist pedagogy: Definition, theory, and professional development. *Journal of Curriculum and Pedagogy, 2*(1), 119–132.

Brousseau, B. A., Book, C., & Byers, J. L. (1988). Teacher beliefs and the cultures of teaching. *Journal of Teacher Education, 39*(6), 33–39.

Brown, A., & Stepler, R. (2016). *Statistical portrait of the foreign-born population in the United States.* Pew Research Center. https://www.pewhispanic.org/2016/04/19/statistical-portrait- ofthe-foreign-born-population-in-the-united-states/.

Casey, K. (1992). Why do progressive women activists leave teaching?: Theory, methodology and politics in life-history research. In I. Goodson (Ed.), *Studying teachers' lives* (pp. 187–208). New York: Columbia University, Teachers College Press.

Cisneros, J. D. (2008). Contaminated communities: The metaphor of "immigrant as pollutant" in media representations of immigration. *Rhetoric and Public Affairs, 11*(4), 569–601.

Conway, M., Elizabeth Grabe, M., & Grieves, K. (2007). Villains, victims and the virtuous in Bill O'reilly's "no-spin zone" revisiting world war propaganda techniques. *Journalism Studies, 8*(2), 197–223.

Costa, J., McPhail, G., Smith, J., & Brisk, M. E. (2005). Faculty first: The challenge of infusing the teacher education curriculum with scholarship on English language learners. *Journal of Teacher Education, 56*(2), 104–118.

Counts, J., Katsiyannis, A., & Whitford, D. K. (2018). Culturally and linguistically diverse learners in special education: English learners. *NASSP Bulletin, 102*(1), 5–21.

Dabach, D. (2014). "I am not a shelter!" Stigma and social boundaries in teachers' accounts of students' experience in separate "sheltered" English learner classrooms. *Journal of Education for Students Placed at Risk, 19*, 98–124.

Dixon, T. L., & Williams, C. L. (2015). The changing misrepresentation of race and crime on network and cable news. *Journal of Communication, 65*(1), 24–39.

Fitts, S., & Gross, L. A. (2012). Teacher candidates learning from English learners: Constructing concepts of language and culture in Tuesday's tutors after-school program. *Teacher Education Quarterly, 39*(4), 75–95.

Foxen, P., & Mather, M. (2016). *Toward a more equitable future: The trends and challenges facing America's Latino children.* National Council of La Raza. http://publications.nclr.org/handle/123456789/1627

Fuligni, A., Tseng, V., & Lam, M. (1999). Attitudes toward family obligations among American adolescents with Asian, Latin American, and European backgrounds. *Child Development, 70*, 1030–1044.

Gil de Zuniga, H., Correa, T., & Valenzuela, S. (2012). Selective exposure to cable news and immigration in the U.S.: The relationship between FOX news, CNN, and attitudes toward Mexican immigrants. *Journal of Broadcasting & Electronic Media, 56*, 597–615.

Gramlich, H. (2017). Hispanic dropout rate hits new low, college enrollment at a new high. *Pew Research Center.* https://www.pewresearch.org/fact-tank/2017/09/29/hispanic-dropout-rate-hits-new-low-college-enrollment-at-new-high/.

Grissom, J. A., & Redding, C. (2015). Discretion and disproportionality: Explaining the underrepresentation of high-achieving students of color in gifted programs. *Aera Open, 2*(1), 1–25. https://doi.org/10.1177/2332858415622175.

Gudmundsdottir, S. (2001). Narrative research on school practice. In V. Richardson (Ed.), *Fourth handbook for research on teaching* (pp. 226–240). New York: MacMillan.

Guo, L., & Harlow, S. (2014). User-generated racism: An analysis of stereotypes of African Americans, Latinos, and Asians in YouTube videos. *Howard Journal of Communications, 25*, 281–302.

Guzman, G. G. (2018). Household Income: 2017. *American Community Survey Briefs.* https://www.census.gov/content/dam/Census/library/publications/2018/acs/acsbr17-01.pdf.

Jackson, S. A. (2002). A study of teachers' perceptions of youth problems. *Journal of Youth Studies, 5*(3), 313–323.

Kanno, Y., & Kangas, S. (2014). "I'm not going to be, like, for the AP": English language learners' limited access to advanced college-preparatory courses in high school. *American Educational Research Journal, 51*, 848–878.

Karabenick, S. A., & Noda, P. A. C. (2004). Professional development implications of teachers' beliefs and attitudes toward English language learners. *Bilingual Research Journal, 28*(1), 55–75.

Krogstad, J. M. (2016 July 28). 5 facts about Latinos and education. *Pew Research Center*. https://www.pewresearch.org/fact-tank/2016/07/28/5-facts-about-latinos-and-education/.

Ladson-Billings, G. (1994). What we can learn from multicultural education research. *Educational leadership*, *51*(8), 22–26.

Lee, S. J., and M. R. Hawkins. (2015). Policy, context and schooling: The education of English learners in rural new destinations. *Global Education Review*, *2*(4), 40–59.

Levy, H. O., & Perdue, B. (2017). America's hidden gems: Rural, Latinx and gifted students. *Real Clear Education*. https://www.realcleareducation.com/articles/2017/10/12/americas_hidden_gems_rural_latinx_an d_gifted_students_110213.html.

Liams, M., Shafer, J., & Walker, A. (2004). Not in my classroom": Teacher attitudes towards English language learners in the mainstream classes. *NABE Journal of Research and Practice*, *2*(1), 130–160.

Lowenhaupt, R. (2015). Bilingual education policy in Wisconsin's new Latino diaspora. In E. T. Hamann, S. Wortham, & E. G. Murillo Jr (Eds.), *Education policy in practice: Critical cultural studies* (pp. 245–262). Charlotte, NC: Information Age Publishing.

Martinez, R. O. (2011). *Latinos in the Midwest*. East Lansing, MI: Michigan State University Press.

Martin, P. L. (2016). Election of Donald Trump and migration. *Migration Letters*, *14*(1), 161–171.

Massachusetts Department of Elementary and Secondary Education. (2019). *State and District Profiles*. http://profiles.doe.mass.edu/search/search.aspx?leftNavId=11238.

Massachusetts Education Equity Partnership. (2018). *Number 1 for Some: Opportunity and Achievement in Massachusetts*. https://number1forsome.org.

Mastro, D. E., Behm-Morawitz, E., & Kopacz, M. A. (2008). Exposure to television portrayals of Latinos: The implications of aversive racism and social identity theory. *Human Communication Research*, *34*(1), 1–27.

Matute-Bianchi, M. (1991). Situational ethnicity and patterns of school performance among immigrant and nonimmigrant Mexican-descent students. In M. Gibson & J. Ogbu (Eds.), *Minority status and schooling* (pp. 205–247). New York: Garland.

Meskill, C. (2005). Triadic scaffolds: Tools for teaching English language learners with computers. *Language Learning & Technology*, *9*(1), 46–59.

Moen, T. (2006). Reflections on the narrative research approach. *International Journal of Qualitative Methods*, *5*(4), 56–69.

Moll, L. C., Amanti, C., Neff, D., & Gonzalez, N. (1992). Funds of knowledge for teaching: Using a qualitative approach to connect homes and classrooms. *Theory Into Practice*, *31*(2), 132–141.

National Center for Education Statistics. (2019). *Status and Trends in the Education of Racial and Ethnic Groups 2018*. https://nces.ed.gov/pubs2019/2019038.pdf.

Nieto, S. (2017). Becoming Sociocultural Mediators: What All Educators Can Learn from Bilingual and ESL Teachers. *Issues in Teacher Education*, *26*(2), 129–141.

Nithyanand, R., Schaffner, B., & Gill, P. (2017). *Online political discourse in the Trump era.* https://arxiv.org/pdf/1711.05303.pdf.

Palmer, D., & Martínez, R. A. (2013). Teacher agency in bilingual spaces: A fresh look at preparing teachers to educate Latina/o bilingual children. *Review of research in Education, 37*(1), 269–297.

Paris, D. (2012). Culturally sustaining pedagogy: A needed change in stance, terminology, and practice. *Educational Researcher, 41*(3), 93–97.

Reeves, J. (2004). "Like everybody else": Equalizing educational opportunity for English language learners. *Tesol Quarterly, 38*(1), 43–66.

Reeves, J. R. (2006). Secondary teacher attitudes toward including English-language learners in mainstream classrooms. *The Journal of Educational Research, 99*(3), 131–143.

Salkind, N. J. (Ed.). (2010). *Encyclopedia of research design* (Vol. 1). Thousand Oaks, CA: Sage.

Shavelson, R. J., & Stern, P. (1981). Research on teachers' pedagogical thoughts, judgments, decisions, and behavior. *Review of Educational Research, 51*(4), 455–498.

Sommeiller, E., & Price, M. (2018). The new gilded age: Income inequality in the U.S. by state, metropolitan area, and county. *Economic Policy Institute.* https://www.epi.org/publication/the-new-gilded-age-income-inequality-in-the-u-s-by-state- metropolitan-area-and-county/.

Stepler, R., & Lopez, M. H. (2016). *U.S. Latino population growth and dispersion has slowed since onset of the Great Recession.* Pew Research Center. https://www.pewhispanic.org/2016/09/08/latino-population-growth-and-dispersion-has-sl owed- since-the-onset-of-the-great-recession/.

Stern, P., & Shavelson, R. J. (1983). Reading teachers' judgments, plans, and decision making. *The Reading Teacher, 37*(3), 280–286.

Sugimoto, A. T., Carter, K., & Stoehr, K. J. (2017). Teaching "in their best interest": Preservice teachers' narratives regarding English Learners. *Teaching and Teacher Education, 67,* 179–188.

Sui, M., & Paul, N. (2017). Latino portrayals in local news media: Underrepresentation, negative stereotypes, and institutional predictors of coverage. *Journal of Intercultural Communication Research, 46*(3), 273–294.

Umansky, I. M., Thompson, K. D., & Díaz, G. (2017). Using an ever–English learner framework to examine disproportionality in special education. *Exceptional Children, 84*(1), 76–96.

United States Department of Education. (2017). National Center for Education Statistics State *Nonfiscal Survey of Public Elementary/Secondary Education.* https://nces.ed.gov/ccd/stnfis.asp.

United States Department of Education (n.d.). *Our Nation's English Learners.* https://www2.ed.gov/datastory/el-characteristics/index.html.

United States Census Bureau (2017). *The Nation's Older Population Is Still Growing,* Census Bureau Reports. https://www.census.gov/newsroom/press-releases/2017/cb17-100.html.

Valdes, G. (1998). The world outside and inside schools: Language and immigrant children. *Educational Researcher, 27*(6), 4–18.

Valdés, G. (2001). *Learning and not learning English: Latino students in American schools*. New York, NY: Teachers College Press.

Vollmer, G. (2000). Praise and stigma: Teachers' constructions of the "typical ESL student." *Journal of Intercultural Studies, 21*, 53–66.

Wallace Jr, J. M., Goodkind, S., Wallace, C. M., & Bachman, J. G. (2008). Racial, ethnic, and gender differences in school discipline among US high school students: 1991–2005. *The Negro Educational Review, 59*(1–2), 47.

Wheeler, S. C., Jarvis, W. B. G., & Petty, R. E. (2001). Think unto others: The self-destructive impact of negative racial stereotypes. *Journal of Experimental Social Psychology, 37*(2), 173–180.

Yosso, T. (2005) Whose culture has capital? A critical race theory discussion of community cultural wealth, *Race Ethnicity and Education, 8*(1), 69–91, DOI: 10.1080/1361332052000341006.

Zong, J., & Batalova, J. (2018). *Mexican immigrants in the United States. Migration policy institute.* https://www.migrationpolicy.org/article/mexican-immigrants-united-states.

Chapter 6

A Funny Thing Happens on the Way to the Classroom

Positioning Latinx Students, Families, and Teachers as Knowers while Promoting Cultural Competence for Culturally Relevant Pedagogy through Study-Abroad in Chile

Kenneth Fasching-Varner

According the Pew Research Center (Radford, 2019), immigrant groups, including those from Latinx backgrounds represent about 14% of the U.S. population and over 40% of immigrants; Latinx represent slightly more than 13 million school-aged students identified as Latinx (National Center for Education Statistics, 2017). The United States reflects increasing engagement with Latinx populations concurrent with a significant rise in xenophobic vitriolic racism targeted at Latinx communities. Since 2014 the rise in anti-Mexican and anti-Latinx rhetoric promulgated by Donald Trump has been matched by ultra-right fear and loathing of Latinx students and families with a palpably negative effect on the living-learning landscape that Latinx populations face. These statistics beg the question of how well teachers are prepared to engage with populations of students where ethnicity, racial, and language differences may intersect, given that the U.S. population that is white and non-Latinx is at over 60% (Radford, 2019).

Engagement with Latinx populations is increasingly urgent given the jingoistic sentiment in popular media and political rhetoric (Ben-Ghiat, 2017; Raghunathan, 2018), federal policy changes, public, organized displays of xenophobia (Lopez, 2017) and overt racism (Astor, Caron, & Victor, 2017; Spencer & Stolberg, 2017). Universities have released statements regarding immigration policy changes and attempted bans; "not one statement was issued in favor of . . . ban[s], instead emphasizing that bans strike directly at the global and open exchange of values and ideas" (Braaten, 2017, p. 8).

Researchers are vocal in response to the implications of recently implemented nationalistic policies and rhetoric on teacher education and education in general (Dougherty, 2017; Green & Castro, 2017; Murphy, 2017; Rubin, 2018). Barrow (2017) notes, "We are inextricably interconnected, and building walls or isolating ourselves in the name of nationalism will not change this fact" (p. 164). It would be irresponsible, and historically inaccurate, to imply that issues with nationalism first surfaced during the lead-up to and the first year and months of Trump's presidency (Williams, Pillai, Deptula, Lowe, and McCombs, 2018; Haidt, 2016; Antonsich, 2017). The current climate of heightened awareness surrounding these long-standing issues, instead, gives a sense of urgency to educators. This chapter draws upon empirical data from a 15-year longitudinal research engagement with a study-abroad experience to show how our work in Chile positions Latinx students, their families, and teachers in the positions of knowers and power brokers.

PROGRAM BACKGROUND

The Teaching in Chile program has lived in some form since 2004, so at the time of this chapter roughly 15 years. From its inception through today the program centers on having a group of between 10 to 25 participants from the United States engage in a 120-hour internship in a Chilean PreK-12 school. Participants draw from populations of both pre-service and in-service educators including Bachelor, Master, and Doctoral students as well as practicing educators with varying levels of experience. Participants are paired with a Chilean teacher with opposite experience. U.S. participants with less teaching experience are paired with Chilean teachers who have more teaching experience and vice-a-versa. During the school day the U.S. participants and Chilean teachers engage in a variety of co-teaching and shared classroom interactions and participate in twice weekly after school professional development led by both the K-12 partner school leadership and the U.S. university program leaders.

When not in school, participants live with host families from the school. In each household there is at least one 12- to 17-year-old adolescent who speaks both Spanish and English. The program generally brings monolingual English speakers (though there are occasional Spanish speakers who come), and the parents in the household generally do not speak English (though there are occasional host families where the parents speak English). The goals of the homestay are dynamic and multiple: (1) to empower the adolescents as the language brokers in the exchange between participants and their host families, (2) to help participants understand the complexity of student family and life outside of school in a way that they are not afforded when in their own home community, and (3) to encourage the participants to live in community with a family where they are not the dominant group, or in other words to reveal the position of the Chilean families as the dominant group and the position of U.S. participants as the nondominant player within the relationship. While outside of the school U.S. participants are a visiting member of the family and only interact with other U.S. participants outside of school in the circumstance that the host families are friends and may spend time together.

RESEARCH METHODOLOGY[1]

The data that support our thinking in this piece comes from a larger longitudinal examination of this study-abroad program. Regardless of their decision to participate in the longitudinal study, participants complete a preinterview and beliefs survey to gauge baseline understandings. During the experience, participants engage in a daily one-hour dialogue meeting, write in a two-way journal with program leaders, document their experience through a shared blog, and are informally interviewed during the experience. The interviews are pedagogical tools for the program leaders. Those continuing as research participants complete postexperience interviews and yearly surveys and/or interviews focusing on their current work with links to the program experience. Research participants' interviews are all transcribed and member checked for accuracy.

Participants

There have been 221 participants from 2004 through 2017. Eighty-seven percent of program participants ($n=192$) are female, whereas 13% of participants ($n=29$) are male. This gender imbalance is somewhat greater than the 67% female—33% male split seen in the most recent Open Doors national study-abroad demographic data (Witherall, 2016). The female/male ratio is more in line with national teaching demographics that estimate the teaching force to be 76% female and 24% male (NCES, 2015); the ratio almost is in-sync with our institutional demographics for pre-service teachers. In terms of race, 73% ($n=162$) of participants identified as white whereas 27% ($n=59$) of participants identified as not being white, again in line with Open Doors data. A particular breakdown of racial and ethnic identity revealed that 19% ($n=42$) of participants identified as Black or African American, 4.5% ($n=10$) identified as Latina, and 3% ($n=7$) identified as Asian. Approximately 5% ($n=11$)

of participants were not from the United States; seven participants came from countries in Asia and four were from other countries in the Americas including two Chilean-origin students.

From the total set of participants, nearly 56% (n=124) had never left the United States and just over 26% (n=57) of participants had never been on a plane before this experience. About 29% (n=63) of the participants were first-generation college//university attendees. Table 6.1 provides an overview of the program participants over the 14-year time span.

Some broader themes of the longitudinal research include heightened discussion of communication with families, teachers, and students upon return to the United States, overcoming resistances to unfamiliar pedagogical practices, pushing through homesickness, questioning difference, abandoning assumed hierarchical roles, and developing a commitment to the community.

RESULTS

Latinx students, families, and teachers as knowers and power brokers: Challenging U.S. monolingual educators' beliefs and perspectives.

The first area of focus here is the way that the program serves to position Latinx students and their families as well as the teachers as knowers and power brokers within this experience. Immigrant families, and in particular

Table 6.1 Program Participants over Time

Year	Participants	Female	Male	First Time Outside US/Plane	White/Not-white	First Generation
2017	22	19	3	14 / 5	16 / 6	8
2016	25	20	5	12 / 4	17 / 8	7
2015	20	18	2	12 / 5	16 / 4	10
2014	21	18	3	9 / 6	15 / 6	6
2013	24	20	4	14 / 4	19 / 5	7
2012	18	17	1	11 / 5	9 / 9	3
2011	19	17	2	11 / 7	15 / 4	6
2010	Program suspended for 2010 Concepción Chile earthquake.					
2009	15	12	3	8 / 3	12 / 3	2
2008	13	13	0	9 / 4	10 / 3	3
2007	10	9	1	6 / 4	8 / 2	3
2006	13	11	2	7 / 3	9 / 4	3
2005	11	10	1	5 / 2	8 / 3	3
2004	10	8	2	6 / 5	8 / 2	2
Totals	221	192 (87%)	29 (13%)	124 / 57 (56%) / (26%)	162 / 59 (73%) / (27%)	63 (29%)

Latinx families, in the United States whose children attend public schools are not met with a landscape that favors who they are, what they know, or how their base of knowledge contributes to the larger learning landscape. Even at its best many school systems adopt a model aimed at helping these families acclimate and acculturate to the United States based on a perception that English is the default language and that immigrant status is a less than position relative to U.S.-born students. Schools often do not have language-abled staff to interact with families, and given that demographics of the U.S. teaching force most immigrant children will experience identity disconnects with their teachers that intersect race, ethnicity, and language at a minimum. The sentiment around immigrant status is also complex, particularly given the rise of xenophobia described in the introduction of the chapter. What teachers see, even when well-meaning, are children very different from who they are; teachers are positioned with dominant group advantage. Teacher preparation programs do not have the capacity or scope to address the engagement of difference, particularly in landscapes where programs are either asked to cut credits and reduce time spent in preparation or teacher candidates chose accelerated alternative education programs where little time, if any, considers the unique engagement of difference with respect to learning.

When asked about the role of immigrant students in their classrooms, prior to the trip, data from most participants reflect well-meaning but vague and uninformed perspectives on working with these families. Agatha, a participant in the early iteration of the program, said, "Look I mean, I know they are there but I am not really sure what to do, they don't understand what I am saying and it's not like it's my fault." The idea of fault that Agatha expressed is interesting as it implies that a student's first language is a problem that requires blame. Jennifer, a more recent participant, shared, "I want to be helpful to students but sometimes I really don't even know where to start and I do not feel like I was prepared to even know what to do." Peter, a participant in 2016, during the height of pre-election Trump-driven xenophobia, shared, "All you hear all day long is that people are invading the country and, I mean, it's not like I believe it really but it's so overwhelming that it makes working with these kids difficult." Over time nearly 80% ($n=189$) of participants have articulated perspectives that combine some perspective of lacking preparation, being unsure how to engage, or feeling overwhelmed, as expressed by the sentiments of Agatha, Jennifer, and Peter.

During our time in the program, however, participants see what engagement looks like with Latinx teachers, students, and families firsthand, and they simultaneously are able to critically transfer their own lack of preparation and feeling of overwhelming as a dominant group to contemplating the emotional and psychological state of the students given their positionality within the Chilean context, where being the underrepresented groups is a first time of marginalization for many of the participants. Where Agatha established a level of fault before the trip, toward the end of her experience she shared

> no one here ever missed an opportunity to make sure I was included and they never seemed to not know what to do with me. It makes me think that even if I am not sure exactly what to do it shouldn't stop me from trying and making the extra effort.

Whereas Jennifer focused on her lack of preparation before the trip she shared at the end of the experience,

> I think what I learned here most is that you have to ask and engage and just keep coming back to the table, I think that I have been frustrated that no one told me how and here I learned that there isn't a manual and you just have to reach out and connect.

And, Peter shared.

> I can never look at an immigrant student the same way—in Chile no one was ever like "let's ignore Peter cause he's an invader," everyone just wanted to get to know me and in that process I realize like hey this kids dream is almost the same as what I dream about and like we are so much more in common. When I get home and I hear this bullshit about invasion like I am ready to go after it because it's just ignorant, we are all hoping for something in life. The thing is too I am way older than the kids I was working with in Chile but they had so much to teach me and I had so much to learn. So in my classes when I heard, you know, that no one is a blank slate this showed me that but so much more, it wasn't just that they had something, they had really important knowledge to teach me and that was something I didn't really think would have been what happened.

Peter's extended response shows not only his ability to see the humanity of the people he worked with in this different contact from his, but that the people he was seeing as different had very valuable knowledge to share. The context of this program provides an experience with Spanish speakers which particularly relevant given the outright marginalization that Latinx populations experience in the United States.

Maria Paz, a mentor teacher in the Chile program, shared her thoughts about the program and how her own understandings have evolved. Maria Paz says,

> so early on I was intimidated because you are taught that somehow what you know and do as an outsider to the "Americans" as US people is not quite good

enough when you are the "American" Chilean. We have, as a country, looked up to the United States and struggle because we see ourselves as American too. And I think for so long I wondered what do I have to share. Over time what I realize is that our way has a lot of value and that the teachers who come here say things like "I had never thought about that" and even years later still ask for support and advice.

This sentiment has been echoed by a vast majority of the mentor teachers when asking them about their relationship with U.S. participants. Jose Gabriel, another mentor teacher, stated,

> I am not sure I would have seen our strengths without the differences presented by this program. In your own world you do not see yourself as too good or too bad, but I appreciate that my colleagues and I know a lot about working with kids that our counterparts don't know as easily and that especially for Spanish speakers many teachers from the US are sort of lost. It has also helped me see how to enhance what I know with the things that they know and that makes it, I guess, cool the way ideas and experiences go back and forth.

An administrator at the school Raul shared that

> seeing how confident our teachers have become and how willing to share has had a positive impact on our school community. Not in any sort of arrogant way, but in a reassuring way, we have seen teachers stronger about how they value their own work and how they communicate with the students, families, and bigger community.

Many U.S. participants enter the experience feeling that they will have to serve as the knower or teacher to their Chilean partner for two principal reasons: their own improperly informed assumptions and based on how the partner teachers communicate prior to the experience. Sarah is an example of the first time of conceptualization. After her experience Sarah shared that

> it was totally wild, because I just assumed that being not the US they would be like really behind or something. And looking back like wow, that's just so stupid, but I definitely thought "well I have been teaching 15 years and I am sure this will be a great opportunity for me to teach someone else all the great things we do." What I realized so quickly though was that Joesfina has been teaching a long time too and she dances circles around me in a lot of ways. I have never seen a teacher be able to connect with kids the way she does and make it relevant to the learning. And in working with her I not only was able to see it but she walked me through how she comes to do what she does and

that dialogue was so important and it was like she was better than any professor I ever had.

Jill, a U.S. pre-service teacher participant, shared about the conflict between the Chilean partners pre-dialogue and the actual experience. Jill said that

> after emailing and WhatsApping for a while before the trip I was worried because Margarita (the Chilean partner) kept telling me that she was so happy to host me and learn from me and that she was not a great teacher probably like how they "make them in the US." So I thought yikes this is going to be a lot of pressure because what do I know. What I found though was this huge opposite. Margarita has such a kind and humble nature I think she downplayed who she was and what she knew. I had already had three practicums to that point and had a lot of classes with so called experts who couldn't do the things that Margarita did. And what I loved was that she was never like "take it from me," she did her work and she was good at is and I learned so much. Toward the end when I shared what I had taken away from working with Margarita she said "you really learned all this in our time?" and the truth of the matter was that it is what happened. It's like a funny thing happens on the way to the classroom—I spent so much time trying to get something from my US experience but it was in Chile where I learned what I couldn't at home and it was because of Margarita that I pride myself now in supporting my students for whom English is second or even third or fourth language.

Again, these extended responses get at the heart of a significant transformation for participants. And, as it turns out the teachers in Chile too have significant take aways. After the experience when interviewing Margarita about her experience she shared,

> I never really thought about myself as teaching other adults about how to do the work we do. I try to work on my own teaching but this experience gave me the confidence to start sharing with colleagues. When Jill shared what she learned I felt so proud because these were things that I take great care with but never felt like I should share that with others.

Positioning Latinx families and students as well as teachers as knowers and power brokers at the same time that participants' beliefs are challenged is a powerful antidote to the deficit perspective pervasive about this population in the United States. Interestingly, having Latinx knowers and power brokers in this experience also supports participants engagement with students and families across the spectrum of difference in a way that might not have been likely to register without a profound and meaningful experience with difference.

CULTURAL COMPETENCE AND CULTURALLY RELEVANT PEDAGOGY

We would be remiss in this work if we did not discuss at least some meaningful aspect of culturally relevant pedagogy linked to the work we do in Chile. It is important to note that over the past 25 years, there have been various considerations regarding culturally relevant, culturally responsive, and culturally sustaining approaches to education that might serve as antidotes to the often-disengaging pedagogy that most public school students receive, particularly those from historically underrepresented and marginalized populations. Since Ladson-Billings introduced the concept of CRP a number of scholars have attempted to explain, unpack, situate, or otherwise make known the three principle tenets of CRP explained earlier: high expectations for achievement, cultural competence, and sociopolitical commitment (Cochran-Smith, 2004; Cook-Sather, 2002; Fasching-Varner & Dodo Seriki, 2012; Fasching-Varner & Mitchell, 2013; Fasching-Varner, 2013; Gutiérrez & Orellana, 2006; Howard, 2013; Ladson-Billings, 2006, 2013; Nieto, 2003; Noguera, 2003; Villegas & Lucas, 2002; Windschitl, 2002).

Much of the literature on these culturally engaging approaches either focuses at a theoretical level to the exclusion of practice or demonstrates a desire to implement engagement-based pedagogies through practice with little comprehensive and cohesive enactment of the theory themselves. Large gaps persist between students from historically over- and underrepresented groups in participation, achievement, persistence, reported behavior, and educational outcomes (Aud, Fox, & Kewal Ramani, 2010). Ongoing disproportionality in special education (Tefera, Thorius, & Artiles, 2013), gifted education (Ford, 1998; Ford & Russo, 2016), and disciplinary measures (Raufu, 2017; Gregory, Skiba, & Mediratta, 2017; Gregory, Skiba, & Noguera, 2010) further indicates a disconnect between the theory and praxis of culturally relevant and culturally responsive pedagogy.

Recently identified inconsistencies between self-reported and observed culturally proficient teaching practices imply that even teachers who are intent upon addressing the unique needs of their culturally diverse students lack the training, insight, and experience to do so effectively (Debnam, Pas, Bottiani, Cash, & Bradshaw, 2015). Naturally consistent disparities suggest a closer look at challenges to CRP, including that of cultural competence.

One of the three principle components of CRP is developing cultural competence. In other work from researchers on this team (Fasching-Varner & Dodo Seriki, 2012; Fasching-Varner, 2013) we learn that the perception that cultural competence in the culturally relevant framework is often misinterpreted to mean that teachers attending to their perceptions (however false those perceptions may be) of student culture and either acknowledging or "doing" something with their perceptions is sufficient to be engaged in a culturally relevant way. We argue that the first consideration of cultural competence that needs to be engaged with is the cultural competence a teacher has about her/his own identity culturally. So while understanding and working within the complex sets of cultural identities a teacher should be competent with respect to their students, but we often fail to see that enactment at least in part because teachers often do not have the opportunity to reflect upon and critically engage with their own cultural identity and the perceptions, beliefs, and interactions that ensue.

In our Chile program we have shown that Latinx students, families, and teachers are knowers, but to do that we have also revealed that this engagement comes through a process of the teachers being challenged by their own beliefs and their own perceptions of difference. In essence, we are able to get at something that is difficult to get at when your experience is decontextualized from kids' life as most local practicum and teacher experiences are. We argue that pre-service teachers and classroom teachers can engage in relevant and/or responsive methods, as they begin seeing themselves "emerging as sociocultural conscious teachers who are able to identify critical issues" (Ramirez, Jimenez-Silva, Boozer, & Clark, 2016, p. 27) and we see the opportunities for facilitated dialogue and 360-degree engagement in our program, in embedded community contexts, as helping to facilitate the stance that leads to critical introspection.

The importance of active listening in effective communication both in and out of the educational setting has been established in the research literature (Barker, 2017; Wise, Hausknecht, & Zhao, 2014; Ladson-Billings, 2016; McNaughton, Hamlin, McCarthy, Head-Reeves, & Schreiner, 2008), but it carries even more weight in the context of intercultural dialogues in which we engage during our program and in our participants' future classrooms. Listening, and the requisite processing skills, is of vital importance for second language learners to make meaning (Kuhl, Stevenson, Corrigan, van den Bosch, Kan, & Richards, 2016; Rost & Candlin, 2014). Given that English is used for communication with both the school partners and students, listening more (and providing the requisite wait time and silence) models helps ensure that conversations are as rich as possible and that both sides are making meaning given that in any interaction with a Chilean partner, their use of English is not in their first language.

Cultivating the space for dialogue is particularly important in a landscape within the United States, as described in the early part of this chapter, that is jingoistic and xenophobic where both of those elements grow and infest in large part because of fear. Fear of other and fear of difference present prominently in the U.S. national dialogue allowing "cultures of domination [to] rely on the cultivation of fear as a way to ensure obedience," with the rhetoric and ensuing actions of fear, loathing, and hate. This context, lamentably, prompts many educators to decontextualize from their own reality and their own identity ironically in the name of intending engagement all the while separating themselves from others; the fear of the unknown in difference "promotes the desire for separation" (hooks, 2000, p. 83), and ultimately never allows an educator the opportunity to fully engage with the cultural competence aspect of culturally relevant pedagogy.

Robin was a hesitant and skeptical participant at first; she tried to avoid journal writing and sat seemingly non-participatory in group conversation time at the beginning of the program. When we look at her pre-trip writing and even clues in her early journals, she entered the space willingly but full of so much fear it paralyzed her ability to understand how she has come to see the world let alone engage with others about their cultural values and perspectives. Her journal entry from the last Friday of the program, however, conveyed a newly perspective on the critical need for communication and her own competence. Robin wrote,

> So, talking and listening are becoming my new favorite forms of thinking. I learned so much more about others and my own understandings from talking, listening, and writing. And I'm so glad I now have my journal and blogs to go reread anytime. I think I sort of believed things for lots of reasons that didn't have much to do with what I really think; I never have had to think that much but kind of just echo others. In this program I learned that if I am going to work with kids the frame can't be if I think they are similar or different to me—I need to keep working at the balance between figuring myself out and letting them introduce and guide me as to who they are, how they see their reality, and how multiple realities can interact together.

Through communication and the growth of community partnership, participants learn to see strength of others by first engaging one's self as mechanism to build caring bonds with their future students (hooks, 2000). Active listening becomes a crucial component of a pedagogy that values cultural competence of self and others (Larson & Murtadha, 2002). Over 15 years we see significant moments of introspection for participants and community partners, all important to consider in any context where one is interested in the culturally relevant or responsive preparation of educators.

CONCLUDING THOUGHT

Institutions are called upon to develop and sustain means for transforming experiences and interactions that conceptualize ways for teachers to be culturally relevant. We recognize that the proposition of study-abroad is not the only method, nor is it a quick fix to address issues presented by systemic oppression. The purpose of this chapter was not to say that study-abroad in itself is a solution to anything. Instead, the context of this longitudinal program has placed a focus on seeing Latinx students, families, and teachers as whole, complete, and a value-added set of partners to U.S. educators. That recognition comes from positive and meaningful sustained interaction over multiple weeks as well as through dialogue. The pathway to combat systems of oppression, we would argue throughout history has always come through individual and collective experiences, and through the focus of working to comprehend the tensions between the local of a context within systems of existence in the bigger world (Forsey, Broomhall, & Davis, 2012; Brooks & Pitts, 2016). Having Latinx students, families, and teachers positioned as knowers, in and of itself has value that is not easily dismissed, but coupled within an active communication approach, we believe that the positioning works at the often-difficult idea of developing cultural competence which is a known key component of culturally relevant pedagogy. Our hope is that across the scholarly community more narratives, cases, and accounts of the engagement and positioning of Latinx individuals and communities will permeate the barrier between fear and generosity that influences the living learning landscape for so many in the United States.

NOTE

1. The methodology section is borrowed completely from our previous work:
Fasching-Varner, K. J., Denny, R. K., Stone, M. P., Stewart, L. M., Albornoz, C. F., Mora, R., . . . & Denny, M. A. (2018). Love in a "glocal" world: Living and learning to teach through study-abroad. *Multicultural Perspectives*, *20*(3), 135–147.

This language is reprinted with the permission of *Multicultural Perspectives* Editor Kevin Roxas. Reviewers for this piece wanted a fuller methodology; using the previously written methodology for our study made the most sense as that has not changed. We wish to thank Kevin Roxas and *Multicultural Perspectives* for their generosity in letting us reuse our methodology section from that article essentially as is.

REFERENCES

Antonsich, M. (2017). The return of the nation: When neo-nationalism becomes mainstream. *Environment and Planning D: Society and Space*, 1–4. Society and Space: http://www.societyandspace.org.

Astor, M., Caron, C., & Victor, D. (2017, August 13). A guide to the Charlottesville aftermath. *The New York Times:* https://www.nytimes.com.

Aud, S., Fox, M. A., & Kewal Ramani, A. (2010). *Status and trends in the education of racial and ethnic groups.* Washington, DC: National Center for Education Statistics.

Barker, L. M. (2017). Under discussion: Teaching speaking and listening: Beyond "rock and roll": How teachers reimagine their responses during classroom discussion. *English Journal, 106*(3), 87.

Barrow, E. (2017). No global citizenship? Re-envisioning global citizenship education in times of growing nationalism. *The High School Journal, 100*(3), 163–165.

Ben-Ghiat, R. (2017). Donald Trump's cult of personality. *Huffington Post.*

Braaten, D. B. (2017). Higher education in the age of Trump. *Intersections, 45,* 6–11.

Brooks, C. F., & Pitts, M. J. (2016). Communication and identity management in a globally-connected classroom: An online international and intercultural learning experience. *Journal of International and intercultural Communication, 9*(1), 52–68.

Cochran-Smith, M. (2004). *Walking the road: Race, diversity, and social justice in teacher education.* Teachers College Press.

Cook-Sather, A. (2002). Authorizing students' perspectives: Toward trust, dialogue, and change in education. *Educational Researcher, 31*(4), 3–14.

Debnam, K. J., Pas, E. T., Bottiani, J., Cash, A. H., & Bradshaw, C. P. (2015). An examination of the association between observed and self-reported culturally proficient teaching practices. *Psychology in the Schools, 52*(6), 533–548.

Dougherty, D. M. (2017). From the classroom to the streets: Trump, DeVos and the denial of racism. *Mid-Atlantic Education Review, 5*(1), 8–11.

Fasching-Varner, K. & Mitchell, R. (2013). CRT's challenge to educators' articulation of abstract liberal perspectives of purpose. In M. Lynn and A. Dixson (Eds.) *Handbook of critical race theory in education* (pp. 375–387). Routledge.

Fasching-Varner, K. J. (2013). "Uhh, You Know," Don't You?: White racial bonding in the narrative of white pre-service teachers. *Educational Foundations, 27,* 21–41.

Fasching-Varner, K. J., Denny, R. K., Stone, M. P., Stewart, L. M., Albornoz, C. F., Mora, R., Olave, P., Yacoman, M. & Denny, M. A. (2018). Love in a "glocal" world: Living and learning to teach through study-abroad. *Multicultural Perspectives, 20*(3), 135–147.

Fasching-Varner, K. J., & Dodo Seriki, V. (2012). Moving beyond seeing with our eyes wide shut. A response to "There is no culturally responsive teaching spoken here". *Democracy and Education, 20*(1), 1–6.

Ford, D. Y. (1998). The underrepresentation of minority students in gifted education: Problems and promises in recruitment and retention. *The Journal of Special Education, 32*(1), 4–14.

Ford, D. Y., & Russo, C. J. (2016). Historical and legal overview of special education overrepresentation: Access and equity denied. *Multiple Voices for Ethnically Diverse Exceptional Learners, 16*(1), 50–57.

Forsey, M., Broomhall, S., & Davis, J. (2012). Broadening the mind? Australian student reflections on the experience of overseas study. *Journal of Studies in International Education*, *16*(2), 128–139.

Green, T. L., & Castro, A. (2017). Doing counterwork in the age of a counterfeit president: Resisting a Trump–DeVos education agenda. *International Journal of Qualitative Studies in Education*, *30*(10), 912–919.

Gregory, A., Skiba, R. J., & Mediratta, K. (2017). Eliminating disparities in school discipline: A framework for intervention. *Review of Research in Education*, *41*(1), 253–278.

Gregory, A., Skiba, R. J., & Noguera, P. A. (2010). The achievement gap and the discipline gap: Two sides of the same coin? *Educational Researcher*, *39*(1), 59–68.

Gutiérrez, K. D., & Orellana, M. F. (2006). At last: The "problem" of English learners: Constructing genres of difference. *Research in the Teaching of English*, *40*(4), 502–507.

Haidt, J. (2016). When and why nationalism beats globalism. *Policy: A Journal of Public Policy and Ideas*, *32*(3), 46.

hooks, B. (2000). *Feminism is for everybody: Passionate politics*. Pluto Press.

Howard, T. C. (2013). How does it feel to be a problem? Black male students, schools, and learning in enhancing the knowledge base to disrupt deficit frameworks. *Review of Research in Education*, *37*(1), 54–86.

Kuhl, P. K., Stevenson, J., Corrigan, N. M., van den Bosch, J. J., Can, D. D., & Richards, T. (2016). Neuroimaging of the bilingual brain: Structural brain correlates of listening and speaking in a second language. *Brain and Language*, *162*, 1–9.

Ladson-Billings, G. (2016). And then there is this thing called the curriculum: Organization, imagination, and mind. *Educational Researcher*, *45*(2), 100–104.

Ladson-Billings, G. (2006). From the achievement gap to the education debt: Understanding achievement in US schools. *Educational Researcher*, *35*(7), 3–12.

Ladson-Billings, G. (2013). Stakes is high: Educating New Century Students. *The Journal of Negro Education*, *82*(2), 105–110.

Larson, C. L., & Murtadha, K. (2002). Leadership for social justice. *Yearbook of the National Society for the Study of Education*, *101*(1), 134–161.

Lopez, G. (2017, December 15). The past year of research has made it very clear: Trump won because of racial resentment. *Vox*: https://www.vox.com.

McNaughton, D., Hamlin, D., McCarthy, J., Head-Reeves, D., & Schreiner, M. (2008). Learning to listen: Teaching an active listening strategy to preservice education professionals. *Topics in Early Childhood Special Education*, *27*(4), 223–231.

Murphy, J. P. (2017). Defending "all this Diversity Garbage": Multidimensional coalition-building in the age of Trump. *Mid-Atlantic Education Review*, *5*(1), 12–18.

National Center for Education Statistics. (2017). *ACS 2013–2017 dataset profile*. Washington, DC: National Center for Education Statistics.

Nieto, S. (2003). *What keeps teachers going?* Teachers College Press.

Noguera, P. A. (2003). The trouble with Black boys: The role and influence of environmental and cultural factors on the academic performance of African American males. *Urban Education, 38*(4), 431–459.

Radford, J. (2019). *Key findings about U.S. immigrants*. Pew Research Center: https://www.pewresearch.org.

Raghunathan, S. (2018). Trump's xenophobic vision of America is inciting racist violence: Attacks against Muslim, South Asian, Sikh, Hindu, Arab, and Middle Eastern communities in the US were up a staggering 45 percent in 2017. *The Nation*: https://www.thenation.com.

Ramirez, P., Jimenez-Silva, M., Boozer, A., & Clark, B. (2016). Going against the grain in an urban Arizona high school: Secondary preservice teachers emerging as culturally responsive educators. *Multicultural Perspectives, 18*(1), 20–28.

Raufu, A. (2017). School-to-prison pipeline: Impact of school discipline on African American students. *Journal of Education and Social Science, 7*(1), 47–53.

Rost, M., & Candlin, C. N. (2014). *Listening in language learning*. New York, NY: Routledge.

Rubin, J. (2018). The Trump candidacy: Implications for curriculum. *Interchange, 49*(2), 153–160.

Spencer, H., & Stolberg, S. G. (2017). White nationalists march on University of Virginia. *The New York Times*: http://www.nytimes.com.

Tefera, A., Thorius, K. K., & Artiles, A. J. (2013). Teacher influences in the racialization of disabilities. In H.R. Milner (Ed.), *Handbook of Urban Education* (pp. 256–270). Routledge.

Villegas, A. M., & Lucas, T. (2002). Preparing culturally responsive teachers: Rethinking the curriculum. *Journal of Teacher Education, 53*(1), 20–32.

Williams, E. A., Pillai, R., Deptula, B. J., Lowe, K. B., & McCombs, K. (2018). Did charisma "Trump" narcissism in 2016? Leader narcissism, attributed charisma, value congruence and voter choice. *Personality and Individual Differences, 130*, 11–17.

Windschitl, M. (2002). Framing constructivism in practice as the negotiation of dilemmas: An analysis of the conceptual, pedagogical, cultural, and political challenges facing teachers. *Review of Educational Research, 72*(2), 131–175.

Wise, A. F., Hausknecht, S. N., & Zhao, Y. (2014). Attending to others' posts in asynchronous discussions: Learners' online "listening" and its relationship to speaking. *International Journal of Computer-Supported Collaborative Learning, 9*(2), 185–209.

Witherell, S. (2016). *IIE releases open door 2016 data*. Institute of International Education: http://www.iie.org.

Section III

VOICES OF TEACHER EDUCATORS

Introduction

The Journey from Student to Teacher to Teacher Educator: A Cry for Change

Ofelia Castro Schepers

As I pulled up to the parking lot of Sandoval Elementary School on Wednesday, November 9, 2016, a wave of despair overcame me. I sat in the car for a few extra minutes, regulating my breathing and wiping away the tears streaming down my face.

Months of listening to painful and hostile rhetoric aimed at the Latinx community engendered my pain. This rhetoric seemed to bolster portions of the U.S. population that either vehemently agreed with those allegations, with little regard to truth, or were apathetic to the pain it caused our community, not concerning themselves with what they deemed identity politics. Yet, this painful time impacted and continues to affect many Latinx teachers and students. Because many of the students at Sandoval worried about their parents and even their futures in this country, the impending teacher observation's particulars seemed inconsequential. Walking the hallways and seeing children would be a difficult task for me. I shared the same sense of sadness and uncertainty that many of them were noticeably feeling. Further, my knowledge that many of the students at Sandoval were academically and emotionally unsupported led me to believe that some of their teachers were dismissing their fears and worries. While I think that most of Sandoval's teachers genuinely care about their students, very few of them knew what these students were going through that day. Some even felt that students' feelings around fears of deportations were unwarranted. Further, in a predominantly white profession, the few Latinx teachers faced similar fears and despair, likely lacking support from peers and administration.

Yet this pain and these fears are understandable. Ther are rooted in the direct aim at the character and right to exist in this country that the Latinx community regularly faces. In this sociopolitical context, teachers in schools dress up as Trump's Border Wall and as Mexicans. There are teachers that tell students that their parents will be deported and they will be put into foster care. Those that publicly call for support from the federal government to remove all undocumented students from their schools. Many that actively tell students they should "go back to their country" (regardless of country of origin). Imagine being a Latinx student and how difficult it is to learn and to thrive. Or what it must feel like to look around and not see many teachers that understand you or worse, some that mock or threaten you.

This hostile rhetoric is not isolated to K-12 classrooms. It was and continues to be experienced by students and faculty of color in primarily white institutions of higher education. This narrative about Latinx communities is not new, as can be seen in the anti-immigration rhetoric within U.S. history primarily aimed at communities of color and mostly focused on Latinx folks. However, the 2016 election cycle proved to embolden people who align with these negative narratives, and as a result, schools became increasingly difficult spaces for Latinx students and teachers. These negative sentiments and toxic environments in schools may explain why there is a failure to recruit and retain Latinx teachers, further isolating Latinx students.

I went into teaching because, growing up, I longed to visualize myself in the teachers who led my classes. I wanted to know that someone understood my perspectives and characteristics and saw them as strengths rather than deficits or weaknesses. I wanted to see that I was not perceived as someone who needed to be fixed or saved. As an immigrant from Mexico, being a U.S. K-12 public school student proved to have many challenges. Though I was able to persevere, this narrative only served to continue to marginalize other students by tokenizing stories of success without attention to the hardships faced or supports offered. In elementary school, I was segregated under the guise of language acquisition classes. In middle school, I faced similar scrutiny. School administration forced me to drop my electives to take additional language courses (regardless of testing out or having grades in literacy courses that mirrored those of monolingual students). I was tracked out of accelerated English courses in high school, even though I met the requirements to be in the classes. These are not experiences that I have faced in isolation. Numerous students face these barriers. These students have educators who either do not understand them, misunderstand them, or believe the fatalistic rhetoric about them. Often, these teachers enforce exclusionary practices. Students' experiences, and my experience, bring to light how they traverse an education system that is wrought with a political divide. Further, when one's immigration status or ethnicity and race are under scrutiny, the toxicity of the experience can become unbearable. Latinx youth continue to have one of the highest dropout rates in the nation. Though reform efforts have proven that teacher representation makes a difference in retaining students in school and students' success, it has not proven easy to recruit and retain Latinx teachers into teacher education programs.

While representation is key in supporting Latinx youth, my own teacher preparation program proved to be lacking in the representation of Latinx people. I was the only Latina, out of the three cohorts of students, who had enrolled and was accepted into the program that year. The 60 plus students across all three cohorts were largely homogenous in their race, gender, and socioeconomic status. The candidates that were considered "diverse" were almost all in the same cohort, except one or two students. This lack of diversity and representation at the collegiate level was difficult, especially as a first-generation college student. Yet, I was fortunate enough to be enrolled in educational opportunity programs that provided additional support through affinity spaces. These particular groups were essential in providing cultural and emotional supports during times of extreme racial tensions.

After college, my own teaching experiences proved to be equally difficult, especially around politically charged conversations. Unfortunately, there were no affinity groups to support me through these tense times. Furthermore, a colleague and I, the only two Latina faculty at the school, faced extensive scrutiny from parents and often from other colleagues as well. The teachers' lounge was filled with negative rhetoric about "those students" and "those families" as white, affluent teachers decided to move into whiter communities when their children turned school-aged. Yet, "those students" and "those families," primarily Latinx youth and families, were the same students they were supposed to teach and care about in their classrooms. This experience was isolating and defeating for me, and after five years in the classroom, it was apparent to me that one teacher cannot change the system. This realization led me to pursue a Ph.D. program in Educational Equity and Cultural Diversity. I wanted to shift systems that had historically marginalized the Latinx and People Of Color experience and continue to do so both implicitly and overtly.

My journey to becoming a teacher educator allowed me to dissect each experience as a Latinx individual at each level of the educational continuum. These experiences led me to become a teacher educator with a mission: to help dismantle institutional racism and build systems that support pre-service Latinx students and academic allies to become educators that support Latinx students and their communities. My progression, and that of millions of others through the U.S. K-12 and higher education systems, reinforces the pressing need to move away from the inaccurate belief that education is apolitical and that everyone will be treated equally. What would it look like to have an educational system in which a Latinx person would feel supported? We must prepare more Latinx educators and more educators who understand how to help Latinx students see themselves in the curriculum, in positive interactions, and as future educators and leaders. Higher education must examine policies, structures, practices, and curriculum so that the Latinx students who want to be teachers are supported socially, emotionally, and academically so that they make it through to teach all students, including Latinx students, in affirming and culturally sustaining ways. State and local education agencies must better define their role in this process in supporting Latinx students, teachers, guardians, and support staff. We must take on an abolitionist teaching mindset so that no more Latinx educators need to wipe tears away before entering a school building. No more Latinx students need to fear their teachers; no more Latinx colleagues need to face added scrutiny. We need better recruiting, retaining, and supporting sustainable structures for Latinx teachers now. In the end, we need all levels of the education system to work in partnership to close the feedback loop so that we have a sustainable avenue for students as they advance K-12 education to higher education and eventually highly supported educators.

Chapter 7

Educating Teachers to Work with Latinx Children and Families in Challenging Sociopolitical Contexts and Times

Eleonora Villegas-Reimers

INTRODUCTION

In the Spring semester of 2017, one of my undergraduate students, completing his first elementary education teaching practicum under my guidance, shared this observation during one of our student-teaching seminars: a child in his second-grade classroom was crying, quietly, in a corner of the room; when my student approached to ask the child what was going on, the child shared that she was scared because ICE was going to go to her house and take her parents away, and she did not know where she would go after school. My student said he tried to calm the child, assuring her that she would be OK, but realizing he could not say the parents wouldn't be picked up by ICE that day or in the near future, as he had learned her parents were in this country without proper documentation. He asked the seminar members and me how to handle that situation in the future, as he knew this would happen again given that this girl was not the only student of undocumented parents in his classroom. Before I began to answer, another student, also in practicum, followed with this question, "And what should we do when we hear a student or a group of students tell other students, usually Latinx, in anger, that they should go back to their own country, regardless of whether those students do actually come from another country?"

I remember sitting down, quietly, and looking at these two students, surprised, and then the others, and just asking, "How many of you are experiencing these kinds of events in your practicum classrooms?" and all hands went up. Pause. While thinking about how to respond, one of my two Latinx students in that group said, "I had a child tell me that I could not tell her what to do because, not only was I not her 'real' teacher, but also that I was in this country 'illegally.' When I explained that I had been born in this country, just like she was, she said that was not possible as I could not be an American like her because of my name and my skin color."

This kind of conversation, which has been repeated often with some variance in my student-teaching seminars in the past three years, points to how increasingly difficult the current sociopolitical and cultural contexts where teachers teach have become as a result of the changing policies, politics, dialogues, and practices that have transformed the U.S. society from one that celebrated differences in most places and welcomed immigrants with open arms, to one that presents all immigrants and children of immigrants as people who do not belong, who are not welcome, and who just should "go back" to where they came from (Varela, 2018). This is particularly emphasized for teachers of Latinx students and for Latinx teachers themselves, as the Latinx community has been one of the most targeted groups in the recent political discourse. How do we, then, prepare teachers who need to respond to these issues effectively? How do we prepare teachers to not only offer support and understanding to children who are either causing or experiencing these circumstances, and more importantly, to prepare all students, including Latinx students, effectively so that they can become successful members of society who contribute in effective ways to its well-being and who help make this a more open, respectful, accepting society?

The need to prepare effective teachers to work with Latinx children and families in this country today should be priority for all teacher preparation programs, not only because the number of Latinx children continues to increase in the United States (Flores, 2017) but also because indicators of their success in school show that their academic performance is, on average, at the lowest rates when compared with any other group of students (Musu-Gillette et al, 2017). This trend has been going on for many years, but it has intensified in the current sociopolitical and cultural context, where Latinx groups are constantly labeled as not belonging, being social deviants, and a burden to society, and where children are experiencing higher levels of stress due to constant bullying, insults, threats to their security, and fears that relatives will be asked to leave the country with no warning (Miller, 2017).

In this chapter, I will describe what we know about Latinx students and teachers today, followed by the current sociopolitical contexts, and educational experiences and outcomes of Latinx students, and, finally, will present best teacher education preparation practices to educate effective teachers (both pre- and in-service) to work with Latinx children and families in the current contexts.

WHO ARE THE LATINX STUDENTS IN THE UNITED STATES AND WHO ARE THE TEACHERS WHO TEACH THEM?

Contrary to the general perception that all Latinx students in the United States come from very homogenous communities, making them similar to one another, all English language learners, and all from under-resourced families with little or no formal education, the community of Latinx students in the United States is a very diverse in terms of country of origin, English proficiency, Spanish/Portuguese proficiency, family level of education, racial background, religious background, political views, and socioeconomic status, to just mention a few sociocultural characteristics. The diversity is so deep that there is even some disagreement among members of the community on the appropriate label to use to identify them as a group. Some prefer to be identified as "Hispanos" (highlighting the Spanish roots, and the common language that they share, but leaving Brazilians out, for example); others prefer Latinos or Latinas (highlighting their countries of origin regardless of language spoken), and yet others prefer Latinx to highlight the inclusivity of all gender identities. Some opponents of the use of "Latinx" consider that the "x" is a "linguistically imperialist term," (as reported by Griffin, 2018), imposing American values onto the Spanish language which has a grammar rule that all nouns have a gender, usually ending in "a" for females and "o" for males. What this very diverse group of students has in common is that their ancestors or themselves were born in one of the many countries of Latin America (each with unique cultural characteristics), and thus share similar cultural roots, including the languages that their ancestors, and *sometimes* themselves, speak, and a few other characteristics such as the way they value family and community.

The Latinx population in the United States reached 59.9 million in 2018, up 1.2 million from the previous year according to the U.S. Census Bureau population estimates (Flores et al., 2019). They represent 17.6% of the total U.S. population (Gándara, 2017), which makes Latinx the largest ethnic minority population in the United States today. Despite these numbers, the Pew Research Center (Noe-Bustamante et al., 2020) reports that the U.S. Latinx population growth has slowed down in the last 10 years. After Asians, however, the Latinx community is still the largest growing ethnic minority population in the country. Latinos are among the youngest racial and ethnic group in the United States, with a median age of 30 years (Flores, et al., 2019). Flores (2017) reports that 37% of Latinx in 2015 were born in the United States.

Of the students in K-12 public schools, 25% (or one in four students) are Latinx (Gándara, 2017). According to the National Center for Education

Statistics (NCES), by 2024 Latinx students will be about 29% of the total public K-12 populations (Clontz, 2018). Contrary to popular belief, however, more than 90% of the school-age Latinx population was born in the United States; they are U.S. citizens (Gándara, 2017).

With regard to the total enrollment in K-12 schools and colleges in the United States, Latinx students were nearly 18 million in 2016, up from 8.8 million in 1996 according to Census Bureau data. Also, despite the fact that Latinx students have the highest high school dropout rate of any ethnic group in the country, that rate dropped from 34% to 10% between 1996 and 2016 (Paterson, 2019).

When looking at country of origin for the students and/or their families, two-thirds are of Mexican origin, and about 10% are of Puerto Rican origin. The rest come from a variety of countries from South and Central America (Gándara, 2017). The majority of the students come from under-resourced communities and from families with low levels of formal education. Many Latinx students (and teachers) come from different racial backgrounds: some identify as White, others as Black, others as Indigenous, and many as mixed; Black Latinx individuals are usually identified by others as African American, and Asian Latinx are usually identified as Asian. The reality is that the Latinx community is truly mixed given its historical origins, and teachers, therefore, need to address the very different needs of this very diverse community.

Unfortunately, on average, Latinx students are also the students with the lowest academic performance in the United States today. They have the lowest participation in pre-school programs in the country, and thus tend to enter formal schooling lagging behind most of the students from other ethnic and racial groups (Gándara, 2017). According Gándara (2017), data collected by the National Assessment of Educational Progress (NAEP) which tests representative samples of all U.S. K-12 students in math and reading, show that Latinos are consistently among the lowest performing groups despite making some gains in the last few years. But this gain has not been significant; when the gap (23 points) between Latinos and whites is compared between scores obtained in 1992 and in 2007, there is no significant difference (NCES 2019). However, when the graduation rate of Latinx students is compared between 2006 and 2014, it has increased from 61% to 76%, but even with that significant gain, their graduation rate is significantly below that of White students (87%) and Asian students (89%). A recent report (Samuels, 2019) also shows that Latinx students whose mothers were born in the United States attend less racially and ethnically segregated schools than Latinx students whose mothers were foreign born. This is supported by studies conducted by the Civil Rights Project at UCLA which found that White and Latinx students attend the most segregated schools in the country: Latinx students attend schools where 55% of the student population is Latinx too.

Looking beyond the K-12 years into bachelor's degree programs, in 2015 only 16% of Latinx students had completed at least a bachelor's degree by age 29, compared with 43% of Whites, and 66% of Asians (Gándara, 2017). One of many reasons for this gap is that the majority of Latinx students that do attend college choose two-year colleges, thus completing an Associate Degree (Krogstad, 2016).

Many have attributed the low academic performance of Latinx students to lack of English proficiency when they enter school (Gándara, 2017), in particular given the fact that the lowest performing students in most states of the country tend to be the students classified as English Language Learners or Dual Language Learners. However, given that 90% of the Latinx students are born in the United States, and that only 77% of all Dual Language Learners in the United States are Latinx (NCES 2018), and that in 2015, 69% of Latinx students reported that they speak only English at home, or that they speak English very well, many research studies have tried to identify other variables to explain the low academic performance. Research has also found that Latinx immigrants and children of immigrants outperform Latinx students who have lived in the country for many generations (Telles & Ortiz, 2008). For example, U.S.-born adult children of Latinx immigrants have "higher incomes, more are college graduates and homeowners, and fewer live in poverty" (Pew Research Center, 2013, p. 7). As a result, limited language proficiency cannot be the only explanatory variable. Many researchers have identified other more powerful variables to explain the low achievement of Latinx students; poverty, lower levels of formal education of their parents, isolation from English-speaking neighbors and communities, significant placement of Latinx students in low performing schools with low performing teachers or teachers who are teaching subjects not covered in their teaching licenses are among the most common variables mentioned (Gándara, 2017; Kao & Tienda, 1995; Suarez-Orozco & Suarez-Orozco, 1995, Telles & Ortiz, 2008).

In terms of the teachers who teach Latinx students, most are White with no Latinx ethnicity. Only about 8% of teachers are themselves Latinx (Davis et al., 2016). Shapiro and Partelow (2018) report that the widest gap in the number of students and teachers of the same ethnic background is that of the Latinx group. The states with the largest student / teachers gap are those with the largest population of Latinx students; and the four states with the largest gaps (California, Nevada, Arizona, and Texas) include more than 50% of the Latinx student population in the country (Shapiro & Partelow, 2018).

Although there is no specific study that has focused on the impact of this gap on student achievement, there are studies that demonstrate that Black students benefit from having a Black teacher (Partelow et al, 2017), so it could easily be assumed that the same may be true for Latinx students and teachers. Potential explanations for this include that Latinx teachers will have had similar experiences at home, are more likely to have been Dual Language Learners themselves, and will serve as role models to Latinx students who will see that there are professionals who come from their same neighborhoods and experiences and have successfully graduated from college (Shapiro & Partelow, 2018). In addition, Cherng and Halpin (2016) report that high school students in urban settings in the United States, "have more positive ratings of Latino and Black teachers than White teachers after controlling for student demographic and academic characteristics, other teacher characteristics, work conditions and teacher efficacy" (p. 412).

Even though Latinx individuals are among the largest minority ethnic group to be entering the teaching profession (with an increase from 3% to 8% from 1987 to 2012), they are also among the highest percentage of teachers leaving the profession (Griffin, 2018; Casey et al., 2015). Given current political discussions in Washington, there is a risk of having even more Latinx teachers leave the profession. About 20,000 teachers currently working in the United States live legally in this country as recipients of the Deferred Action for Childhood Arrivals or DACA (the initiative that grants temporary protection to undocumented immigrants who were brought into the United States as children). These teachers are at risk of being deported from the country if DACA were to be terminated (Shapiro & Partelow, 2018).

Similar to Latinx students, Latinx teachers also report being bullied, disrespected and discriminated against in their jobs. In a recent study that Griffin (2018) and other colleagues completed, Latinx teachers reported that

> They were often stereotyped as being inferior teachers, or viewed in a limited way as good teachers for Latino students only. This often created situations in which these teachers needed to "prove their worth." Latino teachers in this study also said they were belittled and at times considered to be aggressive when they incorporated Latino culture or Spanish language in the classroom. Teachers particularly reported being viewed this way when they advocated for Latino students. In addition, Latino teachers said that while they often accepted additional roles, most often as a translator, they were frequently overlooked for advancement opportunities. (p. 2)

Many Latinx teachers find themselves playing the role of advocates and translators for students and families, not only translators of language but also of cultural practices and meanings. "They are often taxed with negotiating relationships between parents, students and staff" (Griffin, 2018, p. 9), a role that adds to their already stressful jobs.

CURRENT SOCIOPOLITICAL CONTEXTS AND EDUCATIONAL EXPERIENCES AND OUTCOMES OF LATINX STUDENTS

Recently, the process of teaching and guiding Latinx K-12 students and preparing the teachers who do so has become increasingly difficult, as the current sociopolitical climate generated by the Trump administration has highlighted significant divisions and facilitated negative interpersonal interactions and behaviors that have added to the challenging classroom and school environments where most public school teachers teach today.

In addition to a number of social media public messages that demonstrate the level of disrespect, aggression, and actual bullying that many Latinx students have been reporting (for a sample, check youtube.com videos that can be found when searching "Latino students being bullied"), there are also well-documented cases of aggression and bullying that Latinx students, as young as three years of age, are experiencing with increasing frequency in their communities, in their schools, and on the way to and from home. According to Miller (2017), there have been national reports that cite an increase in hate incidents against Latinx students, and the increase became more pronounced when former President Trump was elected. His campaign highlighted his promise of building a wall between the United States and Mexico, and deporting all undocumented immigrants in the country. Mr. Trump's messages described all Mexicans and people of Mexican and other Latinx origin as thieves, rapists, and criminals (Tobar, 2018; Varela, 2018). Despite the fact that there are a number of undocumented immigrants from other regions of the world, the message was usually descriptive of Latinx individuals, in particular Mexicans and natives of other Central and South American countries. Many educators and other professionals working with youth report that Latinx students are regularly the recipients of comments such as "Go back to your country," "Learn to speak English," "You don't belong here," and "You are not welcome here," regardless of whether they are U.S. citizens or monolingual English speakers who were born in those communities.

As a result of these frequent experiences of bullying and the fear that their parents or other family members may be deported or unjustly accused of crimes, Latinx students are experiencing high levels of anxiety and depression (Staccciarini et al, 2015). In fact, toxic stress has become common in this community given that about five million children in the United States have at least one parent who is undocumented (Gross, 2016).

The National Council of La Raza points to the 2016 election results as the generator of an increase in bullying and harassment against Latinx children. According to Miller (2017), the same report says that "Many young Latinos have been exposed to profound hostility and overt xenophobia in schools and other social spaces" (p. 2). A number of studies (Ramirez, 2017) report that discrimination by peers, teachers, and other members of the school community, exposure to violence, teacher stress, bullying, and poverty are the main community stressors experienced by Latinx youth in the United States. As a result, "Latino youth reported significantly greater symptoms of depression and post-traumatic stress disorder (PTSD) than their White peers" (Ramirez, 2017, p. 2).

It is also well documented that victims of bullying have an increase in anxiety levels, a loss of self-esteem and confidence, an increase in depression, self-harm, and suicidal thinking. "Many young victims increasingly skip school to avoid being bullied, causing their academic work to suffer and their educational aspirations to fade away" (Miller, 2017, p. 3).

In response to these situations, many school districts in the country have either increased existing supports or created new ones. For example, in Boston, Massachusetts, the superintendent has consistently referred families to the Boston Public School's Socio-Emotional Learning and Wellness website which offers a number of resources for Latinx families. The Los Angeles Unified School District school board president alerted families to extra resources that the district is offering to all children who may be experiencing anxiety and fear (Gross, 2016). However, those measures have not been enough.

Given the low number of Latinx teachers, and especially given the current climate in the country, it is essential to prepare teachers from all racial and ethnic backgrounds to work effectively with Latinx students, both recent immigrants and those who have been here for generations. Teacher Education Programs must begin to focus on developing and implementing necessary strategies to prepare new teachers to work with Latinx students and offer in-service teachers effective professional development opportunities to mentor new teachers and work effectively with the increasing Latinx student population in our schools. The next section presents several recommendations.

WHAT CAN TEACHER EDUCATION PROGRAMS AND TEACHER EDUCATORS DO TO EDUCATE EFFECTIVE TEACHERS TO WORK WITH LATINX CHILDREN AND FAMILIES IN THE CURRENT SOCIOPOLITICAL CONTEXT?

In general, the process of educating teachers is complex and challenging, and it is also often misunderstood. Too often people refer to the education of teachers as teacher "training," limiting the depth and extent of the knowledge, skills, behaviors, and dispositions that prospective teachers need to learn, develop, and practice before they are able to successfully educate all children and youth (Villegas-Reimers, 2003). As we have increased our understanding of brain development, how humans learn deep knowledge and develop deep understandings, we have also deepened our understanding of how and what teachers need to learn and develop in their professional preparation in order to facilitate students' learning (Darling-Hammond, 2006).

The sociopolitical context in the United States has not been favorable with regard to teachers, their jobs, careers or their education, and as a result we have seen a recent decline in those interested in becoming teachers, and an increase in licensed teachers who are abandoning the profession (Garcia & Weiss, 2019). Compared to high performing countries, such as the Netherlands and Singapore, where teachers are highly valued and the preparation of teachers is considered as rigorous and challenging as the preparation of other highly valued professions including medical doctors and engineers, teaching in the United States is generally considered an easy profession chosen by low performing high school students. Those common views are affecting the field in negative ways.

Unless these negative stereotypes about teachers, their preparation process, and the work they do change in this country, the future is not very promising for the field, and as a result, for the students of this nation. Delving into all these issues in more detail is beyond the scope of this chapter. My focus here is limited to how teacher preparation can and should be planned and implemented to improve outcomes for all students, and in particular, for Latinx students. Addressing teacher education is a necessary first step that will help begin the process of transforming our society, reducing inequities and discrimination against Latinx students, and improving the overall education level of the population.

It has been well documented that one of the most important factors in improving the academic performance of the students is teacher quality (Goldhaber, 2016). The good news is that there is much research that has helped identify what quality teacher preparation looks like (Darling-Hammond, 2006). The paradox in this country is that the implementation of research recommendations is not universal.

What follows are recommendations for how to equip teachers with the knowledge, skills, behaviors, and dispositions that will help them be truly effective teachers of Latinx students in particular. It is my belief, however, that these recommendations apply to teachers who work with all students.

Among the most basic aspects of teacher preparation that have been identified to be crucial in the education of all teachersare: teachers must know the content they will teach, the pedagogical content knowledge of their particular discipline, and pedagogy in general. They must also know theories, relevant research, and practical applications about teaching, learning, socio-emotional learning, cognition and cognitive science, child and adolescent development, language development, dual language development, culturally relevant pedagogy, anti-racist education, differentiated instruction, education for social justice, curriculum development and lesson planning, Universal Design for Learning, assessment, differentiated instruction, educational technology, classroom and behavior management, and the professional code of ethics. All of these must be learned, implemented, practiced, and assessed until the teacher candidate is proficient. Begining teachers should continue to improve with experience, opportunities for reflective practice, mentoring, and coaching.

This long list, which is not exhaustive with details, is a good starting point to reflect on what excellent teachers of Latinx students need to know and be able to do. Given the current sociopolitical context, I would like to argue that teachers also need more focused education on issues that affect Latinx students directly. In the next few pages, I will go deeper into some of those characteristics and how they are essential for the success of Latinx students.

New teachers must examine, confront, and change their biases and negative beliefs about Latinx students. One crucial element that teachers must develop to be effective educators of Latinx students is a positive perception of these students; in other words, teachers must truly believe in the strong abilities and intelligences of Latinx students, so that they can support their learning, hold and communicate high expectations of their performance, and encourage them to pursue academic and professional excellence (Davis et al., 2016). This is only possible when teachers become aware of their own biases and work to become anti-racist educators. Although this principle has always been necessary, it is a crucial element of the preparation of teachers currently. Studying Anti-Bias Education (Derman-Sparks, 2016), Socio-Emotional learning (CASEL, 2019; Schonert-Reichl, 2017), Culturally Responsive Teaching (Hammond, 2015), Culturally Proficient Instruction (Nuri-Robins et al, 2012), how to develop a growth mindset in themselves and their students (Dweck, 2017), how to promote and strengthen all their students' multiple intelligences (Gardner, 2011), and other such theories and research is just the beginning. However, at a time when teachers have many misconceptions about Latinx students and also English learners (for example, that they can learn English in one year when research shows that they need a minimum of six years to become proficient [Garcia, 2005], or that all of them need to learn English even when most of them are already proficient), teacher education programs must create all kinds of opportunities for pre-service and in-service teachers to understand, confront and change their own beliefs and negative biases.

Unless teachers truly believe that Latinx students are capable of the highest academic performance and achievement, and teach them in a way that reflects those beliefs, their behaviors will not be helpful to these students. Many studies have demonstrated that teachers' beliefs affect teachers' expectations of their students (Pettit, 2011) and thus impact their actions and the way they behave in the classroom (Molle, 2013; Farrell & Ives, 2014). Other studies have shown that the way students perceive their own teachers' judgments of their behavior affects students' behavior and academic achievement (Mantero & McKiver, 2006), as their perception becomes a self-fulfilling prophesy. Specific research about English learners has shown that teachers' negative views about their students have a deep and negative impact on those students (Harper & DeJong, 2009) and on the teachers' approaches to teaching those students (Rizzuto, 2017; Garcia, 2015). In fact, many authors have pointed out that using the term "English learner" highlights what the students lack (English fluency) rather than seeing language as a stength. As a result, many authors are now using "Dual Language Learners" and "Spanish Dominant Learners" as a way to start changing their perception of those students (Mellom et al., 2018). Rueda and Garcia (1996) also report that teachers use their own beliefs as the primary value system to base their judgments of their students' performance. The good news is that studies have shown that teacher attitudes and beliefs can be significantly affected by appropriate professional development and education, and this is especially true when working with Dual Language Learners (Nieto, 2017; Mellom et al., 2018) and other ethnic minority groups, including Latinx students.

New teachers need to learn an assets-based/strengths-based approach to teaching and learning. In order to help pre-service and in-service teachers address their biases and negative beliefs about Latinx students, teacher educators can emphasize the many assets that Latinx students possess. For example, most Latinx students who are immigrants or children of immigrants have a collaborative orientation to learning, strong resilience skills, are bilingual, have a multicultural perspective, and have "immigrant optimism," the belief that with hard work and effort good results are obtained (Gándara, 2017). All of these characteristics, some identified as twenty-first-century skills and foundational of deep learning, are highly sought out by employers today. Employers usually emphasize the needs to have employees who have critical thinking skills, analytic skills, strategies for effective teamwork, and cooperative learning skills. It is well known that many Latinx families tend to emphasize the development of cooperative and respectful family relations which foster cooperative learning among Latinx students (Cox et al., 1991), and teachers can build on those assets.

New teachers must develop the skills of resilience and persistence in themselves and learn how to teach those skills to their students who are the focus of negative stereotypes. Fortino (2017) highlights the importance of helping new teachers develop the skills of resilience. She reports being inspired by Yosso's (2005) concept of a "community cultural background" in her perception of the strengths of the Latinx community, and noticing that Latinx students come with a strong "community cultural background" which teachers must know how to strengthen as each of its components foster resilient behaviors that promote academic achievement, perseverance, and excellence. Yosso's (2005) components of this "community cultural background" are:

> Aspirational capital: "the ability to maintain hopes and dreams for the future even in the face of real and perceived barriers";
> Linguistic capital: "the intellectual and social skills attained through communicating in more than one language or style";
> Familial capital: "the cultural knowledge nurtured within the family that carries the sense of community, history, memory, and identity";
> Social capital "the networks of people and community that support families as they navigate society's institutions";
> Navigational capital: "the ability to maneuver through social institutions by drawing on culture specific skills and experiences"; and
> Resistant capital "the knowledge and skills that foster self-esteem, self-reliance, and the strength to persevere. Promoting and advancing the work of student leadership is central to the mission of teaching and learning."

Teacher educators must help teachers see these assets in their students, their families, and their communities, so that they change from a deficit perspective about Latinx students, to an asset-rich strength perspective, recognizing, and celebrating these capitals that students already possess. Once pre-service and in-service teachers are able to value all these positive characteristics, their attitudes toward their Latinx students should begin to change. Of course, this assumes that teacher educators have this asset-rich strength perspective themselves. Studies show that they, too, can benefit from professional development opportunities that help them uncover unrecognized biases in themselves and/or their programs, and begin to change those program so that they can be more effective in helping pre-service and in-service teachers develop positive attitudes about all of their students (Davis et al., 2016).

New teachers must also learn the skills of culturally relevant, culturally responsive, and culturally sustaining teaching. Teacher educators must also help pre-service and in-service teachers develop their understanding, knowledge, skills, and dispositions toward culturally relevant and culturally responsive teaching practices (Hammond, 2015). This will help teachers learn how to sustain—rather than exchange—students' cultural practices and beliefs, including their home languages, as research shows that those practices are much more effective in building academic skills and academic success (Davis et al., 2016). This will help teachers understand that bilingual and dual language learners should not have to forgo their home language or home cultures to be successful in schools (Gándara, 2017). These practices will help teachers use students' backgrounds, cultures, beliefs, and traditions as assets on which to build excellence, will help them develop culturally appropriate forms of assessment, communication, interactions, expectations, and so on, and in the end will lead to more positive results for students.

New teachers must understand how social ecological systems work and identify their own role in the ecological systems of their students. New teachers also need to learn how to collect data and use research. It is widely accepted that teachers need to know and understand all of their students' dimensions, their developmental characteristics, their backgrounds and contexts, and their cultural traditions. This is not unique to teaching Latinx students, but it is essential for them. The Latinx culture is very diverse, as the countries of origin of the Latinx families, the number of years they have been in the United States, their social class and level of education, among other variables, make a significant difference. Despite this level of variance, there are a few cultural characteristics common to all. Understanding how ecological systems work (see Bronfenbrenner's [1992] theory, for example) will be an excellent addition to the preparation of new teachers so that they can begin to see and understand the impact of the many contexts where their students live and where they and their families come from, and how the interactions among those many contexts (families, schools, communities, society, etc.) impact each individual child. Teacher candidates and new teachers need to have the tools to learn about their new teaching environments, the ecological systems where they will find themselves as professionals, so that they can be ready to teach in any new setting. By developing critically reflective practitioners (Davis et al., 2016), new teachers will be able to use self-inquiry and also collaborative inquiry with students to challenge unexamined assumptions and develop self-determination.

New teachers need to learn how to plan and implement differentiated instruction that understands cultural differences as strengths not deficits. Teachers need to learn how to plan and implement differentiated instruction with Latinx students in mind. Usually, differentiated instruction is conceived of as a technique used in integrated classrooms (general education students and students with identified special needs); however, "the development of differentiated skills and knowledge according to student needs which result in impactful and even transformative education" (Davis et al., 2016, p.2) must be part of any program of quality teacher education. However, it is an essential component when teaching Latinx students, as their unique needs can be met more effectively, regardless of whether they have an identified learning disability or are learning English as a second or third language. Given the current sociocultural environments, new teachers need to learn how to address the trauma and negative experiences of Latinx students through their curriculum and instruction. Trauma-informed teaching can also be an essential form of differentiated instruction that addresses the emotional needs of Latinx students.

New teachers must be prepared to work with all students, including those who are dual language learners, and thus must learn and master techniques that will facilitate their work with Latinx students who are English learners. Although not all Latinx students are English Learners or Bilingual students (Gándara, 2017), teachers educators should be prepared to become teachers who are knowledgeable about language development, bilingual development, and second language acquisition and the content pedagogy that can be used with these learners. These skills will help all address the specific needs of this population and will make them more culturally and individually responsive to all students as well. Teachers need to learn how language develops, both in monolingual and bilingual learners; they must have the skills to teach children in a language they have not mastered yet while celebrating the language(s) they already possess. Understanding that bilingualism is also biculturalism is very important, especially because teachers must be able to communicate openly, respectfully, and in culturally appropriate ways with their students and families. A few researchers (Gándara, 2017, for example), have recommended that all teachers become bilingual, stating that states and school districts must create pathways for young people to become bilingual teachers as that will increase the level of commitment to English learners in their classrooms.

Student-teachers must be provided with opportunities to practice their developing teaching skills in clinical settings that include Latinx students, and must be guided by program supervisors knowledgeable about the needs of the Latinx students and how to teach them effectively. An important aspect of teacher education in general (not specific to Latinx students only) is, of course, the clinical experiences or student-teacher practica in which teacher candidates must be properly supervised and guided through the teacher preparation program. Given the current sociopolitical contexts, these clinical experiences are even more important than before in order to educate all teachers about the realities of schools and student experiences today. Every effort should be made to have teacher candidates complete these clinical experiences in settings where student-teachers interact with Latinx students (and, ideally, Latinx teachers), and where they can learn how to teach these students effectively. Having several (vs. one) of these opportunities during their teacher preparation program (Davis et al., 2016) will help student-teachers develop effective teaching skills and will more likely change any potential stereotypical view about Latinx students they may hold. This will require, of course, not only the exposure to this population but also strong mentorship to help teacher candidates develop positive views of Latinx students and question their own biases and blind spots. A few research studies (Guha et al., 2017) have shown that clinical practices aligned with teaching residency models are quite effective when working with Latinx students and other groups which are mostly concentrated in urban settings. These models usually include a full academic year (as a minimum) of student-teaching, during which the student-teacher works and learns side by side with strong mentorteachers. To prepare teachers to work with Latinx students effectively, these models are especially helpful when the clinical sites include a significant number of Latinx students as well as Latinx mentor-teachers who know how to work with this population effectively.

There are other, more macro-level, measures that teacher educators and teacher education programs must plan and implement to prepare teachers who are effective in reaching, teaching, keeping, and lifting the success of Latinx students.

Teacher education programs must recruit more Latinx students to the teaching profession. Recruiting more Latinx teacher candidates into the profession is key. "Diversifying the teacher workforce improves student outcomes and supports students of color" (Shapiro & Partelow, 2018). In addition, "Research has shown that students' perceptions of teachers are associated with motivation and achievement and that having a more diverse teaching force can help close longstanding racial achievement gaps" (Cherng & Halpin, 2016, p. 417).

The large gap between the number of Latinx students in our schools and the small and decreasing size of our Latinx teachers is something that must be addressed directly and urgently. Particularly in this sociocultural context, having teachers who can serve as Latinx role models, not only for Latinx students but for all students who are constantly bombarded with very negative stereotypes about this population, is key. In order to do this, teacher preparation programs must examine their policies and practices which facilitate or hinder the addition of Latinx candidates to their programs (Davis et al., 2016). Large research universities must also help teacher preparation programs in their institutions be recognized, celebrated, and valued. They, too, have a responsibility to elevate the value of teachers and their education in our country. The recruitment of diverse students into the profession will not be as effective (Davis et al., 2016) without their support.

Griffin (2018) argues that an increase in Latinx student-teachers and teachers is essential as they are the professionals who can understand the Latinx student population better, can serve as role models for all, and can create classrooms where everyone feels welcome, including the families of the Latinx students. Many believe that the Latinx teachers are better prepared to teach and support the community of Latinx students as they may share many of the same characteristics. For example, they may have found themselves in schools where they could not understand the language, may have experienced discrimination, micro-aggressions, bullying, and some of them may have come into this country as undocumented immigrants. As a result of these experiences, they may have the skills, understandings, and dispositions to help Latinx students succeed academically. Griffin (2018) also reports that Latinx teachers believe that they are better prepared to honor the Latinx culture, which in turns honors and values the students' home cultures and lives. They are better able to include a curriculum rich in Latinx content and meaning, and are more open to encouraging students to speak Spanish, a practice that is often highly criticized by other teachers and administrators, and yet gives students an opportunity to celebrate their background, community assets, and identities.

Gándara (2017) also emphasizes the need to recruit more men into the teaching profession, especially Latino men. This is based on studies that have found that having more Latino male teachers improves the academic performance of Latino males in significant ways (Howard et al., 2016). Gándara et al. (2013) also report that "In our research we have found, based on national data, that Latinas are more likely to attend college if they have Latino teachers (male or female). In fact, the more of these teachers they encounter, the more likely they are to attend college" (Gándara, 2017, p. 10).

The retention of the few Latinx teachers in the field is essential too. In addition to recruiting, the field must also work to retain those teachers, as the number of Latinx teachers who abandon the profession continues to grow. One way to help with the retention in the field is to create induction programs; they are helpful to all new teachers, and essential to Latinx teachers who may enter communities where they may be the only ones from this ethnic group and where it would be quite easy to feel isolated (Davis et al., 2016). In this current climate, feeling welcome, appreciated, and professionally effective is very important.

Develop and fund wrap-around schools in under-resourced communities. Another research-based macro recommendation is to support Latinx students and teachers in our schools (Gándara, 2017) with wrap-around services for all students and families living in poverty, which will include some members of the Latinx population. This will require that educators (particularly administrators, but also teachers and teacher candidates), be willing to staff these services, work collaboratively with other professionals who also serve the Latinx population and others, and be supportive of these endeavors. This measure, although not directly related to teaching the Latinx population or preparing teachers to do so, does speak to the need to address the difficult and challenging effects of poverty which permeate into the classrooms and the work of teachers. The same can be said about offering more access to quality early childhood education programs which can improve the preparation of Latinx children for school (Gándara, 2017). Again, this is not directly related to teacher education, but having teachers advocate for these kinds of services as part of their commitment to social justice could definitely make a difference in the lives of many Latinx children and families, particularly in this very difficult sociopolitical context.

Develop inter-institutional partnerships. In order to be successful in creating and addressing these macro-level recommendations, it is essential that both teacher educators and their programs model the establishment of partnerships and professional collaborations among different institutions; this will help improve the services offered to Latinx students and families, and will also model for teacher candidates and in-service teachers the importance of these partnerships to support the well-being of the Latinx communities and other student communities in their midst (Davis et al., 2016).

CONCLUSION

The preparation of teachers is key for the future success of the next generations in every country. The United States is in a situation at the moment that requires us to be open-minded, respectful, anti-bias, and anti-racist leaders who can lead the country to success for all students. Teacher preparation is one of the strongest tools we have to change the trajectory the country seems to be following at the present time. The Latinx community is strong, values cooperation and hard work, has a familial orientation in life, and is ready to make a significant and positive impact in our world for the benefit of all. Teachers who can harvest those positive values, that optimistic energy and resilience, and prepare the next generation for success will, literally, help to change the world for the better. Teacher educators are called to be among the leaders in this movement. We know how, we now need the commitment to do it well.

REFERENCES

Bronfenbrenner, U. (1992). Ecological systems theory. In R. Vasta (Ed.), *Six theories of child development: Revised formulations and current issues* (pp. 187–249). London, England: Jessica Kingsley Publishers.

CASEL. (2019). *Framework for systemic social and emotional learning.* The Collaborative for Academic, Social and Emotional Learning (https://casel.org/what-is-sel/)

Casey, L., DiCarlo, M., Bond, B., & Quintero, E. (2015). *The estate of teacher diversity in American education*. Washington, DC: Albert Shanker Institute.

Cherng, H. S., & Halpin, P. (2016). The importance of minority teachers: Student perception of minority versus White teachers. *Educational Researcher, 45*(7), 407–420.

Clontz, C. (2018, Oct. 2). *Equity in education to Latino students and teachers*. University of Pittsburgh: Panoramas Scholarly Platform.

Cox, T. H., Lobel, S. A., & McLeod, P. L. (1991). Effects of Ethnic Group Cultural Differences on Cooperative and Competitive Behavior on a Group Task. *Academy of Management Journal, 34*, 827–847.

Darling-Hammond (2006). *Powerful teacher education: Lessons from exemplary programs*. San Francisco: Jossey-Bass.

Davis, J., Hernandez, A., McHatton, P. A., Sapien, B. B., Shanley, D., & Terjeson, K. (2016). *Developing quality teacher preparation programs that serve the needs of Hispanic students* (White Paper). Washington, DC, White House Initiative on Educational Excellence for Hispanics.

Derman-Sparks, L (2016). What I learned from the Ypsilanti Perry Preschool Project: A teacher's reflections. *Journal of Pedagogy, 7*(1), 93–106.

Dweck, C. (2017). The journey to children's mindsets and beyond. *Child Development Perspectives, 11*(2), 139–144.

Farrell, T., & Ives, J (2014). Exploring teacher beliefs and classroom practices through reflective practice: A case study. *Language Teaching Research, 19*(5), 594–610.

Flores, A. (2017, Sept. 18). *How the U.S. Hispanic population is changing*. Pew Research Center (retrieved Feb 22, 2019 from http://www.pewresearch.org/fact-tank/2017/09/18/how-the-u-s-hispanic-population-is-changing/).

Flores, A., Lopez, M. H., & Krogstad, J. M. (2019). "U.S. Hispanic Population Reached New High in 2018, but Growth Has Slowed." Pew Research Center. Retrieved September 13, 2019. https://www.pewresearch.org/fact-tank/2019/07/08/u-s-hispanicpopulation-reached-new-high-in-2018-but-growth-has-slowed/.

Fortino, C. (2017). Why supporting Latino children and families is Union work. *American Educator, 41*(1), 14–30, 44.

Gándara, P. (2017). The potential and promise of Latino students. *American Educator, 41*(1), 4–11, 42.

Gándara, P., Oseguera, L., Huber, L. P., Locks, A., Ee, J., & Molina, D. (2013). *Making Education Work for Latinas in the U.S.* Los Angeles, CA: Civil Rights Project.

Garcia, E. (2005). *Teaching and learning in two languages: Bilingualism and schooling in the United States*. New York, NY: Teachers College Press.

Garcia, E., & Weiss, E. (2019). *The teacher shortage is real, large and growing, and worse than we thought*. Washington, DC: Economic Policy Institute.

Garcia, O. (2015). Language policy. In J. D. Wright (Ed.), *International encyclopedia of the social & behavioral sciences* (2nd ed., Vol. 13) (pp. 353–359). Oxford, UK: Elsevier.

Gardner, H. (2011). *Frames of mind: The theory of multiple intelligences*. New York, NY: Basic Books.

Goldhaber, D. (2016). In schools, teacher quality matters most. *Education Next*, 16(2), 56–62.

Griffin, A. (2018). *Our stories, our struggles, our strengths: Perspectives and reflections from Latino teachers*. Washington, DC: The Education Trust.

Gross, N. (2016, Nov. 11). Schools offer counseling as many Latino students face bullying, uncertainty after Trump win. Education Writers Association (https://www.ewa.org/blog-latino-ed-beat/schools-offer-counseling-many-latino-students-face-bullying-uncertainty-after)

Guha, R., Hyler, M. E., & Darling-Hammond, L. (2017). The teacher residency: A practical path to recruitment and retention. *American Educator, 41*(1), 31–34, 44.

Hammond, Z. (2015). *Culturally responsive teaching and the brain: Promoting authentic engagement and rigor among culturally and linguistically diverse students*. Thousand Oaks, CA: Corwin.

Harper, C., & DeJong, E. (2009). English language teacher expertise: The elephant in the room. *Language and Education, 23*(2), 131–151.

Howard, T. C., Tunstall, J., & Flennaugh, T. K. (Eds.) (2016). *Expanding college access for urban youth: What schools and colleges can do*. New York: Teachers College Press.

Kao, G., & Tienda, M. (1995) Optimism and achievement: The educational performance of immigrant youth. *Social Science Quarterly, 76*, 1–19.

Krogstad, J. M. (2016, July 28). *Fact tank, news in the numbers: Five facts about Latinos and education*. Washington, DC: Pew Research Center.

Mantero, M., & McVicker, P. (2006). The impact of experience and coursework: Perceptions of second language learners in the mainstream classroom. *Radical Pedagogy, 8*(1), 1–23.

Mellom, P. J., Straubhaar, R., Balderas, C., Ariail, M., & Portes, P. R. (2018). "They come with nothing:" How professional development in a culturally responsive pedagogy shapes teacher attitudes towards Latino/a English language learners. *Teaching and Teacher Education, 71*, 98–107.

Miller, A. (2017, Feb.8). *Latino kids being bullied more amid political controversy, groups say*. Georgia Health News (www.georgiahealthnews.com)

Molle, D. (2013). Facilitating professional development for teachers of English language learners. *Teaching and Teacher Education, 29*, 197–207.

Musu-Gillette, L., de Brey, C., McFarland, J., Hussar, W., Sonnenberg, W., & Wilkinson-Flicker, S. (2017). *Status and Trends in the Education of Racial and Ethnic Groups 2017 (NCES 2017-051)*. U.S. Department of Education, National Center for Education Statistics. Washington, DC. Retrieved Feb 22 2019 from http://nces.ed.gov/pubsearch.

National Center for Education Statistics. (2018). *English Language Learners in public schools*. Washington DC: NCES.

National Center for Education Statistics. (2019). *The condition of education 2019*. Washington, DC: NCES.

Nieto, S. (2017). Becoming socio-cultural mediators: What all educators can learn from bilingual and ESL teachers. *Issues in Teacher Education, 26*(2), 129–141.

Noe-Bustamante, L., Lopez, M. H., & Krogstad, J. M. (2020). U.S. Hispanic population surpassed 60 million in 2019, but growth has slowed. *Fact Tank News in the Numbers*. Washington, DC: Pew Research Center.

Nuri-Robins, K., Lindsey, D., Lindsey, R., & Terrell, R. (2012). *Culturally proficient instruction: A guide for people who teach* (3rd ed.). Thousand Oaks, CA: Corwin.

Paterson, J. (2019). Nine colleges recognized for supporting Latino students. *Education Dive*. www.educationdive.com

Partelow, L., Spong, A, Brown, C., & Johnson, S. (2017). *America needs more teachers of color and a more selective teaching profession*. Washington, DC: Center for American Progress.

Pettit, S. K. (2011). Teachers' beliefs and English language learners in the mainstream classroom: A review of the literature. *International Multidisciplinary Research Journal*, 5(2), 123–147.

Pew Research Center. (2013). *Second-Generation Americans: A Portrait of the Adult Children of Immigrants*. Washington, DC: Pew Research Center.

Ramirez, A. (2017, Sept. 11). Mental health research: Latino community and school issues. *Salud America*. https://salud-america.org

Rizzuto, K. C. (2017) Teachers' perceptions of ELL Students: Do their attitudes shape their instruction? *The Teacher Educator*, 52(3), 182–202.

Rueda, R., & Garcia, E. (1996). Teachers' perspectives on literacy assessment and instruction with language-minority students: A comparative study. *The Elementary School Journal*, 96(3), 311–332.

Samuels, C. (2019, July 30). *Segregation of Latino students from White peers increased over a generation, study finds*. Education Week.

Schonert-Reichl, K. (2017). Social and emotional learning and teachers. *The Future of Children*, 27(1), 137–155.

Shapiro, S., & Partelow, L. (2018). *How to fix the large and growing Latinx teacher-student gap*. Washington, DC: Center for American Progress.

Stacciarini, J. M. R., Smith, R., Garvan, C. W., Wiens, B., & Cottler, L. B. (2015). Rural Latinos' mental wellbeing: A mixed-methods pilot study of family, environment, and social isolation factors. *Community Mental Health Journal*, 51, 404–413.

Suárez-Orozco, C., & Suárez-Orozco, M. (1995). *Transformations: Immigration, Family Life, and Achievement Motivation among Latino Adolescents*. Stanford, CA: Stanford University Press.

Telles, E. E., & Ortiz, V. (2008). *Generations of Exclusion: Mexican Americans, Assimilation, and Race*. New York: Russell Sage Foundation.

Tobar, H. (2018, Dec. 12). Trump's ongoing disinformation campaign against Latino immigrants. *The New Yorker*. https://www.newyorker.com/news/daily-comment/trumps-ongoing-disinformation-campaign-against-latino-immigrants

Varela, J. R. (2018, Dec. 28). Trump's border wall was never just about security. It's meant to remind all Latinos that we're unwelcome. NBC News. https://www.nbcnews.com/think/opinion/trump-s-border-wall-was-never-just-about-security-it-ncna952011

Villegas-Reimers, E. (2003). *Teacher professional development: An international review of the literature*. Paris: UNESCO International Institute for Educational Planning.

Yosso, T. (2005). Whose culture has capital? A critical race theory discussion of community cultural wealth. *Race, Ethnicity and Education, 8*, 69–91.

Chapter 8

What Counts as Official Knowledge?
Pursuing Accreditation in a Post-Truth Era

Jaclyn Caires-Hurley, Andrea M. Emerson,
Anne Ittner, and Carmen Cáceda

INTRODUCTION

Culturally responsive pedagogy, for many, is an elusive construct. For the authors of this paper, we know that preparing culturally responsive teachers requires, at its core, an understanding that individuals cannot put down their cultural and historical consciousness as they enter institutionalized spaces in pursuit of standardized ways of knowing and learning. Nonetheless, as we pursue the re-accreditation of our Educator Preparation Program (EPP), we are situated in a negotiation room tangled in conversations about what counts as official knowledge. While it is our charge to "determine how best to make use of the diversity (we) already have" (CAEP, 2018, p. 51), it is also our obligation to align outcomes for curriculum, clinical experiences, and recruitment and retention to predetermined standards. This chapter documents our first steps at setting curriculum goals for our EPP related to diversity outcomes. In this chapter, we aim to identify the knowledge, skills, and dispositions that our students will need to teach in a diverse PK-12 school system in a way that not only meets certain standards but that is grounded in and values our students' diverse ways of knowing and learning.

CONTEXT

As an accredited EPP, the way we construct and enact principles for preparing culturally responsive educators is delimited by and situated within The Council for the Accreditation of Educator Preparation's (CAEP) cross-cutting theme of diversity. CAEP defines *diversity* in terms of individual (e.g., personality, interests, learning modalities, and life experiences) and group (e.g., race, ethnicity, ability, gender identity, gender expression, sexual orientation, nationality, language, religion, political affiliation, and socioeconomic background) differences. CAEP also claims "to best serve America's students, EPPs must show respect for the diversity of candidates; provide experiences that support the candidates' commitment to diversity; and prepare candidates to design and enact equitable and excellent experiences for all PK-12 students" (CAEP, 2018, p. 51). Additionally, there are 10 standards from the Interstate Teacher Assessment Support Consortium (InTASC) to which we must align our curriculum, clinical experiences, and recruitment and retention practices. Each of the 10 InTASC standards contains lists of performances, essential knowledge, and critical dispositions that every pre-service teacher should gain. In order to make claims as to how these standards are met, CAEP suggests that institutions interpret diversity for themselves and consider how they "make use " of the diversity among their programs, experiences, faculty, and pre-service teachers in order to best-prepare teachers to serve "all" students in America's classrooms. However, we acknowledge that this process does not occur in a vacuum. The CAEP *Handbook for Initial-Level Programs* (2018) suggests each institution has their "own unique contextual conditions that surround preparation," and that we need to "analyze (our) own situation," and "set challenging goals that move further toward the diversity found in America's PK-12 classrooms" (p. 51).

As such, in making these determinations, it is critical that an EPP take an affirmative step to consider the biases held by the individuals who are interpreting diversity for the purposes of accreditation. This study takes place at a regional EPP in the Pacific Northwest. We are the oldest public university in our state with a total enrollment of approximately 5,000 students. According to the 2019 Oregon Educator Equity Report[1], our EPP has a total enrollment of 142 students in their final year of their degree program with 13 students (1%) identifying as Hispanic or Latino and 111 students (78%) identifying as white. Likewise, our faculty is made up of 34 tenure, tenure-track, or non-tenure-track professors of which 6 identify as faculty of color (15% total or 14% Latinx specifically) and 85% identify as white. Furthermore, none of the administrators (dean or division chair) in our school of education are administrators of color. The ethnic and racial disparities among faculty and students are relevant because we know that students' identities shape their perceptions of the campus racial climate (Griffin, Cunningham, Mwangi, & Chrystal, 2016; Harper & Hurtado, 2007; Rankin & Reason, 2005; Suarez-Balcazar, Orellana-Damacela, Portillo, Rowan, & Andrews-Guillen, 2003) and feelings of being accepted by faculty (Hurtado & Ponjuan, 2005; Stebleton, Soria, Huesman,& Torres, 2014; Stebleton, Rost-Banik, Greene, & DeAngelo,

2017). It is also important to consider that in the 2018–2019 school year, 38% of PK-12 students in our state were ethnically diverse. While, statewide, 25% of EPP completers in our state identify as ethnically diverse, only 10% of teachers employed identify this way (Oregon Equity Advisory Group, 2019). This means, more ethnically diverse teachers complete EPPs than are hired and retained in the profession. While the number of ethnically diverse teachers increased in recent years, the disparities between students and teachers in our state persist.

PROBLEM

Due to the increasing number of culturally and linguistically diverse PK-12 students, there is incredible pressure for institutions of higher education to look inclusive and equitable, yet the question of whether or not an EPP is addressing diversity effectively is multifaceted. CAEP leaves the interpretation of the interactions among all the individuals teaching and learning in the EPP as well as diverse learners in PK-12 schools up to individual institutions. The production of this kind of evidence is problematic for a number of reasons. There are inherent pitfalls of first defining one's own EPP diversity and responsiveness outcomes, then measuring them, and later speaking for the strength with which you support typically marginalized groups. Left to our own interpretations of how to be responsive, our own biases threaten to blind us, as well as withhold an awareness of our impairment (e.g., we don't know what we don't know), as we prepare evidence for accreditation review. Moreover, a number of authors have noted the risk that EPPs will assert a commitment to diversity as a tool for denying future discrimination (i.e., *how can we be accused of discriminating when we clearly state that in this document that we believe in inclusion and equity?*) (Ahmed, 2007; Diangelo, 2018). As an EPP endeavoring to study the ways we make use of diversity, we critically questioned the legitimacy of a self-study of diversity and the production of evidence. As a result, we decided to begin this treacherous endeavor by considering whose voices carried the truths about diversity at our own institution.

We see this work as embedded within the context of the post-truth era. The oscillation between objective facts (or lack thereof) and emotional appeals that plagues our current political landscape is also present in conceptions of diversity performance within institutions of higher education. Divides may exist between administrative and faculty intention and the student experience with regard to diversity and equity of opportunity. The Oxford dictionary defines *post-truth* as "relating to or denoting circumstances in which objective facts are less influential in shaping public opinion than appeals to emotion and personal belief." In a post-truth era, emotion and personal belief are more influential than objective facts, and these emotions tend to shape opinions and even begin to sound like truth for those who are influenced (Peters, 2017). What does this mean for an EPP? For those institutions pursuing accreditation, the understanding that we live in a post-truth era means we are juxtaposed, left to discern what counts as official knowledge, which, we argue, may not reflect the *pedagogies of the home* shared by our pre-service teachers. The challenge, then, is to discern which data, facts, and opinions matter the most within a self-study of diversity.

PURPOSE

In an effort to conduct an authentic self-study of diversity, we began by positioning student voices as the main source of official knowledge at our institution rather than the predominately white faculty's perceptions of diversity and equity of opportunity. We sought to understand student experiences and attitudes toward difference, equity of opportunity, and inclusion within this EPP. Their stories from home and school cast new light on the responsive actions necessary from faculty to truly "make use" of our diversity.

Commencing our accreditation journey with an analysis of student voices allows our students to self-identify and to co-construct the definition of diversity by which our self-study will be grounded and our EPP will be evaluated. In this way, student voices become the data through which we form a baseline understanding of who the diverse pre-service teachers are and if their pedagogies of the home are reflected, considered, or even welcomed as we prepare them to be culturally responsive teachers. As EPPs pursue accreditation, InTASC standards are to be considered institutional knowledge, but in order to attend to the cross-cutting theme of diversity, we argue that students' cultural knowledge base should be privileged and counted as official knowledge in our interpretation of the standards. This will allow our students to become creators of the knowledge shared within their EPP, rather than become mere recipients of discrete knowledge and skills that faculty (in isolation) determine that they should acquire.

THEORETICAL FRAMING

The authors of this chapter believe that the standards for teacher education are subject to interpretation. In thinking about our Latinx[2] pre-service teachers, our interpretation of our standards (InTASC) will be grounded primarily in Chicana epistemologies which are rooted as much in cultural-historical (Rogoff et al., 2014) as in critical perspectives (Anzaldúa, 1987). Specifically, our work is framed around Delgado Bernal's (2001) concept of pedagogies of the home, which can be defined as a "cultural knowledge base that helps students survive and succeed within an educational system that often excludes and silences them" (p. 623). Just as PK-12 public schools are laden with power and politics, so too, are EPPs. We recognize, as Rogoff et al. (2014) explain, that schools are settings for children, but controlled by adults. Likewise, in higher education, standards often are designed to drive what counts as official knowledge, which must be transmitted in a systematic way to our students. It is our role, as culturally responsive teacher educators, to interpret these standards in ways that will encourage our students to carry what they learn from home into their educational journey (Delgado Bernal, 2001). We believe that this approach will not only remove challenges to education faced by Latinx pre-service teachers, but it will also model how all of our pre-service teachers should teach to affirm the culturally and linguistically diverse students in our PK-12 public school communities.

Critical Perspectives in Teacher Education

Given the requirements set by our accreditation process, we understand and name the dissonance of working within a system of teacher education standards and programming that has historically been a space for perpetuation of whiteness. We also are aware of the call to recognize the absence of the experiences and voices of teachers of color in issues of policy in teacher education (Haddix, 2017). We are reminded by scholars (e.g. Sleeter, 2016; Salazar, 2018) who have applied critical perspectives to the endeavors of teacher education that historically teacher education programs have been situated within white and Eurocentric standards and mindsets. In fact, teacher education programs may perpetuate these standards of whiteness while attempting to "teach" diversity. Gorski (2009) suggests that the teacher education program accreditation goals may "meet" diversity standards, but in actuality, they miss opportunities to engage teacher candidates in authentic multicultural education. In another critique of perpetuating the status quo in the standards and accreditation, Beyerbach & Nassoiy (2004) find a lack of explicitness in "teaching for diversity and critical equity practice" (p.39). As we name the historic whiteness curriculum and "sensibilities" (Sleeter, 2016) that has shrouded teacher education programs and accreditation, we attempt to take this problem and act toward shifting the narrative.

METHODS AND ANALYSIS

Methodology and Research Design for the Accreditation Self-Study

We collected the data used in the present chapter during the baseline data collection phase of our self-study for the purposes of accreditation. We used a convergent, mixed-methods approach in our self-study assuming that multiple methods will provide a more complete understanding about the nature of our EPP as it relates to the cross-cutting theme of diversity. Mixed methodology assumes that all methods have bias and limitations, and that one way to improve the internal validity of all designs is to combine the approaches. In this way, we use a variety of data sources such as performance assessments, surveys, questionnaires, interviews, classroom artifacts, and observations to explain findings and/or inform the development and/or improve the use of instruments for the examination of the cross-cutting theme of diversity (Creswell & Creswell, 2018). As evidenced by the present chapter, in convergent methods, qualitative and quantitative data can be analyzed separately while results are eventually converged so that robust interpretations can be made about a phenomenon (Creswell & Creswell, 2018). Additionally, we selected this methodology because the convergent approach can be expanded for use within a single-case study design. A convergent, mixed-methods single-case study design relies upon a more complex methodology and is an alternative to a typical case study that draws upon qualitative approaches more exclusively. Furthermore, according to Yin (2014), all case studies can include either a singular unit of analysis (i.e., holistic design) or multiple units of analysis (i.e., embedded design). The larger self-study for the purposes of accreditation will include an analysis of diversity themes as determined by CAEP as well as how we construct our own definition of diversity across curriculum, clinical experiences, recruitment, and retention practices within our EPP. For this reason, with the unit of analysis being our EPP, we used a holistic design to collect data for the accreditation self-study.

Qualitative Data Sources and Participant Description for the Present Study

During a qualitative analysis of baseline data that occurred during the 2018–2019 academic year, we wanted, first, to explore the cultural knowledge base of Latinx pre-service teachers. In order to place our students' voices at the center of what we count as official knowledge, we generated the following research question:

Research Question: What is the cultural knowledge base of Latinx pre-service teachers in our EPP?

The data analyzed for the present chapter included student autobiographies of all Latinx identifying students collected as student work samples, written as part of the required work for the course *ED 446 (D): Environments for Diverse Learners*. This course is the requisite diversity course offered during students' first term of the final year of their EPP. A primary outcome of this course is for students to examine their positionality. This is accomplished through a number of assignments called "Introspectives," as well as in-class activities and simulations. The autobiographies are a summative assessment of learning for the first few weeks of the course. The assignment description is as follows:

<u>Autobiography Paper (5 pages maximum) (20 points) due week 4</u>
To begin, students will read and reflect on Peggy McIntosh's essay "White Privilege: Unpacking the Invisible Knapsack." Then, students will craft a paper where, in part I, they will provide a description of their cultural backpack. Elements will include a discussion of home language, family history, familial structure, holidays, religious beliefs, music, activities, politics, experiences etc. Overall, students are reflecting on their multicultural selves. In part II, students will provide a description of their education experience where they reflect on two questions: What out of school factors contributed to my success in school? What out of school factors negatively impacted my success in school?

Student work samples analyzed for the present study came from students entering our EPP in the winter 2019 cohort. There were two classes with a total enrollment of 39 students. For our sample, we drew autobiographies from 100% of students who self-identified as Latinx in their autobiographies ($N = 6$). We then randomly selected six students who did not identify as Latinx to serve as a comparison group by choosing every third name on the roster if the student met the criteria for the assignment, which would ensure we had a detailed and reliable assessment to analyze. Of the six Latinx students, two self-identified as male, Carlos and Juan and four self-identified as female (Paola, Consuelo, Celia, and Claudia). All names used are pseudonyms. Of the 6 non-Latinx students, 1 self-identified as male and 5 self-identified as female. While we initially analyzed all 12 samples, we delimited our final sample to the 6 Latinx students in order to conduct a more in-depth analysis of their reported experiences. We asked students' permission to analyze their autobiographies; three of the four authors of this chapter also serve as professors to these students in the EPP. During this participant enrollment phase, we de-identified the autobiographies and gave students the opportunity to revise or edit their autobiographies in order to exclude any personal information that they chose not to share for the purposes of our research.

Data Analysis

The four authors of this chapter served as multiple raters of the autobiographies. Three raters coded a selection of the 12 autobiographies. Following Saldaña's (2013) method of first-cycle and second-cycle coding, we first used process coding (e.g., identifying lines of diversity, hedging, describing/ defining upbringing, justifying description of upbringing) as well as descriptive coding (e.g., out of school factors, dispositions toward diverse learners, microcultures) where we analyzed student writing by assigning the writing into data chunks. In the second cycle of coding, we generated pattern codes consisting of theoretical constructs related to Chicana epistemologies (e.g., order of identity, borderlands, acts of resistance, and socialization). Next, we summarized the data with narrative descriptions where we elaborated on our patterns using data as supports (Miles, Huberman, & Saldaña, 2014). Through several meetings between the authors of this chapter, we examined the patterns and were able to cluster the data. We describe our findings from this analysis in the following section.

FINDINGS

Familismo

The cultural knowledge included within our Latinx students' autobiographies emanated from their strong ties to family. Familismo literally means familism which is a social structure prioritizing the collective needs of the family over any single individual. It is more than the notion of family. The distinction is necessary to highlight familismo as a theoretical framework rather than simply a personal value or the state of being committed to one's family. Familismo is a framework that prioritizes "more collective, family-based decision-making, and responsibility for, and obligation to ensuring the wellbeing of family members" (Smith-Morris, Morales-Campos, Alvarez, & Turner, 2013, p. 3). Familismo is a term used in this study to highlight the value of family experiences as central to pedagogies of the home. More specifically familismo "is typified by strong feelings of loyalty, unity, solidarity, commitment and reciprocity . . . interdependence, cooperation and affiliation [in which] the family needs precede individual needs" (Gloria et al., 2004, p. 169). This conception of family values positions family as more than structural but instead an all-encompassing support and teacher. Excerpts from the Latinx pre-service teachers' autobiographies highlight the unique ways the centrality of family supported them to survive and taught them to succeed in a variety of contexts. These unique funds of knowledge underscore what could be unique ways our Latinx pre-service teachers develop dispositions toward difference and have learned through observation at home.

Claudia describes how she grew up in an apartment complex made up of diverse tenants. She writes about how she observed and participated in cultural exchange alongside her mother at a community event in the complex. This is a rich representation of familismo as it highlights the ways that our Latinx students' family experiences instill values of work and generosity through modeling. She recalls:

We cooked the traditional mole and served it to our neighbors with tortillas. As I was being praised for the delicious food I helped cook, I taught my neighbors a few words from my mother's native language. It was all very new and exciting because my neighbors got to experience my culture through food, and I experienced theirs through music, arts, crafts, and movies. I learned something from each one of them. Alina was our deaf neighbor and from her, I learned American Sign Language. Mrs. Jones taught me how to play chess and Arbula taught me how to dance to islander music.

Her family experience highlights the development of positive dispositions toward difference learned through observation and practice. Similarly, Paola begins her autobiography by describing her immediate family with six members. Followed closely by a descriptive summary of her large extended family:

My mom has 9 siblings, and my dad has 6 siblings. All of my aunts and uncles have children, so I have many cousins. I'm not even counting second or third cousins or aunts and uncles. It's nice to have such a big family.

This pre-service teachers' choice to emphasize the size of her family in detail not only stresses the centrality of family in her life but also alludes to skills collaborating with large groups inherently including differences of opinions. Other research has considered how this cultural emphasis on family, misaligns with higher education contexts where family is typically not included (Gloria & Segura-Herrera 2004; Hernandez, 2000). It is important for us to acknowledge the unique role and value of family for our Latinx students when reflecting upon our responsive practices. Moreover, the household knowledge of and the ability to negotiate diversity or difference is already evident within the Latinx communities of our pre-service teachers described, whether in the navigation of "huge family" gatherings or the open-exchange with a diverse community. Delgado Bernal (2001) connects pedagogies of the home with funds of knowledge passed down between generations of families. "Community and family knowledge is taught to youth through such ways as legends, *corridos*, storytelling, and behavior" (Delgado Bernal, 2001, p. 624). The familial behaviors described in our pre-service teachers' autobiographies reflect a rich familismo experience that teaches them to embrace difference and negotiate collaboratively through observation and experience.

Acts of Resistance

In this chapter, acts of resistance are defined as transformational resistance (Delgado Bernal, 1997), which include "positive strategies used by Chicana and Chicano students to successfully navigate through the educational system" (Delgado Bernal, 2001, p. 625). These strategies are learned in the home and become part of an individual's cultural knowledge base that can be used throughout the educational experience. As Rogoff et al. (2014) found, much can be learned through observation as in communities where children are expected to work or conduct chores alongside their parents and other adults. In our study, we found that when Latinx students reported an observed obstacle faced by their families, they also reported a certain learned behavior that subsequently helped them (see Table 8.1).

It is important for teacher educators to recognize these acts of transformational resistance because we need to be aware of these instances as ongoing, not as events that happened in the past that our students already overcame. As our students engage in our classes, they may be overcoming linguistic barriers, and vying to learn by observing, to make independent decisions about their learning, and to be seen as hard-working people. As teacher educators, we can be responsive to acts of transformational resistance considering the relevance of the content that we teach, *as well as* considering the ways in which we teach. Villegas and Lucas (2002) list factors that prevent teachers from becoming culturally responsive. This includes institutional factors (e.g., hierarchical and bureaucratic nature of the educational system), as well as lack of personal understanding of oppression and empathy for those who are oppressed (p. 56). Thus, to model culturally responsive teaching, teacher educators should ensure that acts of transformational resistance are seen, that we address issues of equity, and that we practice "empathy for students from diverse backgrounds" (Villegas & Lucas, 2002, p. 59). It is by modeling these practices, our students will learn, by observing, how teachers can affirm the diversity in their classrooms.

Borderlands

Some pre-service teachers clearly expressed a sense of being in between, *I have always felt like I am too Mexican for my white friends and too "whitewashed" for my Hispanic friends. It always made me feel like I did not fit anywhere I tried to be (Consuelo)*, which alluded to the borderlands concept. To capture Anzaldúa's (1987) words "borderlands denotes that space in which antithetical elements mix, neither to obliterate each other nor to be subsumed by a larger whole, but rather to combine in unique and unexpected ways" (Cantu & Hurtado, 2012, p. 6). That is, a person realizes that s/he does not "fit" in a new environment because his/her practices are different from the "imagined" normal ones (Anderson, 2006) of the community of practices of which they become members (Wenger, 1998). For example, academic settings would typically ask pre-service teacher to write a five-paragraph essay instead of telling a story about a chosen topic. Latinx pre-service teachers do not have a choice but to perform such practices; in doing so, they cross borders: culturally and linguistically. For pre-service teachers who live in borderlands, it is not an easy feat, and they are sometimes not understood by majority teacher educators because they do not know how to act or use language in the new context of which they become members. As such, they may not perform as well as any majority pre-service teacher, and in the educators' eyes, pre-service teacher may not be college material or do not have the needed skills to be a teacher. Not having the needed teaching skills connects to their socialization process (Park & King, 2003) because some pre-service teachers cross other borders.

Race and Culture. When crossing borders, at times, students may feel segregated so they look for strategies to ease such crossings. As Carlos wrote,

I know that when [I was] in elementary, I really wanted to identify with who I was and because I lived in a rural area where out of twenty students in my class, only about three of them were of brown skin so that is who I always hung out with.

Carlos recalls that there were 20 students in his elementary class, but he (initially) made friends with only three of them due to sharing one salient feature, in his words, "[a] brown skin." It is in the early grades when students realize about differences because they have experienced them or because someone has pointed it out, as it is happening in the United States as we write this piece. Moreover, in crossing, pre-service teachers' experiences are a mix, *Many good times, many times of confusion, and many times of frustrations*, as Carlos stated. He later added:

Table 8.1 Examples of Transformational Resistance

Pseudonym	Observed Resistance	Transformational Resistance
Paola	At home I do speak Spanish because my parents still struggle with English even after all these years in the United States. My mom does understand English if it is spoken clearly, but has a hard time responding back in English. My dad on the other hand doesn't speak English at all. He doesn't understand what people are saying unless it is a short simple phrase. **It's hard to see them struggle with a language that people say they should have learned by now because it's not that easy for everyone to learn it.** My mom has attended English classes at the community college, or when they are offered in the elementary or high school, and it's just very hard for her to get the grasp of all the rules. It's upsetting when people say that people who are not originally from the United States don't try and learn English because I have seen not just my mom but many other people try and learn, but it's a hard language to master.	Talking about school I struggled through a few years of school because I came from a home that spoke only Spanish. Especially during the time that I was moving into 3rd grade. Up until that year I was in a bilingual classroom, so I was able to do things in Spanish. When I went into 3rd grade it was all in English and I had no practice other than ELD during the first few years of school. Since I was the first child I didn't have any older siblings that I could look up to or practice my English with. This is something that I would say had a negative impact on my success in school just because of the situation I was in. **My mom didn't let that stop me though.** She would take me to reading nights at school, enrolled me in programs, and other things that would help me improve my English.
Celia	I was very excited to start school because I was the youngest and had never experienced being in a classroom. **For my mom it was difficult letting me go, but she was also very busy working full time as a housekeeper.** Around the same time, my mom decided to enroll into evening classes at a community college to develop her English language skills. **This new commitment limited her time with my siblings and I.**	Having her away so often gave my siblings and I freedom to make our own decisions at a very young age.

Carlos	I come from a family of migrant workers who in the 1980's moved to America to find a better life, "a land of opportunity" as my dad always said . . . **My parents are hard workers and work is all they have known all their lives.** When they met in Los Angeles California at a factory they continued their relationship together traveling up north to Washington to work in the apple fields. . . . My parents from there migrated to Oregon where they found a place to work in the fields harvesting and cultivating berries. **I can still sometimes smell the freshness of the berries in my hands as I tagged along for the all work day. I basically grew up on the fields.** . . . In my household everyone had their place. As a boy I always went with my father to help with work activities and my mother was followed by my sister who was in the kitchen either cooking or washing dishes sometimes even watching my other little siblings.	Some factors from out of school that contributed to my success in school I think was the **work ethics that my parents instilled in me.** I knew that to achieve my goals would mean that I had to put in the work and effort in order to succeed. That was one thing my teachers always talk to me about, the fact that I always tried my best even though sometimes I might have felt lost. Being able to come from a humble background allowed for me to really value my things in school, my materials, my engagement especially the fact that I got the opportunity to learn something new every day and know that I had privileges that my **hard-working parent** never did have.

Some of my favorite foods are: tamales picaditas, salsa roja, chilaquiles, pozole, barbacoa, tacos, tortas, mariscos, pan dulce and much more. I thank my mother for all these types of foods which is why I took many cooking classes in high school but was disappointed that I didn't learn Mexican traditional dishes.

Understanding that being in borderlands (e.g., using English instead of Spanish or vice versa) is a part of their identities as bilingual and bicultural people is paramount. Thus, the role of EPPs should be to be aware of such crossings and to infuse such knowledge in our lessons, task, and assessments so that tough crossings are minimized. As a result, we will enact more responsive practice and recruit, retain, and graduate more diverse pre-service teachers.

Bilingualism. Most pre-service teachers who identified as Hispanic/Latinx stated that Spanish was their home or heritage language, which mirrors the linguistic context of most U.S. schools at present. The majority of them, 76% (Wright, 2015), are emergent bilinguals as they started their PK-12 trajectory. Many pre-service teachers did not initially recognize such linguistic differences until they heard or saw English so their only choice was to cross linguistic borders: Use one language at home, another language at school, and another one with their (bilingual) peers. For some pre-service teachers, their linguistic crossings had been painful because they (and some of their teachers) did not comprehend the differences. Juan described instances where he struggled using the language of schooling, which was Spanish when he lived in Mexico and English when he returned to the United States.

After arriving to Mexico I missed a year of school because I had to learn Spanish, but even after learning Spanish I did not speak almost at all to the point that my peers had to call me "the new kid" for some time because I was going through the silent phase that I child has after they put in a different environment with a different language.

After arriving to the United States, I discovered that I did not know as much English as I thought. During my years in Mexico my mom put me in English classes, so I did not forget about it, but the classes were, for the most part, basic because it was only textbook and short sentences use. I say they were basic because when I started speaking English here, I noticed that the classes I took did not prepare me for an environment where English is everywhere. The moment when I realized that was when I when to the theater with my step sister and her friends. I would listen to them talk and at the time it seemed as they were talking really fast, but fortunately enough they all understood Spanish, but they just did not want to speak it themselves for some reason or another.

Juan's excerpt showcases that in both countries, his linguistic repertoires did not support a smooth crossing due to various factors (e.g., the silent period that any learner experiences as s/he transitions to a new language) or that he was not taught academic English to even be a peripheral learner in his new community (Wenger, 1998). His account easily connects to what most emergent bilingual learners experience as they transition from home to the PK-12 educational system. One way to minimize such transition is that teachers act as bridges and use the pre-service teachers' home languages to make them feel welcome and send the message that their language is appreciated, valued, respected, and that it is an asset or resource not a "deficit" as some have been led to believe (Ruiz, 1984).

More importantly, once pre-service teachers realized that their languaging practices at school would be different; they chose to hang to it and nurtured it to the best of their knowledge with their parents' support. Most pre-service teachers are painfully aware of the need to translanguage (Garcia & Wei, 2014), merge, and juxtapose to succeed academically. Until EPPs value not only the dominant culture and language (i.e., the official knowledge stated by educational institutions) with which pre-service teachers are socialized, but also the pre-service teachers' familial knowledge they bring to EPPs, their recruiting, retention, and graduation will continue to be a challenge.

Immigration. In most pre-service teachers' communities, it is typical to converse about immigration issues because they have close connections to it. Celia wrote:

> *Throughout my childhood I attended May Day marches with my mom regarding immigrant rights. If I asked ahead of time, sometimes she will pull me out of school so that I could attend. My mom illegally immigrated to the United States at age 16, so at a very young age I became aware of what being undocumented meant. My oldest sister was also undocumented, so we feared our family getting deported, but we did not allow it to impact our daily happiness.*

Since Celia was a child, she was aware of the difference in immigration statuses in her own family, starting with her mother and then her older sister. In her excerpt, she uses concepts such as illegal, undocumented, deported, immigrated, immigrant rights which connect to the discourse that we are exposed these days. The final remarks capture the sentiment that no matter what, as a family they look for happiness even in troubling times as we are living at present.

Identity

According Delgado Bernals's (2001) conceptualization of pedagogies of the home, identity and culture work as strong sites of negotiation in the education journey of the Chicana student. As the students in the study reflected on their multicultural selves within the context of their educational journey, we found that as they identified themselves, there was consistency among their identifiers. When describing who they were and how they identified, Latinx students tended to explicitly stated ethnicity first in their descriptions Claudia stated, *I was born in Baja California Mexico but my family is from Oaxaca* and Consuelo identified *I am Mexican-American. I am also a third generation, meaning my grandparents migrated here to the United States from Mexico*. Most explicitly, Juan states,

> *The first thing that I think about my personal history is that I have been in both Mexico and USA. I was born in Mexico and when I was 11 months old, I was brought to the US and I lived here for 7 years.*

Oftentimes, descriptions followed then with the identifier of language, as in student Claudia's statement *Both of my parents were born in Oaxaca and their first language is a dialect from the region. Mixteco is our family primary language that is most often spoken at home.*

We listen carefully to these statements strongly rooted in ethnicity and language as we seek to understand the identity and culture of our Latinx students. The significance of this finding also aligns with notions of identity and their implications for practices in teacher education (Beauchamp & Thomas, 2009). We need to be "centering the narratives" (Ochoa, 2007, p. 8) so as to increase our understanding of the perspectives and experiences of our Latinx students. Doing so has the potential to influence how we build curriculum and programming and talk about race, ethnicity, and language in our EPP.

Simultaneously, we acknowledge that oversimplifying the Latinx experience and identity in the United States is one to be cautious of (Colomer, 2019). One of the Latinx students in our study spoke at length about her family and her pets before she stated that her family was from Jalisco, Mexico and that her first language was Spanish. This illustration reminds us that the Latinx experience is diverse and changing and "the rich diversity of the Latinx panethnic group is often lost when framed by standardized terminology" (Colomer, 2019, p. 195). Nonetheless, as we continue to seek the lived experiences of pre-service teachers, we recognize their primary identifiers that highlight ethnicity and language. Pedagogies of the home forefront the identities and knowledge from the home and communities so as to leverage lived experiences. By privileging ethnic identity, we may better acknowledge the social positions experienced by Latinx students so that their Mestiza consciousness is no longer silenced (Delgado Bernal, 2001).

CONCLUSION AND IMPLICATIONS

The purpose of this chapter was to document how we positioned our students to self-identify and to co-construct the definition of diversity by which our self-study will be grounded and our EPP will be evaluated. The most significant implication of this study is that the evidence of diversity we provided here will serve as objective facts to guide the self-study of our programs so as to mitigate a post-truth educator preparation accreditation process. Further implications include using this study as an example for how an EPP could begin a self-study related to diversity standards. Beginning with listening sessions or a gathering of student voices may mitigate generic goals for what teacher candidates should know and for how an EPP should support the retention of Latinx pre-service teachers. By continuing listening sessions, we may identify authentic ways to improve our program. To close, we highlight the following recommendations for setting our EPPs diversity outcomes based on our analysis:

1. Our EPP should acknowledge and integrate the unique role and value of family for our Latinx pre-service teachers when reflecting upon our responsive practices (Familismo).
2. Our EPP should minimize transitions by acting as bridges rather than thresholds or barriers (e.g., use the pre-service teachers' home languages to make them feel welcome and send the message that their language is appreciated, valued, respected, and that it is an asset or resource not a "deficit" as some have been led to believe (Borderlands).
3. Our EPP should look for and disrupt assimilationist approaches to teacher education (i.e., the language and culture that counts as official knowledge stated by educational institutions) that enforce a socialization process toward a white teacher identity (Borderlands).
4. Our EPP should model culturally responsive teaching by ensuring that acts of transformational resistance are seen, that we address issues of equity, and that we practice empathy for pre-service teachers from diverse backgrounds (Acts of Resistance).
5. Our EPP should center the narratives of our Latinx pre-service teachers so as to increase our understanding of their perspectives and experiences and our valuing of the approaches that affirm their familial and cultural knowledge as we build curriculum and programming and talk about race, ethnicity, and language in our EPP (Identity).

NOTES

1. The 2019 Educator Equity Report uses the term "Ethnically Diverse" or "Ethnically and Linguistically Diverse" while the authors of this paper use Culturally and Linguistically Diverse to describe the same population.

2. Latinx is the term used in this chapter in response to the multiple and intersectional identities of our pre-service teachers and to align with the framing of the book in which this chapter is published.

REFERENCES

Ahmed, S. (2007). 'You end up doing the document rather than doing the doing': Diversity, race equality and the politics of documentation. *Ethnic and Racial Studies, 30*(4), 590–609.

Anderson (2006). *Imagined communities: Reflections on the origin and spread of nationalism*. London: Verso.

Anzaldúa, G. (1987). *Borderlands, la frontera: The new mestiza*. 4th ed. San Francisco: Aunt Lute Books.

Beauchamp, C., & Thomas, L. (2009). Understanding teacher identity: An overview of issues in the literature and implications for teacher education. *Cambridge Journal of Education, 39*(2), 175–189.

Beyerbach, B., & Nassoiy, T. D. (2004). Where Is Equity in the National Standards? A Critical Review of the INTASC, NCATE, and NBPTS Standards. *Scholar-Practitioner Quarterly, 2*(4), 29–42.

Cantu, N., & Hurtado, A. (2012). Introduction to the Fourth Edition. *Borderlands, la frontera: The new mestiza*. (pp. 3–13). San Francisco: Aunt Lute Books.

Colomer, S. E. (2019). Understanding racial literacy through acts of (un)masking: Latinx teachers in a new Latinx diaspora community, *Race Ethnicity and Education, 22*(2), 195.

Council for the Accreditation of Educator Preparation (2018). *CAEP Handbook: Initial level programs 2018*. Washington, DC: Caepnet.org.

Creswell, J. W., & Creswell, J. D. (2018). *Research design: Qualitative, quantitative, and mixed methods approaches*. 5th ed. Thousand Oaks: Sage.

Delgado Bernal, D. (1997). *Chicana School Resistance and grassroots leadership: Providing an alternative history of the 1968 East Los Angeles blowouts*. Doctoral dissertation. University of California, Los Angeles.

Delgado Bernal, D. (2001). Living and learning pedagogies of the home: The mestiza consciousness of Chicana students. *International Journal of Qualitative Studies in Education, 14*(5), 623–639.

Diangelo, R. (2018). *White fragility: Why it's so hard for white people to talk about racism*. Boston, MA: Beacon Press.

García, O., & Wei, L. (2014). *Translanguaging: Language, bilingualism and education*. New York: Palgrave Macmillan.

Gloria, A. M., Ruiz, E. L., & Castillo, E. M. (2004). Counseling Latinos and Latinas: A psychosociocultural approach. In P. S. Richards & T. Smith (Eds.), *Practicing multiculturalism: Internalizing and affirming diversity in counseling and psychology* (pp. 167–184). Boston: Allyn and Bacon.

Gloria, A. M., & Segura-Herrera, T. A. (2004). Ambrocia and Omar go to college: A psychosociocultural examination of Chicana/os in higher education. *The Handbook of Chicana/O Psychology and Mental Health*, 401–425.

Gorski, P. C. (2009). What we're teaching teachers: An analysis of multicultural teacher education coursework syllabi. *Teaching and Teacher Education, 25*, 309–318.

Griffin, K. A., Cunningham, E. L., Mwangi, G., & Chrystal, A. (2016). Defining diversity: Ethnic differences in Black students' perceptions of racial climate. *Journal of Diversity in Higher Education, 9*(1), 34–49.

Haddix, M. M. (2017). Diversifying teaching and teacher education: Beyond rhetoric and toward real change. *Journal of Literacy Research, 49*(1), 141–149.

Harper, S. R., & Hurtado, S. (2007). Nine themes in campus racial climates and implications for institutional transformation. *New Directions for Student Services, 2007*, 7–24. http://dx.doi.org/10.1002/ss.254

Hernandez, J. C. (2000). Understanding the retention of Latino college students. *Journal of College Student Development, 41*, 575–588.

Hurtado, S., & Ponjuan, L. (2005). Latino educational outcomes and the campus climate. *Journal of Hispanic Higher Education, 4*(3), 235–251.

Miles M., Huberman, M., & Saldana, J. (2014). *Qualitative data analysis: A methods source book.* London: Sage.

Ochoa, G. L. 2007. *Learning from Latino teachers.* San Francisco, CA: Josey-Bass.

Oregon Equity Advisory Group (2019). *2019 Oregon Educator Equity Report.* Salem, OR: Chief Education Office.

Park, E., & King, K. A. (2003). Cultural diversity and language socialization in the early years. *ERIC Digest*.

Peters, M. (2017). Education in a post-truth world. *Educational Philosophy and Theory, 49*(6), 5 63–566.

Rankin, S. R., & Reason, R. D. (2005). Differing perceptions: How students of color and white students perceive campus climate for underrepresented groups. *Journal of College Student Development, 46*, 43–61. http://dx.doi.org/10.1353/csd.2005.0008

Rogoff, B., Alcalá, L., Coppens, A. D., López, A., Ruvacaba, O., & Silva, K. G. (Eds.). (2014). Learning by observing and pitching in to family and community endeavors. *Human Development, 57*(2–3), 150–161. [Special issue].

Ruiz, R. (1984). Orientations in language planning. *NABE Journal, 8*(2), 15–34.

Salazar, M. D. C. (2018). Interrogating teacher evaluation: Unveiling whiteness as the normative center and moving the margins. *Journal of Teacher Education, 69*(5), 463–476.

Saldana, J. (2013). *The coding manual for qualitative researchers.* 2nd ed. London: Sage.

Sleeter, C. E. (2017). Critical race theory and the whiteness of teacher education. *Urban Education, 52*(2), 155–169.

Smith-Morris, C., Morales-Campos, D., Alvarez, E. A. C., & Turner, M. (2013). An anthropology of familismo: On narratives and description of Mexican/immigrants. *Hispanic Journal of Behavioral Sciences, 35*(1), 35–60.

Stebleton, M. J., Rost-Banik, C., Greene, E., & DeAngelo, L. (2017). "Trying to Be Accepted": Exploring foreign-born immigrants' interactions with faculty and practitioners. *Journal of Student Affairs Research and Practice, 54*(4), 357–370.

Stebleton, M., Soria, K., Huesman, R. Jr., & Torres, V. (2014). Recent immigrant students at research universities: The relationship between campus climate and sense of belonging. *Journal of College Student Development, 55*(2), 196–202.

Suarez-Balcazar, Y., Orellana-Damacela, L., Portillo, N., Rowan, J. M., & Andrews-Guillen, C. (2003). Experiences of differential treatment among college students of color. *The Journal of Higher Education, 74,* 428–444. http://dx.doi.org/10.1353/jhe.2003.0026.

Villegas, A. M., & Lucas, T. (2002). *Educating culturally responsive teachers: A coherent approach.* Albany: State University of New York Press.

Wenger, E. (1998). *Communities of practice: Learning, meaning, and identity.* Cambridge, UK: Cambridge University Press.

Wright, W. E. (2015). *Foundations for teaching English language learners: Research, theory, policy, and practice.* 2nd ed. Philadelphia, PA: Caslon Publishing.

Yin, R.K. (2014). *Case study research: Design and methods.* 5th ed. Thousand Oaks, CA: Sage Publishing.

Chapter 9

Preparing Bilingual Teachers through a Bilingual Undergraduate Teacher Corps

Nidos de Lengua y Comunidad[1]

Nadeen T. Ruiz, Margarita Jiménez-Silva, and Samantha A. Smith

INTRODUCTION

In the 1980s, the Maori population of New Zealand took action to stop the loss of their indigenous languages by creating the first *language nests*. Essentially, these early language nests were spaces designed and approved by indigenous communities for very young children, from birth to six years old, as one of several ways to promote the use of the Maori language among future generations. In these language nests, often located in homes or other communal spaces, not schools, the children interacted with Maori speaking elders while engaging in a range of activities anchored in the community, for example, food preparation, songs, games, botanical lessons, and so on.

We initially learned about language nests—*nidos de lengua*—in Oaxaca, México, where the first nido was created in the early 2000s by the Mixtec community in Guadalupe Llano de Avispa Tilantongo, Nochixtlán (Meyer & Soberanes, 2009). Indigenous communities in Mexico have now created nidos throughout the country (Perales Espinosa, 2019). In the United States, the Cochiti community in New Mexico has a long-running language nest to pass on the Keres language, as do other indigenous communities in Hawaii, Minnesota, and North Dakota that are committed to the survival and revitalization of their native languages.

In this chapter we examine a unique undergraduate program that has an exemplary record in nurturing future bilingual teachers. A critical link between nidos de lengua and this chapter's focus is the prevalent theme cited by those working with nidos de lengua: "Es una estrategia de recuperación lingüística, y por lo tanto, resistencia cultural" [It is a strategy to revitalize languages, and therefore, it is a strategy of cultural resistance.] (Meyer & Soberanes, 2009, p. 21).

Despite the proliferation of racist and anti-immigrant rhetoric and actions in recent years, a distinctive program for undergraduate students from Migrant backgrounds has persisted since the 1960s: *California Mini-Corps*. The two main criteria for entering California Mini-Corps are a migrant family background and enrollment in a two- or four-year college. Students can major in any subject. Through previous research, including our own recent study of California Mini-Corps (Jiménez-Silva, Ruiz, & Smith, 2021), we have come to see the program as a site of linguistic and cultural resistance for Latinx undergraduate students. Consequently, we believe that California Mini-Corps creates a *nido* for these students, not only of *lengua* (language) but also of *comunidad* (community). In order to shine more light on how California Mini-Corps nurtures future bilingual teachers and helps them resist assaults on their language and cultural identities, we present in this chapter an analysis of survey responses from what we believe is the largest sample to date of Latinx undergraduates who are not enrolled in a credential[2] program (n=249). Here we focus on: (a) the students' identification of important components of their corps program; (b) their self-assessment of their bilingual repertoire, including as it relates to classroom teaching; and (c) their reasons for and against working toward a bilingual authorization on their teaching credential.

We have two principal goals in writing this chapter. The first arises from the paucity of research on Latinx undergraduates *before* they enter a teaching credential program. Researchers contend that it is precisely to this specific population that recruitment efforts should be directed (Briceño, Rodríguez-Mojica, & Muñoz-Muñoz, 2018; Jiménez-Silva, Ruiz, & Smith, 2020; Ocasio, 2014). If research is limited to students already enrolled in teacher preparation programs, where Latinx students are severely underrepresented, we miss an opportunity to reach an additional pool of potential bilingual teachers, and we make limited headway in countering the bilingual teacher shortage (Harris & Sandoval-González, 2017). Taking into account these calls for additional research, in this chapter we report on and make available to our colleagues in bilingual teacher preparation results stemming from a study with a large group of Latinx undergraduates. Our hope is that this information enables and spurs on future comparative research with Latinx undergraduates who may be open to entering the teaching field.

Our second aim in this chapter is to examine from the students' perspectives how the California Mini-Corps program creates nurturing spaces for development of lengua y comunidad. In doing so, we share components of California Mini-Corps that are potentially replicable at other colleges and, in turn, can augment the number of future bilingual teacher candidates.

LITERATURE CONNECTIONS

In our earlier work we have extensively reviewed the available empirical research undertaken with undergraduate Latinx students before they decide to enter a teaching credential program, and thus we refer readers to that detailed summary (Jiménez-Silva et al., 2021). For this chapter, we briefly report the principal findings from that review, and later make connections between the literature and the present study in the results and discussion section. We also summarize here the body of empirical research with California Mini-Corps.

Research with Latinx Undergraduates Before Entering a Teaching Credential Program

A common finding among several studies of undergraduate Latinx students has been their motivation to enter teaching in order to reverse their negative experiences going through the U.S. school system, and to provide a very different education to their future students (Briceño et al., 2018; Irizarry & Donaldson, 2017). A related theme across these studies is the students' commitment to give back to their community, or what Ramírez (2010) calls a "Peace Corps" mentality (Briceño et al., 2018; Irizarry & Donaldson, 2017).

One recent study explored undergraduate Latinx students' knowledge about bilingual education, and the students' perceptions regarding their possible use of Spanish in the classroom (Briceño et al., 2018). Researchers found that the majority of their participants were unaware of the possibility of teaching in a bilingual classroom, nor did they have any knowledge about a special credential authorization to do so. Briceño and colleagues also documented the students' serious doubts about whether they had the "right" Spanish for bilingual teaching, due to years of denigration directed toward what some would consider nonstandard varieties of Spanish, or due to their Spanish language loss in English-only K-12 instruction (Briceño et al., 2018). The negative perceptions, which the students in that study had accumulated over time, stands in direct contrast with a cultural wealth framework (Yosso, 2005). An assets-based framework explicitly recognizes the connection between students' bilingualism and their development as effective teachers of emergent bilingual students (Ocasio, 2014; Jiménez-Silva et al., 2021).

Overview of the California Mini-Corps Program

Modeled after Peace Corps, the California Mini-Corps (CMC) program began in the 1960s (Quezada & Ruiz, 2018). State-funding through a line-item budget continues to support the CMC program to the present. The overarching goal of CMC has been to provide instructional support to K-12 Migrant children through a formation of a corps of higher education students with connections to Migrant family backgrounds, and who are enrolled in either two-year or four-year colleges.[3] Currently, there are 21 CMC sites located in colleges throughout California. Each site has a CMC Coordinator who recruits approximately 20 undergraduate students to tutor Migrant students in elementary and high schools. All CMC Coordinators hold teaching credentials and are former classroom teachers. They are historically overwhelmingly Latinx. For example, for the 2018–2019 group of 21 CMC Coordinators all but one were Latinx.

Corps students can enter the program as first-year college students and continue to participate throughout their undergraduate education. They are paid for their tutoring of Migrant students during the academic year, and for their work in Migrant summer programs. CMC Coordinators hold monthly professional development meetings with their group of Corps students, focusing on instructional methods for assisting Migrant and emergent bilingual students.

Research with Latinx Undergraduates in the California Mini-Corps Program

Several empirical studies have examined the CMC program and the role it has played in preparing future bilingual teachers, and we have reviewed these studies in depth in an earlier article (Jiménez et al., 2021). Here we summarize the main findings of this body of research, including our own recent study.

Research with CMC has documented the importance of the mentoring relationship that Corps students develop with their Coordinators (Ginsberg, Gasman, & Samayoa, .2018; Lomelí, Parks, Basurto, & Padilla, 2006; Quezada & Ruiz, 2018). In particular, researchers have pointed out how Corps students view themselves as part of the CMC cohort at their particular college, and, significantly, also as part of the teaching profession. The sense of inclusion in the professional community of teachers is marked given its overwhelming White-woman majority. Despite those teacher demographics, however, Corps students of color envisioned themselves as part of this professional community. Researchers assigned credit for the Corps students' feeling of inclusion to the forging of a bond with their Coordinator who shared their ethnolinguistic background, and who had classroom experience with emergent bilinguals (Ginsberg et al., 2018; Lomelí et al., 2006). In addition, Ginsberg et al. (2018) documented that both the bond with the Coordinator and the cohort structure of the CMC program, helped Corps students explicitly discuss the injustices that they observed and/or lived within educational contexts, and how to steer their way through obstacles to baccalaureate graduation and beyond.

Other themes that arose from CMC research were benefits afforded Corps students through extended classroom experiences and monthly professional development specially designed to meet the needs of emergent bilinguals (Ginsberg et al., 2018; Lomelí et al, 2006; Quezada & Ruiz, 2018). In addition, regular classroom observations where the Corps students were working, undertaken by the Coordinator and the supervising classroom teacher, emerged as important aspects of the program. Finally, both active CMC Corps students and alumni highlighted how contacts with the Coordinator, the supervising classroom teacher, and peers helped them gain entrée to teacher credential programs, and later, to classroom and educational administrative positions (González, 2012, as cited in Quezada & Ruiz, 2018). As evidence of the affordances of those contacts, Quezada & Ruiz (2018) cite that 60% of the 2011–2012 CMC cohort received one or more teaching credentials.

In spring of 2018, we began efforts to add to the body of research summarized here through a series of studies with CMC Corps students (Jiménez-Silva et al., 2020). Through our initial literature review, we immediately recognized the value in previous research of interviews with small groups of Corps students (e.g., 10 for the Ginsburg et al. 2018 study), but we were particularly interested to hear from more Corps students, if at all possible. It seemed to us especially critical to access the voices of a large group of Latinx undergraduates, given the lack of research with this group. Hence, we were fortunate to be able to administer a survey to many of the 2018–2019 cohort of Corps students, further described in our "Methods" section.

Our first study with this cohort (Jiménez-Silva et al., 2021) focused on open-ended and closed survey responses from 179 Corps students. Our findings supported previous research that CMC constitutes an outstanding pool of future bilingual teachers in terms of their cultural and linguistic assets (Jiménez et al., 2020). Using a cultural wealth framework (Yosso, 2005), we documented that what Corps students offered as potential teachers was unique and vital to meeting the needs of P-12 emergent bilingual students. Results further showed that Corps students had an expressed commitment to work with children and families from diverse backgrounds, including a willingness to return to their own communities so as to "give back" and assist future generations. In this first study we also analyzed Corps students' responses to questions regarding what they would like to see in their credential programs if they decided to pursue teaching. The two most frequent responses were financial support in the form of paid work or scholarships, and continued teaching experience with culturally and linguistically diverse students.

For the present study we focus on different sections of our survey to add to the still-developing picture of how to best recruit potential bilingual teachers who possess some of the impressive cultural and linguistic assets that we have documented among Corps students. In particular, we examined our data for further understanding of how CMC functions as a space for language revitalization and cultural resistance (a nido), with special emphasis on how colleges may be able to implement effective components of a bilingual undergraduate teaching corps.

METHODS AND ANALYSIS

We constructed a survey of 64 items to be distributed across the 21 California colleges hosting a CMC program. Survey items were generated taking into account: (a) our general literature review for this project (Jiménez-Silva et al., 2021; Jiménez-Silva & Ruiz, 2018); (b) our previous work with surveys of teacher candidates working with emergent bilinguals (Ruiz & Lozano, 2010; Ruiz & Lotan, 2007); and (c) replication of several survey items from previous research with Latinx undergraduates (e.g., Athanases et al. 2015; Ramírez, 2010). The survey consisted of five sections: Background, Schooling Experiences, Languages, Mini-Corps Experience, and Future Plans. The survey included both closed and open response items. Following the recommendation of the CMC Coordinators, we made and distributed hard copies of the protocols instead of an electronic version.

Of the 21 CMC Coordinators throughout the state of California receiving a packet of surveys, 15 administered the survey to their current cadre of approximately 15–20 Corps students' resulting in 249 surveys. In this chapter we present descriptive statistics regarding the following closed-item sections of the survey: (a) language backgrounds; (b) bilingual repertoire self-perceptions; (c) ratings of CMC program features; and (d) dispositions toward bilingual instruction. In addition to the responses to these closed-item sections, we also analyzed the results of one open-ended component of the survey: reasons for and against becoming a bilingual teacher. For open-ended items, we employed qualitative research methods to identify initial categories of responses in our first read of the data (Merriam & Tisdale, 2016). In multiple reviews of the data, either separately or in pairs, we made revisions to the initial categories when necessary, ultimately arriving at consensus for both categories and coding of responses. Again, our primary goals in presenting both the quantitative and qualitative data here are to: (1) provide a basis of comparison for future research with Latinx undergraduates and teaching; and (2) explore how CMC creates a nurturing space—a nido—of bilingualism and community for future bilingual teachers.

RESULTS

The average age of our respondents was 22 years, with 86% (n=214) indicating their gender as female, and 14% as male (n=35). The Corps students' average year in college was junior level. In reporting and discussing our results, we begin with a description of our participants' language backgrounds. We next present an analysis of Corps students' identification of CMC program features that were important to them. We then delve further into Corps students' responses related to the profession of bilingual teacher: self-perceptions of dual language skills; dispositions regarding bilingual language use in and out of schools; and their reasons for choosing, or not choosing, to become a bilingual teacher.

Corps Students' Language Backgrounds

Seventy-seven percent of the students (n=192) reported that Spanish was used most of the time in their household. An additional 8% responded that Spanish was spoken at least half of the time, for a total of 85% (n=212) of Corps students growing up with Spanish as the predominant language in their homes.

Corps Students' Ratings of CMC Program Features

In an effort to more fully understand how the CMC program produces such large numbers of teachers (Quezada & Ruiz, 2018), we asked the Corps students themselves to rate the importance of CMC program features. The scale ranged 5 points: *extremely important* (5), *very important* (4), *neutral* (3), *slightly important* (2), and *not important* (1). As shown in Table 9.1, students highly valued all 11 distinguishing program features: the average rating for all components fell between *extremely important* (5) and *very important* (4).

The top two highest-rated features of this undergraduate teaching corps were: (1) *Getting to know people who may be able to help me get a teaching job in the future* (4.78); and (2) *Receiving help from CMC staff/tutors for entrance into a graduate program* (4.76).[4] The next two highest-rated CMC features received equal rating: (3) *Lots of teaching experience as an undergraduate*, and (4) *Learning about special teaching methods to work with English Learner/Migrant students* (both 4.75). To the next most frequently cited the features, Corps students attributed values only slightly below the

Table 9.1 Corps Students' Rating of the California Mini-Corps Experience

Mini-Corps Experience	Average Rating
Getting to know people who may be able to help me get a teaching job in the future	4.78
Receiving help from CMC staff/Tutors for entrance to grad program	4.76
Lots of teaching experience as an undergrad	4.75
Learning about special teaching methods to work with EL/Migrant students	4.75
Receiving feedback on teaching from CMC Coordinator	4.74
Receiving feedback on my teaching from my supervising teacher	4.74
Being mentored by CMC Coordinator who shares my cultural/linguistic background	4.67
Learning about teaching methods in monthly workshops with CMC Coordinator	4.62
Being mentored by CMC Coordinator who taught ELs/Migrant students	4.61
Paid teaching experience	4.52
Being part of a group/cohort for several years during undergrad	4.37

previous program components. They were: *Receiving feedback on my teaching from my CMC Coordinator*, and *Receiving feedback on my teaching from my supervising (classroom) teacher where I tutor* (both rated 4.74).

The next set of responses in terms of frequency were related to Corps students' appreciation of their CMC Coordinators: *Being mentored by a CMC Coordinator who shares my cultural/linguistic background* (4.78); Learning about teaching methods in monthly workshops with CMC Coordinator (4.62); and *Being mentored by a CMC Coordinator who has taught EL/Migrant students* (4.61). These findings suggest that identifying mentors who possess similar ethnolinguistic profiles and classroom teaching experience with emergent bilinguals will be a valued component of an undergraduate teaching corps.

Corps Students' Language Perceptions

Corps students responded to a series of language-related questions in the survey. We first asked them to rate themselves in both English and Spanish along a conversational-academic language continuum. Given that our research has a specific focus on potential bilingual teachers who would teach in both languages, we also included a targeted question about the students' perceptions regarding the particular register of delivering bilingual classroom instruction.

Self-Rating. Students indicated their degree of agreement to a series of statements regarding their use of English, Spanish, and hybrid varieties.

Overall, the results show that the students consider themselves relatively balanced in their Spanish and English language proficiencies. With 5 indicating the highest level of proficiency and 1 the lowest, students' average rating of their conversational Spanish was 4.69, and conversational English slightly higher at 4.71 (Table 9.2). When asked to estimate their proficiency in formal/standard spoken Spanish (described in our survey as "the kind of language you might use with a professional person from that country"), students rated themselves somewhat lower than conversational Spanish, 4.11 for formal/standard spoken Spanish compared to 4.64 for the conversational register. Interestingly, when responding to similar questions about a more formal version of Spanish and English, but this time for *classroom teaching*, there was a wider disparity between the two languages, with the students' 4.65 rating for delivering English instruction, and 4.19 for teaching in Spanish (Table 9.2).

A different pattern from the previous discussion of oral language emerged with students' responses regarding reading and writing in both languages. Here, instead of relatively balanced self-ratings between languages, students rated themselves higher in English reading and writing skills, in both formal and classroom use: 4.51 and 4.61 for English, versus 3.93 and 3.97 for Spanish, respectively (Table 9.3). Most likely the students' perceptions of more proficiency in English reflects that the majority of them received all-English instruction while in U.S. schools.

Dispositions toward instruction in languages other than English. Borrowing items from the *Teacher Education English Learner Survey* (TEELS; Ruiz & Lozano, 2010), we asked Corps students to rate three statements regarding the use of Spanish in the home and at school, along a continuum from *Strongly Agree* (a rating of 5), *Agree* (4), *Neutral, neither agree or disagree* (3), *Disagree* (2), and *Strongly Disagree* (1). Resoundingly, the Corps students

Table 9.2 Conversation and Formal Language Self-Ratings by Corps Students

Language Usage	Average Rating	
	Spanish	English
Speak and Understand—Conversational	4.69	4.71
Speak and Understand—Formal/standard	4.11	4.56
Speak and Understand—Classroom	4.19	4.65

Table 9.3 Conversation and Formal Language Self-Ratings by Corps Students

Language Usage	Average Rating	
	Spanish	English
Read and Write—Formal	3.93	4.51
Read and Write—Classroom	3.97	4.61

showed very positive dispositions toward native language use at home and in schools, and rejected notions of all English use in both education and home settings.

To the first statement—*It's best that English Learners and Migrant students be placed in English-only classes for them to be successful*—students indicated their disagreement with an average rating of 2.12. Put another way, our respondents showed strong support for the use of bilingual instruction—Spanish and English—for children who shared their Migrant background. The next survey item—*All English Learners and Migrant children should have the opportunity to attend bilingual schools where subject matter (math, science, language arts, and social studies) is taught in both English and a language other than English*—lent further evidence for the Corps students' support of bilingual education. This statement elicited a high degree of agreement, 4.52. The item receiving the lowest rating of agreement was: *As a way of helping English Learner and Migrant students, their parents should only speak English in the home.* Here Corps students signaled their disagreement with Spanish-speaking parents changing the language of the home to English by giving the item a rating of 1.85.

Language discrimination. As a way of delving deeper into Corps students' perceptions of their bilingualism, we included and adapted several of our survey items in this section from a study by Athanases, Banes, and Wong (2015). In an undergraduate education class on cultural diversity, the researchers asked 41 self-identified bilinguals (65% Asian; 35% Latinx) to indicate their level of agreement with regarding their experiences with linguistic discrimination and hybridized language use. Though the student population in the Athanases et al. study had a very different ethnolinguistic profile than Corps students, this research afforded the beginning of a comparison and examination of our group's perspectives on a core component of becoming a bilingual teacher, their multilingual repertoire.

The scale in the Athanases et al. study for responses was 5 for *Strongly Agree* and 1 for *Strongly Disagree*, with the same intermediate scale points previously noted. Their bilingual respondents indicated overall agreement with this statement (3.49): *I have felt judged because of the way/s I speak.* For our survey we parsed this notion into two versions, one for Spanish, and the other for English. Corps students indicated a slightly lower incidence of judgment toward their use of Spanish and English than in the Athanases study: 3.05 for Spanish and 2.96 for English. Athanases and colleagues also asked their bilingual respondents to rate a related statement: *I have felt discriminated against because of the way I speak.* Once again, students in the Athanases et al. study reported higher agreement with this negative view of their language use, 3.20, than the Corps students either for Spanish (2.78) or English (2.56).

Athanases and colleagues also examined hybridized language use among their participants, asking them to rate their agreement with three statements. Taking into account that our Corps students may have been first-year college students and not exposed to readings in linguistic diversity as were the students in the Athanases et al. (2015) study, we added a few examples of hybrid languages in the wording of our survey items in order to clarify the term "hybridized." In the following examples, our additions are in brackets.

Broadly comparing the survey results from the two studies, we first provide the rating of the students from Athanases et al. (2015) study, and then findings from our study: *I often speak in one or more hybridized languages* [added in our survey: (*ex.: Spanglish, Chicanx Spanish, code-switching*)] (Athanases et al. 4.05; Corps students 4.17); *I feel comfortable shifting between languages with my friends and family* (Athanases et al.– 4.41; Corps students –4.47); and, *I feel comfortable shifting between languages in professional or academic settings* (Athanases et al. – 3.33; Corps students– 3.94). The level of agreement between the two separate groups is highly similar. Though it is unclear from the Athanases et al. study whether their reported survey results were from the beginning or end of their 10 week course which included multiple readings on language and cultural diversity, it seems that Corps students' perceptions regarding use of their multilingual repertoire, specifically, hybridized language varieties, were similar.

Corps Students' Reasons for Becoming (or not) a Bilingual Teacher

An overwhelmingly large number of participants (93%, n=232) responded affirmatively to the question, *Would you like to be a bilingual teacher, that is, use both English and Spanish in your instruction?* We also asked respondents for their reasoning behind their decision in an open-ended question. Eighty-eight percent of the students (n=219) provided written responses. Overall, the reasons identified by the respondents for becoming a bilingual teacher were distributed among three main categories: (a) provide support for future students and maximize their opportunities (34%); (b) the overall importance of bilingualism (30%); and (c) ensure a safe and comfortable learning environment for emergent bilinguals and Migrant students (19%).

The leading reason from respondents to enter the bilingual teaching profession was to support future students and maximize their potential. As one respondent wrote about her future students, "Being educated in two languages gives them more opportunities." Another explained, "Speaking both languages is a very important skill I have and would like my students to have the opportunity and exposure to other languages." Approximately 30% of respondents indicated that their main drive for becoming a bilingual teacher was their belief in the importance and value of bilingualism. A representative response in this category was: "I believe it's important to learn in both languages since the majority of students' first languages is Spanish. Also, it's important for them to realize that being bilingual is a great skill to have and should be embraced more." Other students were more succinct, for example, "I believe that being bilingual is SUPER important/beneficial!" The third most common reason (19%) as to why Corps students wanted to become bilingual teachers was to ensure a safe and comfortable environment for emergent and Migrant students to learn: "I think that teaching a bilingual class would help students feel more welcome and I think that it would also help students to not be afraid to express themselves." Another student response in this category included consideration of Migrant students' families when stating the reason to become a bilingual teacher: "Make students and parents comfortable to ask questions and communicate with me in the classroom. Have students understand more clearly with both languages in case they didn't understand in one."

A much smaller group of students (4%, n=10) indicated that they did not wish to become a bilingual teacher, and even fewer reported that they were not sure (3%, n=7). Almost half of the individuals who specified they did not want to become a bilingual teacher referenced their perceived insufficiency in Spanish reading, writing, or speaking. Likewise, in the group who stated their uncertainty about becoming a bilingual teacher, several noted their doubts about their reading, writing, and speaking skills in Spanish. Though few in numbers, these responses reflect the Corps students' lower rating of their formal Spanish usage.

DISCUSSION

In our discussion of results, we circle back to our central metaphor for the CMC program as a nido de lengua y comunidad.

Nido de Lengua

This cohort of 249 Latinx students, all enrolled at two-year and four-year California colleges, entered the CMC program with a primary asset for becoming a bilingual teacher: native Spanish language proficiency. Eighty-eight percent of these Corps members grew up speaking Spanish in their homes for more than half of the time. However, it is important to note that these Corps students had previously attended K-12 schools during the most intense repression of bilingual instruction in California during recent times. In 1998, when Corps students were approximately two years of age,

California voters passed Proposition 227, resulting in legislation that severely curtailed bilingual education. The legislation was not reversed until 2018, when this group of Corps students entered college. At that time, California voters approved Proposition 58, now referred to as *California Education for a Global Economy Initiative*, or *CA Ed.G.E.* in state Education Code. The overall impact of CA Ed.G.E. was to lift the previous restrictions on bilingual education programs and spur on a rapid increase of demand for both programs and bilingual teachers, a primary impetus for our own research here.

Results from our survey document that despite scarce opportunities to attend bilingual schools themselves, Corps Students' demonstrated very positive dispositions toward native language use in the home and schools. Without more available research on Latinx undergraduates, it is challenging to definitively claim that these Corps students showed relatively higher support for native language use by parents and in schools than other groups. We do know, however, that their dispositions mirrored ratings by graduate students already enrolled in a bilingual teacher education program and definitely pursuing a bilingual authorization for their teaching credential (Jiménez et al., in 2021). Overall, these results raise the possibility that the CMC program, with its commitment to furthering the education of Migrant children via tutoring in both English and Spanish, provided a protective community where Corps students' bilingualism was functionally recognized as an asset, not a deficit.

Additional survey responses related to students' language perceptions brought about another issue that may warrant further investigation. In comparison to a smaller group of undergraduate bilinguals in an earlier study (Athenases et al., 2015), Corps students felt somewhat less judged or discriminated against in terms of their Spanish and English usage. We certainly need to avoid any strong statements about the different ratings between these two disparate groups of bilingual undergraduates. However, the lower levels of perceived language judgment or discrimination among Corps students may suggest once again that the CMC program provided a nurturing space for bilinguals and their languages, and a greater degree of resistance to outside discrimination directed at their linguistic repertoire.

Before leaving the topic of language, we need to be clear that some nuances about Corps students' language perceptions arose from ratings of their Spanish and English proficiencies along a range of registers, including conversational, formal, and classroom instruction. Corps students assessed their formal English register slightly higher than their Spanish formal register. The difference in dual language ratings then marginally widened for their perception that their English proficiency may be stronger for classroom instruction than their Spanish. We also noticed the same pattern of a moderately higher self-rating for English reading and writing in comparison to Spanish.

Once again, given this group of students' limited access to bilingual instruction during their K-12 studies, some doubts regarding their formal registers of Spanish are to be expected. Among the very small number of Corps students who indicated that they were not going to seek the bilingual teaching authorization, the most commonly cited reason was their doubt regarding their own Spanish language proficiency, similar to what was reported by the 11 Latinx undergraduates in the Briceño et al. study (2018). At the same time, the Corps students did not seem to show the same degree of hesitation to deploy their Spanish language skills as future bilingual teachers relative to participants in Briceño et al. (2018). Until we have additional research on Latinx undergraduates' self-assessment of Spanish academic language proficiency, the data we do have suggest that support for written academic Spanish in the undergraduate years, as well as in bilingual teaching credential programs, will most likely be welcome by students as an opportunity to extend their multilingual repertoires.

Overall, through the Corps students' positive dispositions for bilingualism in home and school settings, and seemingly greater resistance to language discrimination, our results indicate that Corps students' bilingual repertoires were validated by their participation in the CMC program. Furthermore, these undergraduates, themselves nurtured within a cohort structure that prized their bilingualism and bilingual teaching skills, appear prepared to pass on those same dispositions to their future students. Their inclusive stance toward linguistic diversity stands in direct opposition to the anti-immigrant, English-only, border-walls rhetoric of our current political context. As such, we believe that the CMC program creates a "nido de lengua." Paraphrasing Meyers and Soberanes (2009), the CMC program serves as a strategy to revitalize the Spanish language at home and at school, and consequently, embodies a strategy of cultural resistance.

Nido de Comunidad

Our results indicated that in addition to a nido de lengua, the CMC program functions as a nido de comunidad. In this chapter we focus on two specific aspects of comunidad: a professional community of bilingual education teachers, and the Corps students' home communities that they stand ready to support.

Corps students' survey responses provided a relatively detailed outline of what this large group of Latinx undergraduates valued in their formation as tutors of Migrant children, and as prospective bilingual education teachers. First, Corps students clearly linked their participation in CMC with potential assistance for entering the professional community of teaching. In other words, they viewed the structure of this undergraduate corps as both inviting them to consider teaching, and assisting them to walk what Ocasio (2014) very appropriately called *nuestro camino* in becoming bilingual educators (Jiménez et al., 2020, 2021). Second, our data suggest that Corps students highly valued their extensive CMC classroom experience. Previous CMC research pointed out that if Corps students began the program in their first year in college and continued their participation through their senior year, they would enter a credential program with approximately 3,000 hours of teaching experience (Lomelí et al., 2006). By comparison, California teacher preparation standards require only 600 hours of field practice in teaching credential programs. In addition to classroom teaching experience, Corps students called out the benefits of professional development through CMC during their undergraduate years that was specifically tailored to meet the needs of linguistically diverse K-12 students.

Corps students highlighted their appreciation of feedback on their tutoring from the CMC Coordinator and the classroom teacher where they were placed to assist Migrant children. It is true that many universities give opportunities for students not enrolled in a teaching credential program to volunteer and/or intern in classrooms as part of undergraduate coursework. It is much less frequent, however, for students to receive feedback on their instruction and interactions with children, what we have previously referred to as guided experiences working with emergent bilinguals (Ruiz & Lozano, 2010). Our data indicate that an essential component of an undergraduate corps of potential teachers should be integration of an on-going feedback component for the students' tutoring or teaching efforts. In summary, it is vital that we as bilingual teacher educators explicitly reflect upon, first, this large group of Latinx undergraduates' identification of important characteristics of a teacher corps program; and second, the possibilities of recreating these contextual features at other universities.

Examination of our data also highlighted another dimension of community: the Corps students' strong commitment to give back to their home and cultural community. Repeatedly, Corps students asserted that they wanted to support emergent bilinguals and Migrant students like themselves, and ensure that the children's educational environments were nurturing spaces for their bilingualism, and their overall well-being. A substantive number of Corps students also cited their willingness to return to their geographical communities as bilingual teachers. In short, as a nido of comunidad, the CMC program nurtured high numbers of future bilingual teachers with a strong commitment to advocate for the success of the next generation of bilingual and Migrant children.

CONCLUSION

Our respect and admiration for the international work with nidos de lengua inspired us to discern a connection between the language revitalization and cultural resistance of nidos, and the function of a bilingual undergraduate teaching corps that has flourished since the 1960s, the California Mini-Corps Program. The CMC program has served as a nurturing space for Latinx undergraduates' continuation and affirmation of their bilingual repertoire, and their dreams of entering the professional teaching community. It has much to share with bilingual teacher educators working to meet the dramatic need for additional bilingual teachers. We encourage other researchers to join us in further investigating what Latinx undergraduates have to say about their considerations of bilingual teaching as a career. In the meantime, we are deeply appreciative of the guidance that CMC offers us all as we attempt to replicate its highly effective bilingual undergraduate teaching corps at our own universities.

NOTES

1. Language and community nests.
2. Currently in California, most teacher preparation programs are post-baccalaureate. Consequently, undergraduates select a major of their choice for the bachelor's degree, and subsequently enroll in a credential program as graduate students.
3. Participating college students are usually referred to as "tutors" within California Mini-Corps. For purposes of this chapter, especially our urging of our own and other universities to create similar undergraduate corps of prospective teachers, we refer to California Mini-Corps participants as "Corps students."
4. Again, most teacher credential programs in California are post-baccalaureate and are therefore considered part of graduate studies.

REFERENCES

Athanases, S. Z., Banes, L. C., & Wong J. W. (2015). Diverse language profiles: Leveraging resources of potential bilingual teachers of color. *Bilingual Research Journal, 38*(1), 65–87.

Briceño, A., Rodríguez-Mojica, C., & Muñoz-Muñoz, E. (2018). From English Learner to Spanish Learner: Raciolinguistic beliefs that influence heritage Spanish-speaking teacher candidates." *Language and Education, 32*(3), 212–226.

Ginsberg A., Gasman, M., & Samayoa A. C. (2018). It's in your heart: How the California Mini-Corps Program and Hispanic Serving Institutions are transforming migrant student education. *The Teacher Educator, 53*(3), 244–262.

Harris, V., & Sandoval-González, A. (2017). Unveiling California's growing bilingual teacher shortage: Addressing the urgent shortage, and aligning the workforce to advances in pedagogy and practice in bilingual education. *Californians Together,* 4–8.

Irizarry, J. G., & Donaldson, M. (2012). "Teach for America: The Latinization of U.S. schools and the critical shortage of Latino/a teachers." *American Educational Research Journal 49*(1), 155–194.

Jiménez-Silva, M., & Ruiz, N. T. (2018). *Recruiting and preparing the next generation of California's bilingual teachers.* Awardee, California Teacher Education Research and Improvement Network, Research Award Program 2018, University of California.

Jiménez-Silva, M., Ruiz, N. T., & Smith, S. A. (2020). CTERIN Focus: Recruiting and preparing the next generation of bilingual teachers: Exploring the potential of California's Mini-Corps program. *California Teacher Education Research & Improvement Network.* Retrieved from https://cterin.ucop.edu/publications/resources/focusvol1no2.html

Jiménez-Silva, M., Ruiz, N., & Smith, S. (2021). Lessons learned from exploring the potential of California's Mini-Corps tutors as future bilingual teachers. *International Journal of Bilingual Education and Bilingualism,* 1–13. https://doi.org/10.1080/13670050.2021.1904820.

Lomelí, J., Parks, J. Basurto, I., & Padilla, F. (2006). California mini-corps: Developing quality teachers for 40 years. *Education, 127*(1), 100–108.

Merriam, S. B., & Tisdell, E. J. (2016). *Qualitative research.* San Francisco, CA: Jossey-Bass.

Meyer, L., & Soberanes, F. (2009). *El nido de lengua: Orientación para sus guías.* Oaxaca: Colegio Superior para la Educación Integral Intercultural de Oaxaca (CSEIIO).

Ocasio, K. M. (2014). Nuestro camino: A review of literature surrounding the Latino teacher pipeline. *Journal of Latinos and Education, 13*(4), 244–261

Perales Espinosa, A. G. (2019). El nido de lenguas. *Gaceta de Inovación Educativa Intercultural, 8*(3), 16–19.

Quezada, R. L., & Ruiz, E. (2018). Former children of migrant farmworkers: A "secret" pipeline for growing your own bilingual and bicultural teachers. In (C.D. Gist, ed.) *Portraits of Anti-Racist Alternative Routes to Teaching in the U.S.: Framing Teacher Development for Community, Justice, and Visionaries.* Peter Lang Publishing, Inc., 39–62.

Ramirez, A. Y. (2010). Why teach? Ethnic minority college students' views on teaching. *Multicultural Education, 17*(3), 29–35.

Ruiz, N. T., & Lotan, R. (2007). *Development of a survey to track changes in teacher candidates' knowledge and preferences related to the education of English Learners: The teacher education English learner survey (TEELS).* Paper presented at the annual conference of the U.C. Linguistic Minority Research Institute, Phoenix, AZ.

Ruiz, N. T., & Lozano, A. S. (2010). Increasing accountability in the preparation of teachers to work with English Learners: The teacher education English Learner survey (TEELS). *AccELLerate, a journal of the National Clearinghouse for English Language Acquisition and Language Instruction Educational Programs (NCELA), Winter Issue.*

Yosso, T. J. (2005). Whose culture has capital? A critical race theory discussion of community cultural wealth. *Race, Ethnicity, and Education, 8*(1), 69–91.

Section IV

VOICES OF EDUCATION ALLIES

Introduction

Passion, Resilience, Community, and Education: Core Values as Educational Allies

Karen Kay

The 2016 election was concurrent with the year that I was taking Advanced Placement (AP) Government course in high school. Before 2016, I had not paid much attention to politics because I had never felt the direct impact of political outcomes. But as I began to learn about the broken system, I paid more and more attention. At home, my mother would keep up with the polls on Univision, sometimes shedding tears silently and praying, while my dad would turn off the TV after watching CNN, shaking his head. He continued to tell me, "He might not even win, we could get lucky." Trump's slogan, "Make America Great Again," meant creating a barrier in my family, dividing us from our home, and so many other minority groups. The night after he won the election, I had government class in the morning. Our teacher was hopeful, mostly because the rest of us were not. He told us that this was something unprecedented, and he did not know where it would lead. My school was five minutes away from the U.S.-Mexico border, and this election was something that would weigh heavily on our lives for the next four years. I worried for my mother, for my family, for the Dreamers and DACA recipients, and my family and friends who were undocumented. Many of us feared the worst, and we wondered what we could do against someone so powerful. I vowed that I would do something to fight against everything this president stood for. I wanted to search for humanity and unapologetic kindness, and create real change outside of the corrupt and complacent government system. As I continue my journey as an undergraduate at UC Davis working with underserved communities, I hope that I am doing just that.

When I transferred to UC Davis, I wanted to do well, but I also wanted to make a change. My previous two years were at Woodland Community College; I had no idea initially that I was going to a school right behind the Yolo County Juvenile Detention Center. A few previously incarcerated individuals took classes with me, and a few of them were brave enough to share their stories in our sociology classes. They spoke of the mistreatment, the lack of humanity, and the crushing of their spirit in these facilities. Everyone was stunned, unable to fathom the stories about the mistreatment that they had endured. Over the summer, my partner had joined a club at Davis called Tutors for Incarcerated Individuals (TFII). Their work focused on working with students who were currently incarcerated or previously incarcerated. They were working with young boys at the juvenile detention center; many of whom were migrants who came from countries like Honduras. They were taken all the way from the border so close to my home, to where I was now going to school. I had tutored students in high school, many of whom were English Language Learners (ELLs). This cause was something so personal and close to my life that I immediately felt like I needed to get into this line of work. As soon as I sent in my transfer application to Davis, I applied to the tutoring program. After I was accepted, I learned that the group was faced with the challenge of being cleared into the facility and getting time to work with the students. My partner was also dealing with the news that two of his students were being transferred to Virginia and a possible repurposing of the facility. We expanded our work to focus on foster youth who had also been system impacted. We were hit with major setbacks, such as being told that there was no time for paperwork, a lack of responses from the guards, the office, and none of the new members could get cleared for the facility. As I saw the impact this was having on all of the students, I felt angry and resentful that they were not able to receive the same resources simply because of their history. My work with TFII has completely changed my life, my career path, and how I feel about the criminal justice system and its disproportionate punishments on minorities. We need to keep fighting the fight, no matter how hard it becomes. There need to be people who fight for the children that are put into cages and for the Latinx community that does not feel safe in this current political climate.

As TFII and I continue the work, we are often met with setbacks and obstacles. Whether it is pushback from the facilities themselves or cuts in state funding, it can be draining and often challenging. For every yes we are given 10 nos. TFII and I often fight just to get a chance to work with these students. Everyone who joins this group has something and someone that they are fighting for. They are passionate and they are driven, and they want to address atrocities that have been committed against our people and other minority groups by the previous administration. It is through the community-based action that we are demanding and creating change. The group has had a profound impact on my life, our motivation to enact social justice and work toward abolishing the prison industrial complex has given me lifelong friends, a passion for the work we do, and a career in teaching.

Chapter 10

Undocu-Ally Trainings

Reducing Stigma and Prejudice via Educational Interventions

Jesus Cisneros

According to the Pew Hispanic Center, an estimated 16.6 million people live in mixed-status households where at least one parent lacks lawful immigration status (Taylor et al., 2011). Among this group, nearly 700,000 are recipients of Deferred Action for Childhood Arrivals (USCIS, 2019). DACA is an administrative policy that provides renewable work permits and a temporary reprieve from deportation for eligible undocumented immigrants. Whereas undocumented students previously experienced higher education as a revolving door, the announcement of DACA in 2012 enabled beneficiaries to find their way back to various education pathways and achieve greater degree completion rates (Borjian, 2018; Darolia & Potochnick, 2015; Gonzáles et al., 2017). A report by the UndocuScholars Project estimates that there are approximately 200,000 to 225,000 undocumented immigrants enrolled in higher education, accounting for about 2% of all higher education students (Teranishi et al., 2015). Yet, the temporary status conferred by DACA poses challenges for students pursuing a higher education, and for higher education practitioners working with undocumented students.[1]

Higher education represents a space in which undocumented students often encounter the dissonance between the limitations of their social and legal presence and rights. Being required to enroll as out-of-state or international students at some institutions, even when they have lived in the state and country most of their lives, undocumented students are continuously reminded that higher education was not made with them in mind. Although *Plyler v. Doe* (1982) determined that all children, regardless of their immigration status, are entitled to a free K-12 public education, higher education remains unaddressed and is not guaranteed for undocumented students. States retain the discretion to decide whether to include undocumented students in higher education processes and how, if at all, to support them. Denying access to admission, in-state tuition, and state financial aid, for example, limits undocumented students' access to higher education in many states and can lead to premature disengagement from educational pursuits (Dougherty et al., 2010; Flores, 2010; Gonzáles, 2015).

Exclusionary practices in higher education "sustain a climate of antipathy and suspicion toward undocumented students and immigrants of color" (Rincón, 2008, p. 62). Though institutional agents often serve as important resources in accessing higher education, undocumented students often describe uncertainty regarding whom they can trust (Muñoz, 2016; Teranishi et al., 2015). Experiences where students' needs are not met or support is not provided result in a sense of isolation and an unwillingness to seek advisement or help (Pérez, Cortés, Ramos, & Coronado, 2010). Although institutional agents are "well positioned to provide key forms of social and institutional support" (Stanton-Salazar, 2011, p. 1066) and play a crucial role in shifting the campus culture to be more undocu-friendly, there is a lack of training and support available to prepare them to assist undocumented students.

Institutions play a key role in preparing practitioners to help undocumented students navigate issues related to admission, in-state tuition, financial aid, and career opportunities (Pérez et al., 2010). Educational workshops, trainings, and ongoing activities combined with visible support structures have a high potential to develop more positive institutional responses toward students (Payne & Smith, 2011; Ratts et al., 2013; Woodford, Kolb, Durocher-Radeka, & Javier, 2014). Given the need for professional development opportunities that are responsive to the needs of practitioners working with undocumented students, this chapter highlights current approaches within Undocumented Student Resource Centers (USRCs) for delivering undocually trainings across higher education campuses.

UNDOCUMENTED STUDENT RESOURCE CENTERS

USRCs are physical spaces on higher education campuses leading the charge of providing centralized services and resources for undocumented students (Cisneros & Valdivia, 2020). USRCs help streamline resources and institutional responses to exclusionary policies and historical service gaps in higher education. USRCs represent an institutional strategy for embedding support on campus for undocumented students. One aspect of their work regards facilitating interventions for procuring competency and self-efficacy development, as well as prejudice reduction, among students, staff, and faculty (Cisneros & Valdivia, 2020). While such work is identified by different names across campuses (e.g., DREAMzone, AB 540 Ally, Undocu-Peers), the underlining premise of undocu-ally trainings is to induce first-order change efforts at the individual level for participants. Participants are prepared to select and organize awareness, knowledge, contact, and skills into an integrated course of action.

Awareness is conceptualized as consciousness regarding undocumented students. It consists of the attitudes, values, beliefs, and assumptions that shape participants' understanding of immigrants and immigration (Cisneros & Lopez, 2016, 2020; Nienhusser & Espino, 2017). Being self-aware and understanding of the impact that upbringing, life experiences, and cultural worldviews have on perceptions and interpersonal interactions is conceptualized as central to achieving awareness. Likewise, for individuals who have inaccurate, incomplete, or biased knowledge, that information base must be corrected or completed before development can proceed. For this reason, undocu-ally trainings strive to help participants identify stereotypes, biases, or culturally based assumptions that may hinder their ability to appropriately support undocumented students on campus (Cadenas, Cisneros, Todd, & Spanierman, 2018; Cadenas, Cisneros, Spanierman, Yi, & Todd, 2020).

Knowledge refers to the diverse and complex factors and background information that contextualize the intersection of immigration and education. It represents the content knowledge necessary to be able to cognitively understand the experiences of undocumented students (Cisneros & Lopez, 2016, 2020). Knowledge helps participants contextualize what they observe, deepen their understanding, and enhance their ability to work with undocumented students. To achieve this, trainings deliver information regarding the context of immigration, including existing federal, state, local, and institutional policies, in order to highlight the opportunities and barriers to and through higher education from all levels of government (Cisneros & Cadenas, 2017; Nienhusser & Espino, 2017).

Contact links the concepts of social stigma to lived experiences. Having direct contact and dialogue with undocumented students provides participants with opportunities for critical self-reflection, empathy development, and growth toward competence (Cadenas et al., 2018; Cadenas et al., 2020; Cisneros & Lopez, 2016, 2020). Trainings center the voices of undocumented students by incorporating their perspectives and experiences into the curriculum. Student accounts of the campus climate and their educational experiences provide participants with an opportunity to consider a perspective different from their own.

Lastly, skills encompass participants' ability to apply the awareness, knowledge, and contact previously obtained to implement culturally responsive educational practices. Skills regard the abilities individuals need in order to perform cultural competence within practice (Cisneros & Lopez, 2016,

2020). Educational interventions provide participants with tools to begin or continue conversations on how to better support and work alongside undocumented students by streamlining resources and developing a coordinated outreach plan with immigrant youth-led organizations, advocacy groups, and other community-based organizations (Cisneros & Cadenas, 2017; Nienhusser & Espino, 2017).

Conceptualizing awareness, knowledge, contact, and skills as necessary competencies for working with undocumented students, educational interventions such as undocu-ally trainings stress the importance of preparing higher education practitioners to be able to answer questions and respond knowledgeably to the needs of undocumented students. They create a space for practitioners to ask questions, interrogate processes, or incur professional development directly relevant to working with undocumented students. Additionally, through competency and efficacy development, as well as prejudice reduction, such trainings can help participants counter the marginalizing effects of institutionalized status-quo silence (Cadenas et al., 2018; Cadenas et al., 2020; Cisneros & Cadenas, 2017; Cisneros & Lopez, 2016, 2020; Nienhusser & Espino, 2017).

METHODOLOGY

In 2020, there were approximately 59 USRCs across degree-granting institutions of higher education in the United States (Cisneros & Valdivia, 2020). The majority of USRCs were located in California. Others were located in Arizona (2), Colorado (1), Florida (1), New Jersey (1), Oregon (1), Texas (3), Utah (2), and Washington (1). Thirty were at four-year institutions, while the remaining 29 were at two-year colleges. Only one USRC was at a private institution. This chapter uses interview data from 49 of the aforementioned 59 USRCs to describe the work of USRCs in implementing undocu-ally trainings.

With support from the UndocuScholars Project at the University of California, Los Angeles, a group of immigrant scholars identified existing USRCs and contacted personnel via phone and email to schedule in-depth phone interviews. Specifically, we inquired about USRCs' efforts toward developing competency and self-efficacy on campus and reducing stigma toward undocumented students. Interviews were conducted in both English and Spanish, depending on participants' preference, and lasted between 45 and 90 minutes. Though interviews relied on a standardized format, participants retained the discretion to lead the direction of the interview in order to more deeply explore their unique knowledge.

Data analysis occurred concurrently with data collection, allowing for ongoing adjustments to the data collection process as different themes and patterns emerged. The interviewers wrote shorthand notes during each interview and recorded memos following each interview in order to better facilitate analytical thinking. All data (including memos) were transcribed and later analyzed using MAXQDA data analysis software. Initial analytical codes were developed based on reading and re-reading the overall data. Codes were used to construct categories and themes and develop interpretations (Miles & Huberman, 1994). The constant comparative method (Glaser & Strauss, 1967) also supported the identification of emergent patterns and the generation of findings.

RESULTS

Most USRCs operated under the leadership of one full-time coordinator, program manager, or director, while others utilized one or two part-time positions to fulfill similar responsibilities. Only a few were still student run and operated, with the assistance of institutional allies. While all participants described a need for developing competency and self-efficacy on campus and reducing stigma toward undocumented students, not all USRCs had the capacity to lead the work. As one USRC practitioner at a four-year institution shared,

> I try to do as many of these presentations as possible throughout the quarter, throughout the year. Because of my limited capacity in terms of staffing, I want to say that I do maybe three per quarter, but the need is definitely greater. I wish I was more present in more departments and I was doing more student activities where we can continue to change the culture, but just because of our limited capacity and staffing, it limits us to just a few presentations during the quarter.

Task-forces, advisory boards, and undocumented student organizations, in this sense, often took on the responsibility of facilitating trainings. On other campuses, local and regional community organizations were invited to share their expertise and facilitate trainings, as necessary. The following sections describe important aspects of the facilitation of undocu-ally trainings. Findings represent only a snapshot of emerging trends among USRCs in our sample.

Embedding Undocu-Ally Trainings into Routine Professional Development

USRC practitioners leading this work described the importance of undocu-ally trainings for transforming the campus climate. Getting people to understand that support looks different for different student populations, but especially undocumented students, was essential. Approaches to trainings, hence, were either general for the entire campus community, or specific to individual departments and stakeholders on campus. As one USRC practitioner at a two-year institution shared,

> Within these workshops, our goal was for these different departments to learn how to work with undocumented students. Through these workshops, we've provided awareness of what undocumented meant, what were some strategies in working with these students, or what were some of the best approaches. I'm not sure what else we've provided, but our main goal for these workshops was to bring in experts to teach the different departments in how to best support undocumented students.

USRCs targeted specific departments in order to build institutional capacity to work with undocumented students. The ultimate goal was for each functional area of student services to be able to operate independently in support of undocumented students, without intervention from the USRC. However, the ever-changing sociopolitical context required ongoing training and development. As one USRC practitioner at a two-year institution shared,

> One of the things that we're hoping to provide this semester—with everything that we've been hearing about DACA—is just workshops for students to learn more about what are their rights, what is still in place, and for the ones that need to renew also to have that opportunity. We're hopefully going to create DACA workshops and other workshops to continue educating the public in what's coming up, because we hear a lot of things in the news and most of them are not positive. We do want to create more awareness in the college to know what are the current updates with DACA.

Via undocu-ally trainings, USRCs maintained the campus community abreast of changes within the sociopolitical context. Not surprisingly, most undocu-ally trainings lasted between two and six hours. Hence, it was almost impossible for one training to cover the breadth and depth of everything that prepared participants to work with undocumented students. As one USRC practitioner at a two-year institution shared,

> It was very powerful, but it was not enough time. If you're gonna do something like that and if you want it to really be comprehensive, I think it could almost be a two full day training, but we tried to do it in a couple hours. That's something that I feel like, "yeah, we need more time." But that has been our approach.

For this reason, some USRCs structured their trainings according to different levels of allyship, whereby the first level introduced participants to terminology and context, and subsequent levels delved more into policy and critical practice. One challenge that remained for USRC practitioners, however, was training the individuals that needed the training the most. As one USRC practitioner at a four-year institution shared, "Usually when we have ally trainings for anything, it's like you're preaching to the choir. Those that already have the natural inclination go." Hence, several practitioners described the need to embed undocu-ally trainings into routine professional development and job training opportunities, so everyone could be able to support undocumented students within the scope of their positions.

Undocu-ally trainings served the larger purpose of maintaining students and other institutional stakeholders informed of changes in law and policy. USRC practitioners served as content experts for the institution and described being responsible for staying abreast of changes to immigration and education policy and relaying that information to the campus. As one USRC practitioner at a four-year institution shared,

> So I think that our goal though, ideally would be for more people to have that expertise, right? And be able to do that work. I think it's a little tricky and I don't know what sort of, what your view on this or what other people's perspective is, but you know, I think it's tricky because one of the things we talk about in the ally training is, you know, you don't want to provide misinformation, right? You don't want to guess on things. You don't want to tell students something and you're not really sure about the information because, you know, these are very high stakes situations for students and their families.

From participants' perspectives, it was valuable to have USRCs serve as the hub for undocumented student-related information in order to streamline institutional responses to changes in the sociopolitical context. However, that also necessitated USRC practitioners to be institutional experts, which increased their responsibilities across the institution and decreased their capacity, as USRC practitioners were simultaneously expected to be the primary responders when undocumented students' needs were not met or support was not provided. Because USRC practitioners were required to be knowledgeable about different institutional processes and functional areas in order to find solutions to unestablished institutional procedures and incidents of bias, many described their work with undocu-ally trainings as unsustainable—at their current capacity. Hence, the leadership of institutional taskforces, advisory boards, and undocumented student organizations assisted USRC practitioners' ability to address the immediate needs of undocumented students, as well as develop long-term strategies for institutionalizing undocumented student support services.

Centering Undocumented Voices

Despite the importance of preparing practitioners to work with undocumented students, it was not enough to just provide tools, resources, and trainings without addressing issues of the campus climate. Inaccurate, incomplete, and biased knowledge across different functions of USRC practitioners' respective institutions was pervasive. Hence, combating stereotypes, biases, or culturally based assumptions via undocu-ally trainings was essential. As one USRC practitioner at a two-year institution shared,

> I actually typed up real student scenarios onto cards and then they took turns reading the scenario and then talking about how did they feel hearing the scenario, how would they respond if they were the student. Starting by building that basic foundation of empathy and understanding, and then also educating them on the history of immigration.

A muddled understanding of immigration issues, unclear legal and ethical restrictions, and conservative institutional politics often prevented institutional agents from engaging the topic of undocumented students openly; thereby, potentially posing barriers for undocumented students to ask for help. Undocu-ally trainings aimed to help participants develop proactive philosophies for advocating with and for undocumented students within the scope of participants' positions. However, this work necessitated helping individuals challenge their preconceptions of undocumented immigrants and understand the impact that their upbringing, life experiences, and cultural worldview have on their interactions with undocumented students.

Because most USRC practitioners identified as undocumented, formerly undocumented, or members of mixed-status families, they described using their embodied knowledge to tailor undocu-ally trainings to the needs of students. One way in which they were able to do this was by sharing their stories as undocumented, formerly undocumented, or members of mixed-status families, and inviting students on panels to share as well. As one USRC practitioner at a four-year institution shared, "I do invite students to be part of it, because I always feel like the student voice is definitely needed and there's times where I need to take a step back as an ally and a daughter of immigrants." The student voice was critical for facilitating contact and reducing prejudice, but it was also important for empowering students. Personal narratives aimed to empower students to have a voice in their own stories and share their experiences as they felt most comfortable. As one USRC practitioner at a two-year institution shared,

> I think our biggest impact in undocu-ally trainings is we usually have a three to five student panel. Undocumented students who maybe share a little bit of their stories and we encourage open dialog between the staff and faculty attending the trainings and the students. It's always been very successful. The students often leave feeling very empowered and the staff and faculty, I get a lot of response back saying how impactful actually meeting the students and talking to them was. And how sometimes it has changed the kind of idea that they had about what an undocumented student was or looked like, or etcetera.

Empowering students in their own identities and enabling them to dialogue with staff and faculty aimed to improve the ways undocumented students experienced the campus.

While a focus of most undocu-ally trainings was to prepare practitioners, several institutions simultaneously facilitated trainings specifically for students. Such trainings focused on the ways in which students could mobilize to increase support for undocumented students across campus. As one USRC practitioner at a four-year institution shared,

> The other component is undocu-ally training for peers. It's peer led and for peers. Students pretty much take on a very similar approach to the undocu-ally training but they make it. . . . They model it to fit for students. Students that don't identify as undocumented strongly benefit from this training because it's just a good educational overview of what it is to be an undocumented student. Because it's peer led, it's really interactive and much more comfortable.

Providing a platform for students to engage with each other in their capacity as student leaders and members of the student body, undocu-ally trainings served to increase the visibility of support for undocumented students across different constituencies. Such work was important, given how the development of USRCs was often attributed to mobilizations by and on behalf of undocumented students. Long histories of student mobilization led to the development of institutionalized support services for undocumented students across campuses. Creating opportunities for students to organize and become engaged, hence, honored the history of student mobilization on campus.

By encouraging participants to address the needs of undocumented students within existing programs, services, and outreach efforts, USRCs aimed to create more inclusive campus climates. Symbols and placards communicating safe spaces for undocumented students were integral for relaying the message of inclusivity to students. As one USRC practitioner at a two-year institution shared,

> And then we also have a lot of indirect impacts, as students who maybe never join the club or go to the legal clinics see our butterfly, our safe spaces, indications across campus in various locations and different contexts that make it clear that they are welcome here.

Practitioners described how the visibility of allies helped students feel welcomed, engaged, and supported. The availability of undocu-ally trainings similarly provided institutions with an opportunity to form a community of allies. By equipping practitioners with resources and connecting them to a support network of allies, undocu-ally trainings helped increase USRCs' volunteer base and capacity. Hence, undocu-ally trainings served as the biggest outreach method for helping students utilize the resources and services available within the USRC.

DISCUSSION

This chapter situated USRCs within the overall strategy of preparing higher education practitioners to support undocumented students via the delivery of undocu-ally trainings. USRCs play a critical role in delivering interventions aimed at developing higher education practitioners' competency and self-efficacy for working with undocumented students and reducing stigma and prejudice on campus. Drawing from interview data, this chapter highlighted trends regarding the implementation of undocu-ally trainings across 49 institutions of higher education.

USRC practitioners described embedding undocu-ally trainings into routine professional development, and the need to facilitate both general and targeted trainings for different campus constituencies. Such expectations had implications for their capacity and necessitated the support of institutional task-forces, advisory boards, and undocumented student organizations to help deliver undocu-ally trainings. By supporting the undocu-ally work of USRCs, institutional allies' part of these task-forces, advisory boards, and organizations engaged in transformative educational equity work (Chen, & Rhoads, 2016). However, as documented by Southern (2016), this work was often uncompensated and dependent on the personal commitment of institutional allies; thus, leaving individuals feeling isolated, unsupported, and overworked. Such conditions highlight the importance of increasing USRCs' capacity for engaging undocu-ally trainings with adequate staffing and support.

USRC practitioners also described the importance of addressing the campus climate within their approaches to undocu-ally trainings. One way in which they were able to do this was by sharing their stories as undocumented, formerly undocumented, or members of mixed-status families, and inviting students on panels to share their experiences. Student panels have previously been identified as ideal ways to help participants develop supportive attitudes and reduce prejudice (Cadenas et al., 2018; Cadenas et al., 2020; Cisneros & Cadenas 2017; Cisneros & Lopez, 2016, 2020). By centering undocumented voices, undocu-ally trainings served to increase the visibility of undocumented students on campus and increase empathy. However, this work went beyond validating undocumented students' presence and experiences on campus. It produced spaces where students experienced mattering as a result of being intentionally centered and uplifted.

The precarious state of students' immigration status and the lack of funding options available to persist compel institutions to attend more intentionally to the presence and needs of undocumented students by preparing practitioners with competency and self-efficacy development, as well as opportunities for prejudice reduction. Immigrant-hostile sociopolitical contexts have the potential to create anxiety and uncertainty among practitioners, forcing some to support in the shadows of the institution (Chen & Rhoads, 2016). Undocu-ally trainings, as accessible and replicable tools, can help students, staff, and faculty develop competency and self-efficacy for effectuating change and reducing stigma on campus. By acknowledging the important role of institutional agents for responding to the presence and needs of undocumented students, undocu-ally trainings contribute to the generation of practice-related opportunities for enhancing undocumented student support services.

Implications for Practice

Educators should advocate for comprehensive professional development training that is responsive to the intersection of education and immigration policy. Institutions of higher education bear the responsibility of preparing their practitioners to support the needs of all students, regardless of immigration status. One approach toward holding institutions accountable is by supporting educational interventions aimed at increasing participants' competencies and self-efficacy for working with undocumented students (Cadenas et al., 2018; Cadenas et al., 2020; Cisneros & Cadenas, 2017; Cisneros & Lopez, 2016, 2020). Educational interventions, such as undocu-ally trainings, can provide a starting point for institutionalizing undocumented student support services and the development of a USRC (Cisneros & Valdivia, 2020).

Because undocumented students are more likely to stay in school and feel less emotional distress when they feel supported and are able to talk openly about the challenges associated with their immigrant experience (Gonzáles, Suarez-Orozco, & Dedios-Sanguineti, 2013), educational interventions, such as undocu-ally trainings, can help foster a campus environment that supports the academic success, as well as the personal and social growth, of undocumented students. There is potential to create more inclusive campus climates by embedding undocu-ally trainings into routine professional development and job training for all employees. However, such efforts will necessitate increased investments from institutions in order to increase practitioners' capacity to facilitate such work, particularly at institutions without USRCs.

Higher education practitioners can make a significant difference in the lives of undocumented students by changing their administrative practices and policies to be inclusive of undocumented students. Many have the discretionary power to challenge institutional policies and practices that fail to support undocumented students, but lack the training to be able to identify opportunities for transformational change. Because higher education practitioners are uniquely positioned to intervene systemically, they can circumvent the constraints of the broader sociopolitical environment by working toward inclusive campus-based action. Campus-based action serves as an important site of resistance to the relative silence from state policymakers or to normative responses of de facto exclusion by omission (Barnhardt et al., 2017). For this reason, higher education practitioners need to look at how higher education policy and practice influence undocumented students' perceptions of the campus climate and devise creative programmatic and intervention efforts to address the unique set of challenges undocumented students face. Educational interventions, such as undocu-ally trainings, may be useful for engaging institutional agents in such systematic change. Encouraging higher education practitioners to address the needs of undocumented students within existing programs, services, and outreach efforts may also be important for institutionalizing undocumented student support.

Given the influence of policy at all levels of governance, higher education practitioners must be aware and informed about how to best support undocumented students across a broad range of services (Suarez-Orozco et al., 2015). Higher education practitioners who make a concerted effort to be more sensitive to immigration policy issues, for example, can help counter the negative and discriminatory messages students receive (Contreras, 2009; Pérez & Rodriguez, 2011; Pérez et al., 2010). Without understanding the nexus of policy and law that helps shape undocumented students' experiences, higher education practitioners cannot meaningfully respond to undocumented students' needs (Gildersleeve et al., 2010). Undocu-ally trainings serve as available tools for preparing higher education practitioners with competency and self-efficacy for effectuating change and reducing stigma toward undocumented students.

NOTE

1. The term "undocumented" will be used to include individuals both eligible and ineligible for DACA.

REFERENCES

Barnhardt, C., Phillips, C., Young, R. L., & Sheets, J. K. (2017). The administration of diversity and equity on campuses and its relationships to serving undocumented immigrant students. *Journal of Diversity in Higher Education, 10*(1), 1–10.

Borjian, A. (2018). Academically successful Latino undocumented students in college: Resilience and civic engagement. *Hispanic Journal of Behavioral Sciences, 40*(1), 22–36.

Cadenas, G., Cisneros, J., Spanierman, L. B., Yi, J., & Todd, N. (2020). Detrimental effects of color-blind racial attitudes in preparing a culturally responsive teaching workforce for immigrants. *Journal of Career Development*, 1–16. https://journals.sagepub.com/doi/pdf/10.1177/0894845320903380?casa_token=0CenbszdlCEA-AAAA:S2UP0HPODBWTYncO7oqAJTv6eYIhbTrd6mfeO52sh2c0IVA8Ah-JLu obraxoNlngQKeZTKx988vH.

Cadenas, G., Cisneros, J., Todd, N. R., & Spanierman, L. B. (2018). DREAMzone: Testing two vicarious contact interventions to improve attitudes toward undocumented immigrants. *Journal of Diversity in Higher Education, 11*(3), 295–308.

Chen, A. C., & Rhoads, R. A. (2016). Undocumented student allies and transformative resistance: An ethnographic case study. *The Review of Higher Education, 39*(4), 515–542.

Cisneros, J., & Cadenas, G. A. (2017). DREAMer-ally competency and self-efficacy: Developing higher education staff and measuring lasting outcomes. *Journal of Student Affairs Research and Practice, 54*(2), 189–203.

Cisneros, J., & Lopez, A. (2020). Ally competency and self-efficacy: Comparing DREAMzone outcomes at post-, 2-months, and 8-months. *Journal of Student Affairs Research and Practice, 57*(3), 309–321.

Cisneros, J., & Lopez, A. (2016). DREAMzone: Educating counselors and human service professionals working with undocumented students. *Journal for Social Action in Counseling and Psychology, 8*(2), 32–48.

Cisneros, J., & Valdivia, D. (2020). "We are legit now": Establishing Undocumented Student Resource Centers on campus. *Journal of College Student Development, 61*(1), 51–66.

Contreras, F. (2009). Sin papeles y rompiendo barreras: Latino students and the challenges of persisting in college. *Harvard Educational Review, 79*(4), 610–631.

Darolia, R., & Potochnick, S. (2015). Educational "when," "where," and "how" implications of in-state resident tuition policies for Latino undocumented immigrants. *The Review of Higher Education, 38*(4), 507–535.

Dougherty, K., Nienhusser, H. K., & Vega, B. (2010). Undocumented immigrants and state higher education policy: The politics of in-state tuition eligibility in Texas and Arizona. *The Review of Higher Education, 34*(1), 123–173.

Flores, S. M. (2010). State Dream Acts: The effect of in-state resident tuition policies and undocumented Latino students. *Research in Higher Education, 33*(2), 239–283.

Gildersleeve, R. E., Rumann, C., & Mondragon, R. (2010). Serving undocumented students: Current law and policy. *New Directions for Student Services, 131*, 5–18.

Glaser, B. G., & Strauss, A. L. (1967). *The discovery of Grounded Theory*: Strategies for qualitative research. Chicago, IL: Aldine.

Gonzáles, R. G. (2015). *Lives in limbo: Undocumented and coming of age in America*. Oakland, CA: University of California Press.

Gonzáles, R. G., Murillo, M., Lacomba, C., Brant, K., Franco, M. C., Lee, J., & Vasudevan, D. S. (2017, June 22). *Taking giant leaps forward: Experiences of a range of DACA beneficiaries at the 5-year mark*. Retrieved from https://www.americanprogress.org/issues/immigration/reports/2017/06/22/434822/taking-giant-leaps-forward/

Gonzáles, R. G., Suárez-Orozco, C., & Dedios-Sanguineti, M. C. (2013). No place to belong: Contextualizing concepts of mental health among undocumented immigrant youth in the United States. *American Behavioral Scientist, 57*, 1174–1199.

Miles, M. B., & Huberman, A. M. (1994). *Qualitative data analysis: An expanded sourcebook*. (2nd ed.). Thousand Oaks, CA: SAGE.

Muñoz, S. M. (2016). Undocumented and unafraid: Understanding the disclosure management process for undocumented college students and graduates. *Journal of College Student Development, 57*(6), 715–729.

Nienhusser, K. H., & Espino, M. M. (2017). Incorporating undocumented/DACAmented status competency into higher education institutional agents' practice. *Journal of Student Affairs Research and Practice, 54*(1), 1–14.

Payne, E. C., & Smith, M. (2011). The reduction of stigma in schools: A new professional development model for empowering educators to support LGBTQ students. *Journal of LGBT Youth, 8*(2), 174–200.

Pérez, P.A., & Rodríguez, J. (2011). Access and opportunity for Latina/o undocumented college students: Familial and institutional support factors. *Association of Mexican American Educators Journal, 5*(1), 14–21.

Pérez, W., Cortes, R. D., Ramos, K., & Coronado, H. (2010). "Cursed and blessed": Examining the socioemotional and academic experiences of undocumented Latina and Latino college students. *New Directions for Student Services, 131*, 35–51.

Plyler v. Doe, 457 U.S. 202 (1982).

Ratts, M. J., Kaloper, M., McReady, C., Tighe, L., Butler, S. K., Dempsey, K., & McCullough, J. (2013). Safe space programs in K-12 schools: Creating a visible presence of LGBTQ allies. *Journal of LGBT Issues in Counseling, 7*, 387–404.

Rincón, A. (2008). *Undocumented immigrant and higher education: Sí se puede!* New York, NY: LFB Scholarly Publishing.

Southern, K. (2016). Institutionalizing support structures for undocumented students at four-year colleges and universities. *Journal of Student Affairs Research and Practice, 53*(3), 305–318.

Stanton-Salazar, R. D. (2011). A social capital framework for the study of institutional agents and their role in the empowerment of low-status students and youth. *Youth & Society, 43*, 1066–1109.

Suárez-Orozco, C., Katsiaficas, D., Birchall, O., Alcantar, C. M., Hernandez, E., Garcia, Y., ...Teranishi, R. T. (2015). Undocumented undergraduates on college campuses: Understanding their challenges and assets and what it takes to make a undocufriendly campus. *Harvard Educational Review, 85*(3), 427–465.

Taylor, P., Lopez, M. H., Passel, J. S., & Motel, S. (2011). *Unauthorized immigrants: Length of residency, patterns of parenthood*. Washington, DC: Pew Research Center. Retrieved from http://www.pewhispanic.org/2011/12/01/unauthorized-immigrants-length-of-residency-patterns-of-parenthood/

Teranishi, R. T., Suárez-Orozco, C., & Suárez-Orozco, M. (2015). *In the shadows of the ivory tower: Undocumented undergraduates and the liminal state of immigration reform*. Retrieved from http://www.undocuscholars.org/undocuscholars-report.html.

United States Citizenship and Immigration Services. (2019). Approximate active DACA recipients. Retrieved from https://www.uscis.gov/sites/default/files/document/data/DACA_Population_Receipts_since_Injunction_Dec_31_2019.pdf

Woodford, M. R., Kolb, C. L., Durocher-Radeka, G., & Javier, G. (2014). Lesbian, gay, bisexual, and transgender ally training programs on campus: Current variations and future directions. *Journal of College Student Development, 55*(3), 317–322.

Chapter 11

Voces Unidas

Advocating for Emergent Bilinguals while Navigating Arizona's Sociopolitical Context

Ashley Coughlin, Margarita Jiménez-Silva, and Karen Guerrero

INTRODUCTION

Arizona holds a national reputation for its anti-immigrant legislation, policies, and practices that have negatively impacted numerous families and children throughout the state and beyond. Many of these policies have targeted immigrants from Latinx communities (Ayon, 2018). Specifically, Arizona's English-only policies have negatively impacted K-12 students from Latinx homes which comprise 44% of Arizona's K-12 population (Arizona Hispanic Chamber of Commerce, 2019). According to the U.S. Department of Education (2021), 73.3% of K-12 students enrolled in 2016–2017 who were classified by the state as English Language Learners were Spanish-speaking. The passing of Arizona's Proposition 203 in November 2000 by a margin of 63% to 37% (now Arizona Revised Statute (A.R.S.) § 15-751-755, "English for the Children") severely limited all bilingual education in the state and prohibited access to bilingual education programs for students classified as English language learners (ELLs). The term English language learner itself implies a deficit perspective that, in contrast to an asset perspective, does not acknowledge the value of bilingualism and biliteracy for children's cognitive and socio-emotional development (Garcia & Kleifgen, 2018). In recognition of the linguistic capital (Yosso, 2005) inherent in our students, we will use the term "emergent bilinguals" henceforth. Throughout the process of translating the legislated mandates from law to policy to classrooms, the voices of experts on second language acquisition, the voices of teachers of emergent bilinguals, and the voices of families impacted by the mandates were missing.

As bilingual teachers and researchers working in Arizona, we experienced a vacuum of leadership and support networks in our communities to navigate increasingly restrictive policies resulting from Proposition 203. A number of professional organizations at the state level became fractioned, with groups splintering based on political ideologies regarding bilingual education. Some professional organizations disbanded and left the state as a sign of resistance to the restrictive language policies (e.g., Arizona chapter of National Association of Bilingual Education). Working across various schools and districts in close proximity, we found pockets of teachers and administrators duplicating work as they identified resources for supporting emergent bilinguals and their families. For example, two schools within 5 miles of each other were developing third-grade curriculum for their Dual Language (DL) programs addressing identical state standards. The Consortium described in this chapter was conceived and developed as a response to the need for strength through community, networking of resources, and a refusal to stay silent regarding restrictive language policies and the lack of support for teachers and families of emergent bilinguals.

ARIZONA'S SOCIOPOLITICAL CONTEXT

Arizona has a history of complex and restrictive educational policies as they relate to emergent bilinguals. Traditionally, Arizona has made it increasingly difficult for emergent bilinguals to access academic content, bilingual programs, and other educational resources to the same extent as their native English-speaking peers (Lillie et al., 2012). It is important to acknowledge that this is not the result of one specific policy but rather an accumulation of legislative acts and accompanying policies that have disadvantaged emergent bilinguals. Jiménez-Silva, Gomez, and Cisneros (2014) argue that Arizona has created a perfect storm resulting in educational inequities through the following actions at the state level: (a) severely limiting bilingual education through Proposition 203, (b) developing controversial funding solutions, (c) implementing a segregated four-hour English language development block, (d) mandating teacher preparation that focuses solely on structured English immersion, and (e) developing disputed English language learner identification and classification instruments. School districts and their teachers of emergent bilinguals have struggled to work within the constraints of these actions. The voices of these teachers were often absent from the conversations about policy implementation, further restricting the support they could offer emergent bilinguals.

As mentioned previously, Arizona's Proposition 203 all but prohibited access to bilingual instruction for emergent bilinguals. Arizona's Proposition

203, California's Proposition 227, and Massachusetts' Measure 2 are all regarded as part of an English-only movement intent on scapegoating bilingual education in response to general discontent with K-12 schools and anti-immigrant sentiments (Bartolomé & Leistyna, 2006). Under this initiative, the Arizona Department of Education developed a number of policies under the oversight of then Superintendent Tom Horne to enforce Proposition 203. One of the policies mandated the requirement that all students classified as ELLs attend structured English immersion (SEI) classrooms for four hours per day (Rios-Aguilar, González-Canche, & Moll, 2010). The four-hour block model was structured around four areas of language development with specific time allocations required for reading, writing, oral conversation, and grammar. There was no requirement to teach content-area knowledge during this four-hour block, leaving students even further behind in content-area classes when they finally tested proficient on the state language exam and were allowed to move beyond SEI classrooms (Rios-Aguilar, González-Canche, & Moll, 2010). In addition to limited access to content instruction, the SEI program segregated emergent bilingual students from their English-speaking peers for most of the school day (Gándara & Orfield, 2012).

Teachers of emergent bilinguals struggled to find resources that aligned with these new mandates. Further complicating matters, different districts interpreted the mandates differently to varying degrees which resulted in teachers questioning what was actually legislated and what was within each district's purview to interpret (Jiménez-Silva, Bernstein, & Baca, 2016). Currently, California and Massachusetts have passed legislation expanding access to bilingual education for emergent bilinguals while Arizona trails behind in allowing more flexibility within restrictive language policies (Chang-Bacon, 2020; Kelly, 2018). Over the past few years, legislative bills including House Consensus Bill 2005 (HCB 2005), introduced in January 2021, have been proposed to repeal the mandates of "English for the Children" legislation. However, as of March 2021, no bill has been presented to voters. Therefore, there remains a need to provide a space to advocate for more inclusive practices and support for teachers of emergent bilinguals.

BUILDING A CONSORTIUM OF UNITED VOICES ADVOCATING FOR ARIZONA'S EMERGENT BILINGUALS

The context of Arizona's restrictive language policy created a deep need for community support for emergent bilinguals and a mechanism for advocating with *voces unidas* (united voices). Building and sustaining partnerships that are focused on advocating for and supporting more equitable educational experiences for students is a critical and necessary component for mobilizing acquired knowledge among educators, community, and stakeholders. As a strategy for supporting teachers of emergent bilinguals in Arizona's sociopolitical context, the second and third authors of this chapter sought out grant opportunities at the national level. The Teachers of Language Learners Learning Community (TL3C) Project, funded from 2012–2017 by the U.S. Department of Education as a National Professional Development program, initiated the Consortium in Arizona by bringing together administrators, teachers, parents, and community members within DL programs across the state to navigate the use of DL programming, which was limited. The goal was to support language learners through their teachers across the state. The Consortium was one of the most prominent successes of the grant. Following the end of the TL3C Project, the Consortium work continued through a second grant-funded project. The STEMSS CRUISE EL: Science, Technology, Engineering, Math, and Social Studies Content for Relational Understanding and to Integrate Strategies in E-learning for English Learners Project was also funded as a U.S. Department of Education National Professional Development grant that began in 2017 and will run through 2022.

We established and continued the Consortium with several objectives in mind: (a) to bring together a network of advocates to support Arizona's emergent bilinguals; (b) to create awareness of stakeholders' needs and goals; (c) to provide resources to support Local Educational Agencies and K-12 teachers and administrators; and (d) to propose a DL Certificate through the Arizona Department of Education. Our vision was to approach the work of the Consortium as a collaboration amongst key stakeholders throughout Arizona. These stakeholders included students, parents, K-12 pre-service and in-service teachers, school administrators, higher education researchers, community organizers, policy makers, professional organization leaders, and representatives from the Arizona Department of Education. We were intentional about extending invitations to ensure voices were present from across the various roles of stakeholders as well as to provide representation from various geographic areas in the state. While the Consortium work began in 2012 with the first grant, this chapter focuses on the Consortium work supported through our second National Professional Development grant which was funded beginning in 2017. Next, we discuss each of the four objectives driving the work of the Consortium.

Growing a Network of Advocates and Determining Needs and Goals

One of the very first endeavors of the STEMSS CRUISE EL Project funding was to re-engage with as many past Consortium members as possible.

Because of the turnover in personnel between the first and second projects, the record-keeping proved challenging. We also reached out to local professional organizations that had engaged many of our past Consortium members, including the Arizona chapter of Teachers of English to Speakers of Other Languages (AZTESOL), the Arizona Language Association, Language Solutions, the Arizona chapter of the National Association of Bilingual Education, and the Arizona Center for Law in the Public Interest.

In order for us to determine stakeholder needs and interests, we sent out a survey before the first Consortium requesting that each participant identify their first and second highest needs. Four general areas of need emerged: (a) Family Engagement, (b) Resources for Emergent Bilinguals, (c) Professional Development, and (d) DL Certificate. The first Consortium meeting was held in spring of 2018 with 32 participants. Included were voices of representatives from the Arizona Department of Education (ADE), public and private universities, community colleges, K-12 pre-service and in-service teachers and administrators, parents, and community organizers from across Arizona. Agenda items for the meeting included introductions and sharing of the value of the perspectives of the various roles represented in the room as well as the overall objectives of the Consortium outlined in the grant project. We then opened up the conversation, prompting participants to discuss the recent bridges or successes and the barriers they had experienced in their roles supporting emergent bilinguals. Next, we walked our participants through our needs assessment and determined the areas that Consortium members were most interested in addressing. Consortium participants were then asked to join a work group based on the four areas of interest previously mentioned. Working groups were facilitated by the three authors of this chapter and one additional member of our grant leadership team. Each working group shared additional ideas for how the Consortium could support the various stakeholders.

Family Engagement

When discussing Family Engagement, the foci emphasized by Consortium members included engagement with families of indigenous heritage language learners, finding community leaders and advocates to support sustained change, and an emphasis on modeling two-way conversation between schools and communities. The overall goal of the group was to create a flexible and dynamic framework of ongoing culturally sustaining practices that empowered families by valuing all languages through building in- and out-of-school connections.

Another area of focus was to provide space, both physical and virtual, to share resources, provide support, and drive exponential advocacy. It is important to note that within each working group, advocacy and community empowerment were prevalent themes in the discussions. Participants made many suggestions including identifying books for collective book studies, developing community relationships and strong communication, and ways to address individual biases in order to work alongside and in collaboration with the school communities served across Arizona.

The group additionally discussed identifying evidence-based practices and providing professional development that focus on asset-based mindsets and the development of content and language knowledge in tandem. There was an emphasis on two-way communication to include, honor, and address parent and community voices. The need to increase teacher cultural competence and to support culturally responsive practices was woven throughout the discussion as well. The necessary frameworks identified to support this professional development included culturally sustaining pedagogy (Paris & Alim, 2017; Coulter & Jiménez-Silva, 2017) and community cultural wealth (Yosso, 2005).

Consortium participants also emphasized the need to provide specialized teacher preparation focused on the academic, linguistic, and socio-emotional needs of students in Arizona's classrooms serving emergent bilinguals. The proposed requirements were to have at least 18 units of coursework that would focus on content-area instruction using evidence-based practices to support language and academic content development. Participants emphasized the need to provide adequate resources including assessments in a variety of languages representing Arizona's diverse demographics.

Providing Resources to Support Emergent Bilinguals' Teachers and Administrators

The second focus of the Consortium's work tied to objectives in both grants to compile resources in a central database to help support teachers and administrators working with emergent bilinguals. Many of our Consortium members had expressed concern about the disparity in access to resources across schools and districts which imperils support and success. The Consortium provided the space to discuss the needs of various school sites, the resources already in use that might benefit broader groups, and the areas that were lacking in adequate support. The Consortium provided opportunities to further share and cultivate resources in addition to sharing ideas about broader conversations regarding policy implication and advocacy for legislative changes to better support emergent bilinguals in Arizona.

Over the course of our initial meetings, it became evident that we needed to develop a common vocabulary and understanding of commonly-used terms. We developed a Loteria (Bingo) game with key words to share with Consortium members and dedicated time at several of our meetings to ensure that they were all using terms in similar ways. Examples of these terms included DL learners, culturally sustaining pedagogies, and cultural community wealth.

To inform our conversations, we invited a number of guest speakers who presented their academic work at Consortium meetings and then engaged everyone in conversation about the application of their work through our various roles. For example, Dr. Alexandria Silva and Dr. Yalda Kaveh, faculty at Arizona State University, shared their research focused on supporting families of emergent bilinguals in DL programs during the challenge of online teaching in the midst of the COVID-19 pandemic. Dr. Beatriz Arias, vice president and chief development officer for the Center for Applied Linguistics in Washington, D.C. at the time, shared the center's Pillars of DL and possible upcoming changes to the pillars to address translanguaging. Guest speakers also included a representative from the ADE Office of English Language Acquisition Services who provided an overview and answered questions about SEI Models for the 2019–2020 school year. Patricia Fernandez, World Language/DL Immersion Specialist for Mesa Public Schools, was an invited guest in the Fall of 2020 and shared modifications to the four-hour SEI block proposed by her district.

In addition, in collaboration with Consortium members, we were building on four research briefs titled *Benefits of DL Programs*, *Considerations for Administrators in New Dual Language Programs*, *What Teachers Need To Know About ELLs in Dual Language Programs*, and *Resources to Support ELLs in Dual Language Programs* (Mesa Community College, 2021). These briefs were created at the end of our first grant project. Each brief contains a topical reading and listed resources for continued information and support. In addition to these public research briefs, the Consortium organizers have compiled a list of mentioned, used, and possible resources to disseminate in future briefs and as specific needs arise. The briefs and resources have been shared widely by Consortium members with parents, teachers, and administrators. In the spirit of further uniting our voices, we are in the process of writing four additional research briefs that teachers and parents can use to advocate with their school boards for greater support for emergent bilinguals and their families focused on opportunities in science, math, technology, and social sciences.

Dual Language Certificate

Currently, all teachers in Arizona that work with students identified by the state as ELLs are required to hold an SEI endorsement. This can be achieved by taking and passing a state assessment or completing endorsement coursework. Arizona's SEI endorsement requirements currently consist of completing a 45-hour course related to differentiating instruction for emergent bilinguals and understanding how to accommodate the diverse needs of language learners. The coursework covers topics specifically outlined by ADE related to differentiation and modification of work as well as the state compliance requirements for emergent bilinguals. Currently, the SEI Framework requires that the following content be covered: two hours on Arizona's legal and historical context for English learners; three hours on the SEI model; three hours on language acquisition; six hours on the elements of language; and six hours focused on the language domains. The framework then differentiates for elementary and secondary categories, but the time dedicated to the specified topics is identical across the two categories, with 13 hours specified for instructional strategies; three hours for differentiation; three hours for assessment; two hours for the diversity of English learners; and four hours for culturally relevant instruction. Within the four hours dedicated to culturally relevant instruction, family engagement is one of nine topics. The ADE's Office of English Language Acquisition (OELAS) is currently making revisions to the SEI endorsement framework. These basic requirements, while a start, do not provide the level of support and understanding needed to adequately support emergent bilinguals in DL programs and their families (Jimenez-Silva, Gomez, & Cisneros, 2014; Lillie, Markos, Arias, & Wiley, 2012). Professional development provided through and around the Consortium allowed educators, administrators, and other stakeholders' access to a deeper understanding of the complexities within DL settings related to language development, family engagement, and various other research-based and teacher-tested pedagogical practices.

For a number of years, there was miscommunication in the field regarding the value and need for a full bilingual endorsement, which requires specific coursework and language proficiency requirements. The English as a Second Language (ESL) endorsement is similar to the bilingual endorsement sans the language requirement, while the least comprehensive option for teachers working with emergent bilinguals is the 45-hour SEI endorsement. The sociopolitical climate and the restrictive language policies discussed throughout this chapter contributed to the idea that a bilingual or ESL endorsement was unnecessary (Cruze & López, 2020). Many pre-service teachers were steered away from the fuller endorsement that consisted of 21 semester hours of coursework and a student teaching experience in a bilingual classroom.

Consortium participants regularly discussed how the English-only policy in Arizona along with the SEI model lowered the status of the bilingual endorsement. With more recent flexibilities regarding Arizona's time requirements for the SEI model, including the inclusion of DL programs as one of the models accepted by the state, the creation of a DL certificate became a priority for the Consortium. The DL certificate was seen by participants as an opportunity for greater recruitment and retention of more highly qualified and well-prepared teachers for emergent bilingual students across the language groups represented in Arizona classrooms. Given the history associated with the previously established endorsements and the recent push for DL programs, the Consortium believed that a DL certificate would reinvigorate the effort to recruit qualified teachers committed to serving emerging bilinguals. Conversations with the ADE continue regarding this proposal at the time of publication of this chapter.

Professional Development during COVID-19

During the COVID-19 pandemic, the Consortium found ways to work together to advocate for and address complex issues facing culturally and linguistically diverse students in Arizona. The Consortium held three meetings and one collective inquiry discussion virtually during the spring between March 2020 and May 2021. The collective inquiry was focused on discussing relevant articles read by the participants ahead of the gathering. These meetings were intended to create spaces for participants to check in with each other, share resources for virtual teaching, and provide access to professional development opportunities available across the country focused on the needs of emergent bilinguals and their families. We had over 65 participants across our virtual meetings.

The greatest success of the Consortium as we enter the final year of funding has been building bridges across the various participants who represent numerous school districts and stakeholder groups. We believe that this bridge building is critical to the success of emergent bilingual students across the state. While there remain vast differences in educational supports, access to information and resources, and quality and retention of teachers across districts and even individual schools within a single district, these inequities can be better addressed when conversations allow for connections across wider communities where diverse voices engage in authentic dialogue. The Consortium provides a valuable platform for discussion, sharing of ideas and resources, and creative solutions to complex problems. Because these collaborations allow for the sharing of resources and ideas, more energy is available for additional aspects of teaching and learning.

MOVING FORWARD

As mentioned, this past year has posed many unique challenges due to the COVID-19 pandemic. The inherent inequities evident in education are ever more apparent as access to internet, technology, and stable food and housing negatively affect students' abilities to participate fully in their education (Chamberlain, Lacina, Bintz, Jimerson, Payne, & Zingale, 2020). Additionally, it has been challenging for teachers to come together in community due to health and safety restrictions and protocols, as well as the added challenges of teaching virtually while managing their own added responsibilities at home. While we had planned and budgeted through our STEMSS grant a state-level conference originally scheduled for May 2020, the conference has now been rescheduled thrice and is currently planned for May 2022. This conference will bring together various current and past grant participants, Consortium participants, state representatives, classroom teachers, university educators and researchers, and other members of the larger educational community focused on emergent bilinguals.

At the beginning of our Consortium work, various priorities were identified, including creating a compilation of resources, increasing opportunity for networking and discussion, and developing and building systems to better support emergent bilinguals and DL learners. Several areas, while addressed during meetings, still warrant further attention. For example, there has been no follow up specifically addressing the loss of language and heritage amongst the indigenous populations and communities represented in the state. There has also been little done to address college and career readiness goals related to first-generation high school emergent bilingual students planning to apply to and attend university. These areas could continue to move the Consortium forward in meaningful work.

This is the fourth of five years for the STEMSS grant. This work is far from completed, but there has been much learned and gained from the past four years. While adjustments and needs for improvement are evident, we have also been successful in facilitating and fostering collaborative conversations, open discussions, and together, moving toward recognizing and addressing systemic issues that negatively impact emergent bilinguals. The shift to action-based thinking and open, honest discussion about the gaps in teacher preparation, current state and district practices, and the state of education nationally allows for the seeds of change to take root.

REFERENCES

Arizona Hispanic Chamber of Commerce. (2019). *Datos: The state of Arizona's Hispanic market 2018*. https://issuu.com/azhcc/docs/0_datos_az_2019__1_.

Ayón, C. (2018). "Vivimos en jaula de oro": The impact of state-level legislation on immigrant Latino families. *Journal of Immigrant & Refugee Studies*, *16*(4), 351–371.

Bartolomé, L. I., & Leistyna, P. (2006). Introduction: Naming and interrogating our English-only legacy. *The Radical Teacher*, *75*, 2–9.

Chamberlain, L., Lacina, J., Bintz, W.P., Jimerson, J.B., Payne, K., & Zingale, R. (2020). Literacy in lockdown: Learning and teaching during COVID-19 school closures. *The Reading Teacher, 74*(3), 243–253.

Chang-Bacon, C. K. (2020). Who's being 'sheltered?': How monolingual language ideologies are produced within education policy discourse and sheltered English immersion. *Critical Studies in Education*, 1–17.

Coulter, C., & Jimenez-Silva, M. (Eds). (2017). *Culturally sustaining pedagogies: Issues of language, culture, and power*. United Kingdom: Emerald Publishing.

Cruze, A., & López, F. (2020). Equity and excellence among Arizona school leaders: Encouraging integration within a segregative policy context. *Leadership and Policy in Schools, 19*(1), 81–103.

English for the Children, Arizona Revised Statute (A.R.S.) § 15-751-755 (2021) https://www.azleg.gov/arsDetail/?title=15.

Gándara, P., & Orfield, G. (2012). Segregating Arizona's English learners: A return to the "Mexican Room"? *Teachers College Record, 114*(9), 1–33.

García, O., & Kleifgen, J. A. (2010). *Educating emergent bilinguals: Policies, programs, and practices for English language learners*. New York, NY: Teachers College Press.

Jimenez-Silva, M., Gomez, L., & Cisneros, J. (2014). Examining Arizona's policy response post *Flores v. Arizona* in educating K-12 English language learners. *Journal of Latinos and Education, 13*, 181–195. doi:10.1080/15348431.2013.849600.

Kelly, L. B. (2018). Interest convergence and hegemony in dual language: Bilingual education, but for whom and why?. *Language Policy, 17*(1), 1–21.

Lillie, K. E., Markos, A., Arias, M. B., & Wiley, T. G. (2012). Separate and not equal: The implementation of structured English immersion in Arizona's classrooms. *Teachers College Record, 114*(9), 1–33.

Mesa Community Colleges. (2021, January 10). *Research Briefs*. Education Studies. https://www.mesacc.edu/departments/education-studies/tl3c/educators/research-briefs.

Paris, D., & Alim, H. S. (Eds.). (2017). *Culturally sustaining pedagogies: Teaching and learning for justice in a changing world*. New York, NY: Teachers College Press. https://doi.org/10.3102/0013189X12441244.

Rios-Aguilar, C., González-Canche, M., & Moll, L. (2010). *Implementing Structured English Immersion (SEI) in Arizona: Benefits, costs, challenges, and opportunities, 114*(9), 1–18.

United States Department of Education. (2021, January 9). *Languages*. Our nation's ELs. https://www2.ed.gov/datastory/el-characteristics/index.html#two.

Yosso, T. J. (2005). Whose culture has capital? A critical race theory discussion of community cultural wealth. *Race Ethnicity and Education, 8*(1), 69–91. DOI:10.1080/1361332052000341006.

Chapter 12

Preparing Teachers to be Allies in Addressing Mental Health with K-12 Students

Gabrielle Luu

The National Institute of Mental Health (NIMH) (2019) reports that in 2017, 13.3% of adolescents between the ages 12–17 in the United States experienced at least one major depressive episode. While mood fluctuations and negative emotions in response to life's obstacles are expected and typically short-lived, depression presents itself as a much different opponent. From an educator's perspective, this news is distressing as students' depression can negatively affect their school performance (Fletcher, 2010; Lundy et al., 2010), and ultimately, can end their lives. Teachers are often asked to play many roles in the classroom beyond delivering instruction. This study explores pre-service teachers' knowledge about the causes, symptoms, and treatments of depression as well as how pre-service teachers describe teachers' role(s) in supporting students who may be exhibiting signs of depression. While teachers' primary role in the classroom is to provide instruction, they play a critical role as allies in addressing mental health of K-12 students. Given the stigma of addressing mental health issues within various minority communities, including the Latinx community (Corrigan & Penn, 2015), teachers' roles as allies are even more critical.

Addressing issues of mental health is especially important for Latinx students in the currrent sociopolitical context given the targeted derogatory comments against the Latinx community and the significant increase in racially motivated hate crimes, anti-immigrant sentiment, and White nationalism that was documented during the Trump presidency (Daftary, Devereux, & Elliott, 2020). Several researchers have demonstrated that the sociopolitical context that included derogatory language toward and about the Latinx community fueled by the Trump presidency is associated with increased anxiety and negative stigma that has implications for the mental well-being of Latinx individuals, especially youth (Albright & Hurd, 2020; Jones et al., 2021).

Additionally, there are other factors that can impact addressing mental health among Latinx youth including racial, ethnic, and socioeconomic disparities (Bledsoe et al., 2021). These include stigma within Latinx communities with regard to mental health (Corrigan & Penn, 2015), limited access to mental health services (Haak et al., 2016), and increased exposure to community violence (Katoaka et al., 2003). As a result of these disparities and others (Marrast et al., 2016), Latinx youth have 49% fewer visits to psychiatrists and 58% fewer visits to mental health professionals compared to White children. Bledsoe et al. (2021) report that few studies examine the experiences of Latinx/Hispanic students and barriers to proper mental health services for marginalized communities. Thus, increasing anxiety in the Latinx community due to the sociopolitical climate of the Trump and post-Trump era, coupled with the negative stigma surrounding mental health issues in the Latinx community could have long-lasting negative effects. It is imperative, then, to examine what agents and support structures, if any, might be used to better identify, understand, and address mental health issues among Latinx youth. This chapter specifically examines whether pre-service teachers are prepared to identify and address depression among school-aged youth and how teacher preparation programs might want to include courses in their curriculum that provide content related to youth mental health and well-being.

LITERATURE REVIEW

Depression and depressive symptoms among young students have a wide range of consequences. In elementary students, the effects of depression are found to include negative impacts on school performance (Fletcher, 2010) and lower cognitive functioning (Lundy et al. 2010). Kessler (2011) notes that early-onset depression can have broad sweeping implications into adolescence and adulthood including higher rates of education termination. While occurrence of depressive disorder is reportedly low in children and research on the matter is relatively scarce, depressive symptoms are commonly seen and can be a predecessor to the development of depressive disorders later in life (Gudmundsen et al., 2019). It is suggested that management of early-onset depressive symptoms—even sub-clinical symptoms—plays a crucial role in mitigating the negative effects that tend to follow (Lundy et al., 2010; Cunningham & Suldo, 2014). In adolescents, symptoms of depression often mirror that of adults (Thapar et al., 2010). Depression in adolescence is predictive of greater symptomatic severity into adulthood and correlated with increased levels of migraines, low levels of social support, low self-rated health, and higher rates of cigarette smoking (Naicker et al., 2013).

However, though treatment options are available—for example, cognitive behavioral therapy is commonly suggested (Thapar et al., 2010)—the majority of youth experiencing mental disorders do not receive appropriate treatment (Merikangas et al., 2011). When treatment is received, a large portion of those who were treated were reported to have received service in a school setting (Merikangas et al., 2011; Cunningham & Suldo, 2014). Schools are critical to the implementation of mental health services for children and adolescents, given that schools "provide access to students within naturalistic settings whereas they may otherwise be unattainable" (Bledsoe et al., 2021, p. 14). Warner and Fox (2012) noted that many triggers and signs of depression are seen in school while Platt and colleagues (2013) reported that adolescence is also a time of increased susceptibility to depression. Thus, researchers have called for developing effective means for depression identification and intervention within schools (Cunningham & Suldo, 2014; Warner & Fox, 2012; Gudmundsen et al., 2019; Kuo et al., 2013). Additionally, Kuo and colleagues (2013) mention that communication with parents and other members of the school community are key to successful school-based mental health initiatives. Teachers occupy a unique position in that they spend most of their day interacting with and observing students while at the same time they are also connected to students' guardians and other school staff including counselors. For these reasons, teacher nominations have been proposed as an efficient, cost-effective method for identifying students who may need mental health counseling (Gudmundsen et al., 2019; Cunningham & Suldo, 2014; Kuo et al., 2013).

Cunningham and Suldo (2014) investigated the sensitivity and specificity (defined as correctly identifying students with depression and correctly identifying those without depression, respectively) of elementary teacher nominations. They found that teachers have a sensitivity rate of 50.0% and specificity rate of 83.8%; however, participating teachers were not provided with training and 84% stated that they have had little to no prior professional development regarding mental health issues in children. The authors suggested that training may have an influence on the teachers' accuracy. This suggestion is bolstered by the fact that symptoms of many internalizing disorders such as depression can be easily confused with normal developmental changes and as such, require close observation (Gudmundsen et al., 2019; Merikangas et al., 2011). However, Warner and Fox (2012) caution against depending on schools to identify and intervene in regard to students' mental health needs, stating that school faculty and staff may see it as "creating more work." Gathering data regarding teachers' baseline knowledge about depression and their receptiveness to assuming the responsibility of identifying students who may be dealing with depression opens the door for a more tailored and successful training course dedicated to pre-service teachers, resulting in better outcomes for students.

RESEARCH QUESTIONS

1. What is pre-service teachers' knowledge about the causes, symptoms, and treatments of depression?
2. How do pre-service teachers describe teachers' role(s) in supporting students who may be exhibiting signs of depression?

METHODS AND DATA SOURCES

This study used a mixed-methods research design with quantitative and qualitative inquiry from convenience samples. Mixed methods allow for the collection and analysis of a broader range of data. Data were collected from an online survey (N=190) and seven focus groups from October 2016 through April 2017. Participants for the online survey were recruited from 10 course sections of an undergraduate upper-division Bilingual/English as a Second Language (BLE/ESL) Education course. Participants for the focus groups included upper-division pre-service teachers enrolled in the institution's BLE/ESL program.

Participants

The participants in this study were 190 pre-service teacher students in their third or fourth year within a large public university's teacher preparation program in Southwestern USA. In this study, 75% of participants were female (N=143) while 25% were male (N=47). The pre-service teachers ranged in age from 18–59 with a mean age of 23.95 years (SD=6.85). Slightly over three-fourths (75.1%) were between the ages of 18 and 24, while 24.9% were between the ages of 25 and 59. Additionally, participants self-reported race/ethnicity as follows: White (53.1%), Hispanic or Latino (25.79%), Biracial/Mixed (8.42%), Asian (5.26%), Black/African American (3.16%), American Indian/Alaska Native (2.63%), and other (1.58%). This sample of participants is representative of pre-service teachers at this institution.

The pre-service teachers were enrolled in various programs available in teacher education such as Elementary Education (including various specializations) (65.6%), Secondary Education (33.3%), or other programs (1%). This sample of participants is representative of this institution in terms of program enrollment.

Instruments

Quantitative. The primary data source used to test knowledge of depression and its treatments was the Multiple Choice Questions (MCQ) Instrument constructed by Gabriel and Violato (2009). The MCQ was developed in consultation with national and international psychiatry experts based on empirical evidence from an extensive review of the literature and theoretical knowledge. The survey consists of 27 items and is reported as having an internal consistency of 0.68. The instrument's 27 MCQ are broken into the following subscales: definition (5 items), risk of relapse (2 items), etiology (2 items), presentation and symptoms (6 items), and biological and psychological treatments (12 items). Scores on the MCQ range from 0% (no questions were answered correctly) to 100% (all questions were answered correctly). Questions that were not answered were counted as incorrect. Due to a technical difficulty, responses to question number 21 were not recorded and, thus, are not reported in the results. In this study, the MCQ with 26 items was highly reliable ($\alpha=0.764$). Descriptive and inferential analyses were used to examine results of the MCQ and whether there were any differences in MCQ scores by length of time in the pre-service teacher program.

Qualitative. Data were collected through seven focus groups using a semi-structured interview protocol, each lasting between 10 and 35 minutes. Interviews were recorded and later transcribed verbatim. Qualitative data sources were analyzed using induction methods (Miles et al., 2014) to identify common themes across the pre-service teachers' responses to the focus group questions. Data triangulation, peer review, and member checking were used to support the trustworthiness of the data and as a search for negative cases. A descriptive method was used when analyzing the data, which involves a description and interpretation of the phenomenon (Saldaña, 2013; Sandelowski, 2000). An open-ended approach was used to begin examining the information gathered in order to identify patterns within the different codes and formulate categories of data which were further refined (Miles et al., 2014; Strauss & Corbin, 1998). The data were coded by two individuals. Each researcher independently coded 100% of the data which yielded an inter-rater reliability of 92.47% and consensus was reached at 100%.

RESULTS

Quantitative Findings

The data indicated that pre-service teachers had substantial gaps in their knowledge about depression. In this study, being knowledgeable about depression is defined by a score of 80% correct or above on the MCQ, which means that 80% of the questions were answered correctly on the MCQ. Overall scores ranged from 19.23% to 100%. The mean score of correct answers was 72.19% (SD=15.48%) and fewer than 4 out of 10 (37.9%) participants were considered knowledgeable about depression based on their MCQ responses.

An independent samples t-test revealed no significant difference in mean scores of percent correct on the MCQ between pre-service teachers in their third year (M=71.15, SD=16.13) compared to pre-service teachers in their fourth year (M=74.06, SD=14.41), t(186)=−1.26, p=.209, 95%CI [−7.47, 1.65], d=.22. Thus, pre-service teachers' knowledge of depression did not depend on the amount of time spent in the teacher education program.

Areas of knowledge. The 26 items on the MCQ were divided into four constructs: Overview (definition/risk factors/demographics), Causes and Symptoms, Types of Treatment, and Factors of Antidepressants (see Table 12.1). These categories were split in this fashion in order to better understand the baseline knowledge of what depression is, its causes and symptoms, its treatment options, and details about antidepressants. These aspects are of particular importance to pre-service teachers because in order for them to meaningfully contribute to student-depression intervention, they must have a solid understanding of what depression is, who is more likely to be at risk, how to recognize it via symptoms/signs, and what the process of recovery looks like.

Table 12.1 above lists the four constructs and their corresponding MCQ items along with their respective reliability Cronbach's alpha. The *Types of Treatment* construct, with only three items, had the highest reliability (α=0.643) followed by the *Causes and Symptoms* construct with seven

Table 12.1 Constructs Identified

	Constructs Identified		
Construct	MCQ Items	# of Items	Cronbach's Alpha
Overview	1, 2, 3, 4, 5, 6, 11	7	0.126
Causes and Symptoms	8, 9, 10, 12, 13, 14, 15	7	0.642
Types of Treatment	18, 22, 27	3	0.643
Factors of Antidepressants	7, 16, 17, 19, 20, 23, 24, 25, 26	9	0.228

items (α=0.642). The *Factors of Antidepressants* construct with nine items (α=0.228), and the *Overview* construct with seven items (α=0.126) had the lowest reliability indices.

Participants scored higher on the *Causes and Symptoms* construct (M=86.99%, SD=18.04%), but less so on the *Overview* construct (M=67.97%, SD=17.78%) and the *Factors of Antidepressants* construct (M=66.49%, SD=22.00%). Participants scored the lowest on the *Types of Treatments* construct (M=64.56%, SD=27.99%). Likewise, while 79.5% of participants were considered knowledgeable in the *Causes and Symptoms* construct, only 28.4% were knowledgeable in the *Overview* construct, 25.8% in the *Factors of Antidepressants* construct, and 26.3% in the *Types of Treatment* construct. While almost 8 out of 10 of the pre-service teachers could correctly identify causes and symptoms of depression, fewer than 3 out of 10 were familiar with the other dimensions of depression as assessed by the MCQ.

Qualitative Findings

A number of themes emerged from the qualitative data. The overall themes and subthemes are described in a codebook created and used for coding the focus group transcripts. While numerous codes surfaced, for the scope of this study, only the three major themes that directly relate to the research question regarding teachers' roles will be discussed here (see Figure 12.1). This generated a total of 92 coded statements from the focus group data.

Theme 1: Teachers should take responsibility for the whole student. The responsibility of teachers to be attentive and responsive to student depression emerged as one of the themes. This theme included being both an advocate and a support figure for the student. Of the 92 codes, 21.74% of the codes referred to the expectation of teachers to assume this level of care for their students. Comments generally centered around the idea that teachers are responsible for more than just the student's academic success. As Participant A2 stated, "We're not just there to put information into children's heads.

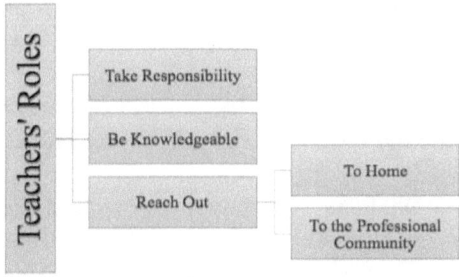

Figure 12.1 Themes and Subthemes Found.

We're obviously there to care about the whole child." Participant B2 believed that the responsibility extends "to advocat[ing] for your students." Some participants stated that at times, teachers find themselves in a position in which they should assume the role of a surrogate parent. This was seen when Participant D3 noted, "[Teachers] have [students] like all day long and [teachers] see them more than the parents sometimes," and when Participant A3 described a student's situation by explaining that his "parents aren't involved with his school life at all. So the teacher would be his only support." Overall, participants believed that teachers should assume responsibility for the whole child—not just their academics.

Theme 2: Teachers should be knowledgeable about depression in general. In addition to caring for their students, another theme that surfaced indicated that teachers should be knowledgeable enough to detect depression within their class. This theme comprised 34.78% of the total 92 codes that were examined in this study. Comments included the importance of knowing the signs and symptoms of depression. For example, Participant E2 believed, "It is important for teachers to be aware of the symptoms so that [they] can notice it and get that child help early on, or whenever possible." Participant F6 agreed, saying, "[A] teacher's role is be[ing] able to detect that symptoms [*sic*] of a student who may be going through depression." Participant G3 broke down the areas in which teachers should be knowledgeable, stating:

> [As teachers,] it is definitely important to recognize the symptoms of depression or even know [what] the true definition [of] depression is and also inform yourself of how to help or [. . .] how to find the right resources for your students.

Participant D3 admitted a disadvantage due to their current level of understanding of depression saying:

> I feel like I would struggle, maybe to even recognize the symptoms, like who knows? Maybe I already have students [who are dealing with depression], but I've never been educated on it, it's not something that they necessarily say like, "Hey, you need to look out for this," so I wouldn't even know how to begin to help.

Participant C3 pointed out that knowledge allows for teachers to be in a better position to assume the level of responsibility described earlier by saying:

> You're going from, "Oh, I don't know what's wrong with this kid. They're just being bad. Or they just don't want to do anything." Instead it's like, "You know, looking at this, I think, they may be suffering from depression. Let's maybe look more into this."

Generally, there was a consensus that part of a teacher's role regarding depression is to be knowledgeable of the subject.

Theme 3: Teachers should reach out. Two subthemes emerged under this third theme: Teachers Should Reach Out to the Student's Home, and Teachers Should Reach Out to the Professional Community. Codes for statements either about reaching out directly to the student or reaching out to an unspecified party accounted for 14.13% of the total number of codes. The subcode about reaching out to the home in particular accounted for 8.70% of the 92 codes, while reaching out to the professional community, such as counselors or medical professionals, comprised 20.65% of all the codes. Participant G1 believed that teachers should reach out to the students, saying, "If they're struggling like this then I can talk to them," while participant D4 stated, "The more tools, more resources we can give them to combat something as dangerous as clinical depression, then the better it is for their success in life."

In terms of reaching out to the home, many felt that teachers had an obligation to connect with the parents of a student who may be battling depression. Participant G1 said, "I think of course confidentiality is important but maybe even reaching out to the parents or to make sure that they know what's going on." More often than not, responses indicated that reaching out both to the home and to the professional community was necessary. Participant C3 believes, "[As teachers,] sometimes you need to be the person that's like, I recognize what's happening with [the student]. We're going to try to get some help happening here between [the student], [the student's] family, and doctors." Similarly, Participant E3 felt, "Recognizing that is just definitely of huge importance, and knowing the resources where students can get help if parents are able, depending on the situation." The participants also acknowledged that resources may exist within the school. Participant F2 states, "[Teachers should] use [the] resources that teachers have to try to help them," and Participant G3 wanted, "[Teachers to] find the right resources, talk about the counselor, [and] talk with a nurse." Predominantly, the pre-service teachers interviewed held the belief that teachers should take the initiative to find help for students who may be impacted by depression, whether that be through the home, through the professional community, or both.

DISCUSSION

The aim of this study was to determine how knowledgeable pre-service teachers are about depression and, in their opinion, what teachers' roles should be regarding student depression. Through this study, it was found that the majority of pre-service teachers believed that teachers have an obligation to intervene in student depression; however, they lack the background knowledge to do so. Given this disconnect, professional development opportunities to educate those going into the field about this topic are vital. We should consider how cultural responsiveness may impact teachers' views and interpretations of the stigma around mental health (Corrigan & Penn, 2015). In addition, teachers recognized the possibility of limited access to mental health services and support in Latinx communities (Haack et al., 2016).

Addressing issues of mental health is especially important for Latinx students in the post-Trump era, in light of targeted derogatory comments against the Latinx community and the significant increase in racially motivated hate crimes, anti-immigrant sentiment, and White nationalism (Daftary, Devereux, & Elliott, 2020). This increase in attacks toward the Latinx community, coupled with the negative stigma surrounding mental health issues in this community could have lasting negative effects. While this study did not explicitly focus on Latinx pre-service teachers or their work with Latinx students, it is imperative that future research intentionally addresses these communities.

Research has documented that depression in children and adolescents can have both short-term and long-term consequences, including greater severity of depression in adulthood (Fletcher, 2010; Lundy et al., 2010; Kessler, 2012; Gudmundsen et al., 2019; Naicker et al., 2013). Independent of this knowledge, the pre-service teachers studied overwhelmingly believed that they have a responsibility to support students with depression. Several participants revealed that they themselves had experienced depression and indicated that when their childhood teachers reached out or made an effort to raise awareness of mental health, it had had a positive impact on them. Teachers who engage with their students at this key stage of their lives have the opportunity to make a lasting impact on their students. Teachers can also act as a liaison to both guardians and the school community—an important factor in school-based mental health programs (Kuo et al., 2013). Thus, teachers occupy a unique position that allows them to play a crucial role in student-depression recovery.

More generally, these pre-service teachers believed that teachers have a commitment to the whole student, including their mental health, rather than being responsible solely for students' academic achievement. This duty to their students is partially spurred by the fact that some teachers may spend more time with students compared to some of their parents. In extreme cases, they even view themselves as surrogate parents, especially when students' guardians at home are less engaged in the students' care. Pre-service teachers acknowledge that due to the amount of time with the students, they are more inclined to notice behaviors of concern that may indicate the presence of depression and therefore, they have the obligation to provide support and reach out to the appropriate parties. Ultimately, they are in an advantageous position to initiate the process for depression intervention.

Although pre-service teachers in this study indicated they wanted to help, they admitted that they were not prepared to do so. When asked about symptoms, causes, and treatment, the participants were able to offer some information, but they largely recognized that they needed to know more about depression in order to detect if any of their students exhibited signs of depression. Specifically, pre-service teachers stated that they needed guidance on what behavioral changes to look for and how to differentiate between a student who is acting out and a student who is grappling with depression. Pre-service teachers went on to say that even if they were able to identify student depression, they would welcome training on how to specifically intervene or what resources to access.

The quantitative data bolsters the argument in favor of a student-depression education program for pre-service teachers. Overall, pre-service teachers surveyed were not considered knowledgeable about depression. More pre-service teachers were considered knowledgeable about causes and symptoms of depression (79.5%), but fewer participants were knowledgeable of what treatment options are available (26.3%), what complications might arise from use of antidepressants (25.8%), and more general facts about depression (28.4%). This parallels what was found in the qualitative results—pre-service teachers could reasonably identify depression symptoms and causes but lacked the knowledge of how to take action. In addition, there was no correlation between length of time in their teacher education program and mean scores of percent correct on the MCQ, indicating that the topic of depression was not effectively addressed before the end of their pre-service education. Therefore, pre-service teachers would benefit from implementation of a student depression intervention training program that emphasizes information about treatment and resources as well as an overview of depression itself. This could include more exploration of specific strategies for addressing stigma and trauma alongside economic, racial, and social disparities that directly impact Latinx community.

While this study provides information about the expectations pre-service teachers have for their future selves regarding student depression and baseline data of their current knowledge of depression, more research is necessary. Future work could examine the structure of the MCQ in order to investigate whether or not the MCQ is multidimensional. The constructs were derived qualitatively, but it may be that quantitative analyses would result in a multidimensional survey whose components stray away from the factors presented in this chapter. A factor analysis or principal component analysis would be appropriate for this type of investigation. In addition to restructuring the constructs, this study could be expanded to include a larger sample of pre-service teachers across a number of universities to find whether the results of this study are consistent. Another possible avenue of investigation is whether the same level of knowledge would be reported if a child-specific depression questionnaire were to be used for pre-service teachers enrolled in the elementary education program. Further, future studies might want to consider asking pre-service teachers whether they completed any psychology courses and distinguishing between courses including general psychology and abnormal psychology to examine if such courses made a difference in their understanding of depression. Finally, it may be beneficial to use the same methods from this study with an in-service teacher population to determine if there is a change in perspective or an increase in knowledge once teachers are in the field.

While the pre-service teachers were in favor of teachers serving as frontline intervention personnel for student depression, their performance on the MCQ revealed the need for depression-specific training prior to assuming that role. Participants agreed that teachers should take responsibility to care for students' mental well-being which includes being knowledgeable and reaching out to appropriate parties. The results from the MCQ found that in order for that to be possible, overall knowledge about depression needs to increase—especially in areas of treatment options, treatment complications, and general facts about depression. Thus, student depressionintervention training for pre-service teachers would be beneficial.

IMPLICATIONS

It is important to note that teachers' primary roles are to educate and address students' academic needs. Furthermore, teachers are typically not qualified to formally diagnose, provide counseling, or prescribe treatment for depression. Focus group participants suggested that teachers' roles regarding student depression should be to identify students who may be struggling emotionally, refer them to the appropriate resources, and provide support through their process of recovery. This is especially noteworthy because it contrasts with the suggestion that teachers may see school-based depression intervention as an unwanted additional burden (Warner & Fox, 2012).

The implementation of a student depression intervention training would allow teachers to be more aware and understanding of students who are demonstrating symptoms of depression. It would also benefit the students since it has been found that early intervention can lower or avoid the serious consequences of depression in young students (Lundy et al., 2010; Cunningham & Suldo, 2014). A previous study examining the impact of workshops on the topic of depression for secondary teachers in Scotland revealed that training from a medical perspective did not improve teachers' accuracy in identifying students with depression (Moor et al., 2007). However, given the results of the current study, it may be worth investigating alternative trainings with education perspectives and conducted in pre-service settings. When teachers are knowledgeable about depression, that understanding can result in appropriate referrals to professional school personnel who are equipped to guide students experiencing depression. Such referrals and subsequent support can produce positive results, impacting teachers' abilities to fulfill their self-imposed expectations along with students' likelihood of recovery.

CONCLUSION

Depression and depressive symptoms are far too common among elementary and secondary students (Gudmundsen et al., 2019; NIMH, 2019)—in fact, adolescents are especially vulnerable to these mental health issues (Platt et al., 2013; Warner & Fox, 2012). Effects of depression and depressive symptoms range from lower cognitive functioning (Lundy et al., 2010) to increased severity of depression and poor self-rated health into adulthood (Naicker et al., 2013). This, coupled with the fact that managing symptoms of depression aids in alleviating accompanying consequences, reveals a strong argument for early identification and referral to intervention resources. While Warner and Fox (2012) highlight the concern about "creating more work" for school faculty and staff, pre-service teachers who participated in this study agreed that they hold a responsibility to be aware, knowledgeable, and active in depression intervention. That said, this study found that fewer than 40% of participants were considered knowledgeable on the topic overall. Though previous researchers have investigated the effectiveness of in-service teacher training programs (Moor et al., 2007), the results of this study suggest that it may be worth revisiting the subject from a less medically centered perspective in a pre-service setting. A program such as this may be beneficial to students as well as allow pre-service teachers to make steps toward the identifier role they hope to assume.

REFERENCES

Albright, J. N., & Hurd, N. M. (2020). Marginalized identities, Trump-related distress, and the mental health of underrepresented college students. *American Journal of Community Psychology, 65*(3–4), 381–396.

Bledsoe, K. G., Lenz, A. S., & Placeres, V. (2021). Mental health symptoms as predictors of school climate evaluations among middle school Latinx/Hispanic students. *Journal of Child and Adolescent Counseling, 7*(1), 13–25.

Corrigan, P. W., & Penn, D. L. (2015). Lessons from social psychology on discrediting psychiatric stigma. *Stigma and Health, 1*(S), 2–17. doi:10.1037/2376-6972.1.S.2

Cunningham, J. M., & Suldo, S. M. (2014). Accuracy of teachers in identifying elementary school students who report at-risk levels of anxiety and depression. *School Mental Health: A Multidisciplinary Research and Practice Journal, 6*(4), 237–250. https://doi.org/10.1007/s12310-014-9125-9.

Daftary, A. M., Devereux, P., & Elliott, M. (2020). Discrimination, depression, and anxiety among college women in the Trump era. *Journal of Gender Studies, 29*(7), 765–778.

Fletcher, J. M. (2010). Adolescent depression and educational attainment: Results using sibling fixed effects. *Health Economics. 19*(7), 855–871. https://doi.org/10.1002/hec.1526.

Gabriel, A., & Violato, C. (2009). The development of a knowledge test of depression and its treatment for patients suffering from non-psychotic depression: A psychometric assessment. *BMC Psychiatry, 56*(9), https://doi.org/10.1186/1471-244x-9-56.

Gudmundsen, G. R., Rhew, I. C., McCauley E., Kim, J., & Stoep, A. V. (2019). Emergence of depressive symptoms from kindergarten to sixth grade. *Journal of Clinical Child and Adolescent Psychology. 48*(3), 501–515. https://doi.org/10.1080/15374416.2017.1410823.

Haack, L. M., Kape, T. L., & Gerdes, A. C. (2016). Rates associations and predictors of psychopathology in a convenience sample of school-aged Latinx youth: Identifying areas for mental health outreach. *Journal of Child and Family Studies, 25*(7), 2315–2326. doi:10.1007/s10826-016-0404-y.

Jones, B. S., Sherman, J. W., Rojas, N. E., Hosek, A., Vannette, D., Rocha, R. R., Garcia-Ponce, O., Pantoja, M., & Garcia-Amador, J. M. (2021). Trump-induced anxiety among Latina/os. *Group Processes & Intergroup Relations, 24*(1), 68–87.

Katoaka, S. H., Stein, B. D., Jaycox, L. H., Wong, M., Escudero, P., Tu, W., Zaragoza, C., & Fink, A. (2003). A school-based mental health program for traumatized Latinx immigrant children. *Journal of the American Academy of Child and Adolescent Psychiatry, 42*(3), 311–318. doi:10.1097/00004583-200303000-00011

Kessler, R. C., (2011). The costs of depression. *Psychiatric Clinics, 35*(1), 1–14. https://doi.org/10.1016/j.psc.2011.11.005.

Kuo, E. S., Stoep, A. V., Herting, J. R,. Grupp, K., & McCauley, E. (2013). How to identify students for school-based depression intervention: Can school record review be substituted for universal depression screening? *Journal of Child and Adolescent Psychiatric Nursing, 26*(1), 42–52. https://doi.org/10.1111/jcap.12010.

Lundy, L. M., Silva, G. E., Kaemingk, K. L., Goodwin, J. L., & Quan, S. F. (2010). Cognitive functioning and academic performance in elementary school children with anxious/depressed and withdrawn symptoms. *The Open Pediatric Medicine Journal. 10*(4), 1–9. http://dx.doi.org/10.2174/1874309901004010001.

Marrast, L., Himmelstein, D. U., & Woolhandler, S. (2016). Racial and ethnic disparities in mental health care for children and young adults: A national study. *International Journal of Health Services, 46*(4), 810–824. doi:10.1177/0020731416662736.

Merikangas, K. R., He, J. P., Burstein, M., Swendsen, J., Avenevoli, S., Case, B., Georgiades, K., Heaton, L., Swanson, S., & Olfson, M. (2011). Service utilization for lifetime mental disorders in U.S. adolescents: Results of the national comorbidity survey–adolescent supplement. *Journal of the American Academy of Child and Adolescent Psychiatry, 50*(1). 32–45. https://doi.org/10.1016/j.jaac.2010.10.006.

Miles, M. B., Huberman, A. M., & Sandaña, J. (2014). *Qualitative data analysis: A methods sourcebook* (3rd ed.). Thousand Oaks: Sage Publications.

Moor, S., Ann, M., Hester, M., Elisabeth, W. J., Robert, E., Robert, W., & Caroline, B. (2007). Improving the recognition of depression in adolescence: Can we teach the teachers? *Journal of Adolescence, 30*(1). https://doi.org/10.1016/j.adolescence.2005.12.001.

Naicker, K., Galambos, N. L., Zeng, Y., Senthilselvan, & A., Colman, I. (2013). Social, demographic, and health outcomes in the 10 years following adolescent depression. *Journal of Adolescent Health, 52*(5), 533–538. https://doi.org/10.1016/j.jadohealth.2012.12.016.

National Institute of Mental Health. (2019, February). *Major depression.* https://www.nimh.nih.gov/health/statistics/major-depression.shtml#part_155031.

Platt, B., Kadosh, K. C., & Lau, J. Y. F. (2013). The role of peer rejection in adolescent depression. *Depression and Anxiety, 30*(9). https://doi.org/10.1002/da.22120.

Saldaña, J. (2013). *The coding manual for qualitative researchers.* London: Sage Publications.

Sandelowski, M. (2000). Combining qualitative and quantitative sampling, data collection, and analysis techniques in mixed-method studies. *Research in Nursing and Health, 23*(3), 246–255.

Strauss, A., & Corbin, J. (1998). *Basics of qualitative research techniques.* London: Sage.

Thapar, A., Collishaw, S., & Potter, R. (2010). Managing and preventing depression in adolescents. *BMJ, 304*(209), 1056–1067.

Warner C. M., & Fox, J. K. (2012). Advances and challenges in school-based intervention for anxious and depressed youth: Identifying and addressing issues of sustainability. *School Mental Health, 4*(4), 193–196. https://doi.org/10.1007/s12310-012-9087-8.

Conclusion

Educational Movimientos: The Imperative to Sustain Relationships and Build Community

Patricia D. Quijada Cerecer and
Leticia Alvarez Gutiérrez

This book began with a story about Joseph Levanos, a sophomore in high school, who describes how he and his mother experienced a city council meeting aimed at discussing how his hometown would align with SB54,[1] a senate bill prohibiting local and state law enforcement from working with federal immigration agencies. Joseph vividly and movingly describes this city hall meeting, which revealed how white supremacy and power come alive in public spaces (Beliso-De Jesús & Pierre, 2020). More pointedly, Joseph reminds us how racism continues to be an endemic social force and a fundamental part of the architecture that shapes U.S. experiences for minoritized students and communities (Hall, 2008). The racist interactions Joseph experienced during the city council meeting reveal how patriarchy, race, class, immigration, and other social forces interact with each other, starkly illustrating how power is an integral force that must be acknowledged as a dynamic that creates social context (Collins,1998; Solorzano & Yosso, 2001). Framing these dynamics from an intersectional lens reveals how racism and discrimination operate to physically and psychologically disempower minoritized communities (Crenshaw, 1990). LATCrit and transformational resistance serve as analytical tools to understand how Latinx youth, families, and communities enact their agencies and resist dominating forces that work hard to silence them, as evident in Joseph's experience at city hall (Solorzano & Delgado Bernal, 2001).

We enter the conversation from distinct geographical locations while supporting family and dear friends who have been impacted by the global pandemic. Like the educators and students in our communities, we too have been impacted by the pandemic. Patricia is Xicana/Cupeño raised by her mother who is from La Paz, Baja California Sur, Mexico. On her father's side, she is Cupeño and Mexican (Sonoran). Leticia is a first-generation Purépecha/Xicana who entered U.S schools as a monolingual Spanish speaker who grew up in a working-poor household along the San Diego-Tijuana border in a mixed-status family. She has attended school in both México and the United States. Our deep connections to community and lived experiences have informed our work as community-based researchers and educators. In fact, we both navigated treacherous political policies and practices common in low-resourced K-12 schools; Leticia in an urban area and Patricia in a rural one.

During the global pandemic we shifted to virtual learning platforms and became part of the "frontline" workforce. While we were in community with educators, we recognize that many of the students and communities we work with and learn from are deemed part of the "essential" workforce, that often become disposable when unable to meet the demands of the workforce (Alvarez Gutiérrez et al., 2020). In fact, we know this all too well since many of our family members are part of the "essential" labor force who became ill while working under unsafe conditions. We, like the authors throughout this book, believe that relationships are important, and take pride in honoring our relations to all beings. During these unprecedented times, negotiating various pandemics and distant learning, relationships are especially important.

The chapters throughout this book vividly illustrate the intricate contradictions and tensions that Latinx students experience within the educational system in the United States. Collectively the authors grapple with the multiple and nuanced ways that Latinx students are positioned in educational contexts (as both teachers and learners) and raise important questions that center on how relationships are formed, nurtured, and sustained. The challenges that K-12 schools experience in forming relationships with students of color and their families are not new, as these multifaceted complexities have been researched extensively (Alvarez Gutiérrez & Quijada Cerecer, 2018; Bajaj & Suresh, 2018; Dryden-Peterson, 2018; Ratliffe & Ponte, 2018). Yet, the incessant struggle for minoritized students to be legitimized as change agents who are actively contributing to knowledge production (Cahill et al., 2019) persists and continues to be a central theme as shared by the authors.

A historical analysis of P-20 educational systems in the United States reveals how colonization, racism, and inequities are foundational to understanding the glaring inequities and educational disparities that are entrenched in the educational trajectory of students of color. Educational policies, for example, have supported educational inequities in P-20 systems in multiple and complex ways, from mandating racially segregated schools (Lomawaima & McCarty, 2006; Orfield et al., 2016; Valencia, 2005), supporting unjust funding formulas (BenDavid-Hadar, 2016), and the unequal distribution of fiscal monies to under-resourced schools serving students of color (Blaisdell, 2016), to disciplining students of color in harsher and punitive ways (Jones et al., 2018; Love, 2019, Lustick, 2017; Morris, 2016; Peguero, 2008; Welch & Payne, 2018). These policies reinforce deficit ideologies that hold individual students responsible for school dysfunction and failure (Fuller et al., 2019; Rodriguez, 2021; Valenzuela, 1999).

The epistemic violence sanctioned upon students of color in schools continues in P-20 systems today and is reinforced and sustained by race-neutral policies that frame students' identities and student success (Saito, 2009). The P-20 school systems are framed around policies and principles that promote assimilationist ideologies and segregate knowledge and learning opportunities for students of color (Valencia & Solórzano, 1997; Valencia, 2010). As a result, a hierarchy of knowledge systems based on class, gender, immigration status, and race have standardized white middle-class sociocultural histories, practices, and values as the norm. These dominant epistemologies are foundational and used to frame how educational institutions position students as learners and as young people. More alarming is how these dominant epistemologies serve as benchmarks in K-12 systems to frame and assess the identities of student learners and their social development. These ideologies (in)form how relationships with students, families, and communities are approached, developed and sustained in most K-12 school settings.

Educational inequities remain rooted in deficit ideologies that shape educational policies, as well as curricular, co-curricular, and campus climates. For example, rather than critically examining how policies and practices in schools diminish access to educational opportunities for minoritized students, interventions center on how to "fix" student behavior by increasing the students' perseverance (Duckworth, 2007). These deficit ideologies, centered on behavior, reveal how educational institutions remain focused on surveilling and controlling the bodies and minds of students through policies and practices (Quijada Cerecer, 2013; Valencia, 1997; 2005; Valencia & Solórzano, 1997).

Given the nationwide context of anti-Latinx rhetoric, we were inspired by how the chapters throughout this book addressed the importance of including the voices and experiences of Latinx young people, educators, teacher educators, and education allies engaging with families in school, neighborhoods, and communities. By centering the voices of students, the authors eloquently highlighted pedagogical practices in and out of classrooms that engaged and legitimized students' cultural practices and inspired students to build a community to learn with and from each other. In Baca's chapter, for example, the "opinion argumentation letters" students authored served as a pedagogical tool for them to engage in critical dialogue about the immigration industrial complex. Similarly, Jacob's chapter revealed how students engaged in letter writing processes that centered students' intersectional identities and affirmed their lived experiences. Through these pedagogical activities the students became researchers, theorists, and activists, critiquing power structures and disrupting colonial student-teacher hierarchies and adult-centric categories that often limit what children and youth can do. Students' intersecting identities were legitimized, empowered, and lifted as they engaged in knowledge production and in liberatory praxis (Freire, 1970). Classrooms became a collective space where students worked with and learned from each other. As thought partners, students engaged in collective forms of resistance and self-care that humanized and modeled what it means to cultivate and sustain relationships.

The collection of chapters powerfully disrupted hegemonic logics that privilege learning that takes place in classrooms by highlighting projects that center the ways in which families and communities generate knowledge. Eloquently woven throughout each chapter are the ways in which students, families, and communities resist oppressive and racist policies and practices by actively joining forces and by being in community with each other. Carreon's chapter inspires hope as it offers an example of how a community of educators, families and students can heal from past mistakes, build trust, and learn with and from each other. Kay's chapter also reminds us of the *ganas* that the community holds to "create real change outside of the corrupt and complacent government system."

Throughout the book, authors share projects that reveal how structural racism, immigration status, patriarchal heteronormative ideologies, and other inequities permeate school systems, yet educators and students engage in transformational resistance (Solorzano & Delgado Bernal, 2001) to uplift the sociocultural linguistic and cultural identities of minoritized students. In combination, the chapters reveal policies and community-centered praxis that lift each other as both teachers and learners demonstrating the power of working with and learning from community stakeholders. As Esqueda reminds us, "It takes intention, patience, and a willingness to go out of the way to create authentic relationships that allow teachers to critically engage in practices that highlight and value the communities in which they serve."

Yet, K-12 educational systems continue to be challenged by how to build relationships with students, families, and communities (Alvarez Gutiérrez & Quijada Cerecer, 2018; Bajaj & Suresh, 2018; Delgado Gaitan, 2012; Ratliffe & Ponte, 2018). We align with scholars who argue that the challenges experienced by K-12 educational systems in forming relationships with students of color are rooted in hegemonic ideologies that frame policies and practices (Beliso-De Jesús & Pierre, 2020; Blaisdell, 2016; hooks, 2006; Madrigal & Acevedo-Gil, 2016). Consequently, structural racism and other inequities permeate school systems and influence how educators frame and form relationships with young people of color in schools (Bajaj & Suresh, 2018; Dryden-Peterson, 2018; Quijada Cerecer, 2013). In other words, the challenges center on educators' perceptions of students and their identities as learners, and as holders and producers of knowledge (Alvarez Gutiérrez & Quijada Cerecer, 2018; Dryden-Peterson, 2018; Hjerm, Johansson Sevä & Werner, 2018, Osorio, 2018). We find inspiration in how the scholarship presented throughout the book center young people not as children or adolescents who are moving through stages of development (Erikson, 1968), but rather as youth who are enacting their own agency, producing ideas and contributing to knowledge production (Lesko, 2001).

We find inspiration also in how scholars throughout the book form and build relationships with students. Authors shed light through their projects on how youths' identities are complex and necessitate an intersectional framing that includes contextualizing historical moments while also accounting for the interplay of power. These chapters interrupt the epistemological violence often enacted upon minoritized students in educational systems, and diverge assimilationist practices that often frame students' identities. School systems in the United States are framed around policies and practices that promote assimilationist ideologies and segregate knowledge and learning opportunities for students of color (Valencia & Solórzano, 1997; Valencia, 2010). These hegemonic patriarchal dominant epistemologies frame the logic used by educational institutions to position students as learners and as young people. More alarming is how dominant epistemologies serve as benchmarks in K-12 systems to frame and assess the identities of student learners and their social development. .

We close by offering our deep gratitude for the opportunity to be in conversation with each of the amazing scholars highlighted in this book. In their unique way, each chapter provided space and pedagogical tools for critical inquiry, reflections, healing, and inspiration. Collectively the chapters remind us that teaching and learning are political (Freire, 1970) and the importance of engaging in culturally sustaining pedagogies (Paris, 2012) that center the lived experiences of communities are foundational to learning. We conclude by returning to Joseph, who expressed how fulfilling it was to use his voice to advocate for justice in his community and reminds us that learning is not confined to school walls. Joseph shared his most sacred gift, and that was his voice. He states: "Looking back at that night, I was still primarily feeling hunger, but I now realize that I felt fulfillment for using my voice, perspective, and data to try to make a difference."

NOTE

1. https://leginfo.legislature.ca.gov/faces/billNavClient.xhtml?bill_id=201720180SB54

REFERENCES

Alvarez Gutiérrez, L., Fukushima, A. I., & Gaytán, M. S. (2020, July 6). *Essential Latinx Educators: Teaching in a Time of Pandemic*. Latinx Talk: Research. https://latinxtalk.org/2020/07/06/essential-latinx-educators-teaching-in-a-time-of-pandemic/

Alvarez Gutiérrez, L., & Quijada Cerecer, P. D. (2018). Resisting invisibility through creative expressions: immigrant students and families' voices and actions. *Journal of Family Diversity in Education, 3*(2), 79–97.

Bajaj, M., & Suresh, S. (2018) The "Warm embrace" of a newcomer school for Immigrant & refugee youth. *Theory Into Practice, 57*(2), 91–98.

Beliso-De Jesús, A. M., & Pierre, J. (2020). Anthropology of white supremacy. *American Anthropologist, 122*(1), 65–75.

BenDavid-Hadar, I. (2016). School finance policy and social justice. *International Journal of Educational Development, 46*, 166–174.

Blaisdell, B. (2016). Schools as racial spaces: Understanding and resisting structural racism. *International Journal of Qualitative Studies in Education, 29*(2), 248–272.

Cahill, C., Quijada Cerecer, D. A., Reyna Rivarola, A. R., Hernández Zamudio, J., & Alvarez Gutiérrez, L. (2019). 'Caution, we have power': Resisting the school-to-sweatshop pipeline through participatory artistic praxes and critical care. [Special Issue: Picturing Care: Re-framing Gender, Race, and Educational Justice], *Gender & Education, 31*(5), 576–589.

Collins, P. (1998). It's All in the family: Intersections of gender, race, and nation. *Hypatia, 13*(3), 62–82.

Crenshaw, K. (1990). Mapping the margins: Intersectionality, identity politics, and violence against women of color. *Stanford Law Review, 43*, 1241.

Dryden-Peterson, S. (2018). Family–school relationships in immigrant children's well-being: the intersection of demographics and school culture in the experiences of black African immigrants in the United States. *Race Ethnicity and Education, 21*(4), 486–502.

Duckworth, A. L., Peterson, C., Matthews, M. D., & Kelly, D. R. (2007). Grit: perseverance and passion for long-term goals. *Journal of Personality and Social Psychology, 92*(6), 1087.

Erikson, E. H. (1968). *Identity: Youth and crisis* (No. 7). WW Norton & company.

Freire, P. (1970). *Pedagogy of the oppressed*. New York, NY: Continuum.

Fuller, B., Kim, Y., Galindo, C., Bathia, S., Bridges, M., Duncan, G. J., & García Valdivia, I. (2019). Worsening school segregation for Latino children? *Educational Researcher, 48*(7), 407–420.

Gaitan, C. D. (2012). Culture, literacy, and power in family–community–school–relationships. *Theory Into Practice, 51*(4), 305–311.
Hall, R. E. (2008). *Racism in the 21st Century: An.* New York: Springer.
Hooks, B. (2000). *Feminist theory: From margin to center.* Cambridge, MA: South End Press.
Jones, K., Ferguson, A., Ramirez, C., & Owens, M. (2018). Seen but not heard: Personal narratives of systemic failure within the school-to-prison pipeline. *Taboo: The Journal of Culture and Education, 17*(4), 49–68.
Lesko, N. (2001). *Act your age!: A cultural construction of adolescence.* Psychology Press.
Lomawaima, K. T., & McCarty, T. L. (2006). *"To Remain an Indian": Lessons in Democracy from a Century of Native American Education.* Teachers College Press.
Love, B. L. (2019). *We want to do more than survive: Abolitionist teaching and the pursuit of educational freedom.* Beacon Press.
Lustick, H. (2017). "Restorative justice" or restoring order? Restorative school discipline practices in urban public schools. *Urban Education, 56*(8), 1–28.
Madrigal-Garcia, Y. I., & Acevedo-Gil, N. (2016). The New Juan Crow in Education: Revealing Panoptic Measures and Inequitable Resources That Hinder Latina/o Postsecondary Pathways. *Journal of Hispanic Higher Education, 15*(2), 154–181.
Morris, M. (2016). *Pushout: The criminalization of Black girls in schools.* The New Press.
Orfield, G., Ee, J., Frankenberg, E., & Siegel-Hawley, G. (2016). *"Brown" at 62: School segregation by race, poverty and state.* Los Angeles, CA: Civil Rights Project-Proyecto Derechos Civiles.
Paris, D. (2012). Culturally sustaining pedagogy. A needed change in stance, terminology, an practice. *Educational Researcher, 41*(3), 93–97.
Peguero, A. A. (2008). Is immigrant status relevant in school violence research? An analysis with Latino students. *Journal of School Health, 78*(7), 397–404.
Quijada Cerecer, P. D. (2013). The policing of Native bodies and minds: Perspectives on schooling from American Indian youth. *American Journal of Education, 119*(4), 591–616.
Ratliffe, K. T., & Ponte, E. (2018). Parent perspectives on developing effective family–school partnerships in Hawai'i. *The School Community Journal, 28*(1), 217–247.
Rodriguez, S. (2021). "They Let You Back in the Country?": Racialized Inequity and the Miseducation of Latinx Undocumented Students in the New Latino South. *The Urban Review,* 1–26.
Saito, L. T. (2009). *The politics of exclusion: The failure of race-neutral policies in urban America.* Stanford University Press.
Solórzano, D. G., & Bernal, D. D. (2001). Examining transformational resistance through a critical race and LatCrit theory framework: Chicana and Chicano students in an urban context. *Urban Education, 36*(3), 308–342.
Solórzano, D. G., & Yosso, T. J. (2001). Critical race and LatCrit theory and method: Counter-storytelling. *International journal of qualitative studies in education, 14*(4), 471–495.

Valencia, R. R. (2010). *Dismantling contemporary deficit thinking: Educational thought and practice*. New York, NY: Routledge.
Valencia, R. R. (2005). The Mexican American struggle for equal educational opportunity in Mendez v. Westminster: Helping to pave the way for Brown v. Board of Education. *Teachers College Record, 107*(3), 389–423.
Valencia, R. R., & Solórzano, D. (1997).Contemporary deficit thinking. (The Stanford Series on Education and Public Policy). In R. Valencia (Ed.), *The evolution of deficit thinking in educational thought and practice* (pp. 160–210). New York, NY: Falmer Press.
Valenzuela, A. (1999). *Subtractive Schooling*: *U.S.-Mexican Youth and the politics of caring*. Alban, NY: State University of New York Press.
Welch, K., & Payne, A. A. (2018). Latino/a student threat and school disciplinary policies and practices. *Sociology of Education, 91*(2), 91–110.

Index

Note: page references for figures are italicized

3 modes of belonging, engagement, imagination and alignment, 12
50/50 model of language immersion, 29
2016 election, xv, 8, 47, 67, 87, 128, 137, 193; resulting increase in bullying and harassment of Latinx children, 137, 138. *See also* Trump, Donald

abolitionist teaching mindset, 130
academic achievement differences, Latinx/ELLs and white peers, 97, 134
active listening, importance of in in intercultural dialogues, 118
advocate/s, advocating, 67, 76, 79, 84, 187, 213
affinity groups, for student cultural and emotional support, 129
agency to become advocates, 21
agents of change, positive social, 8
all hands on deck approach, 60, 62
the American Dream, 90, 91
antidote to the deficit perspective, 116
anti-racist educators, 140
anti-racist practices and pedagogy, 88, 92, 98–99, 103

Anzaldua, 163
argumentative identity-text writing, 8, 14
Arias, Beatriz, Dr., 217
Arizona, 8–9, 12; Department of Education, 213–15; English-only polices, 211–13; Proposition 203, 212–13; Tucson, 48, 51. *See also* HB2281; Mexican American Studies (MAS) program
asset-based perspectives, framework, xvi, 98, 175
asset pedagogies, 10, 50
authentic caring, 50, 52

background knowledge, using students', 100
Bernal, Delgado, 157, 162
Beutel, xv–xvi
biases, 96, 155
bilingualism, 144, 184, 185
bilingual teachers, 174, 183–84
borderlands, 163, 166
borders, cross linguistic, 166
border wall, U.S.-Mexican, 8, 16–17, 19–20
Briceño, 175

CAEP. *See* Council for the Accreditation of Educator Preparation
California, 3, 71, 176
California Mini-Corps (CMC), 174–79, 184
campaign of fear, 47
CDA. *See* Critical Discourse Analysis
challenges for Mexican immigrants in U.S. K-12 schools, 128
change, community-based actions for, 194
Chicana epistemologies, 160
Cinco de Mayo, incident, 48, 51, 53, 55, 59, 61
city council, 3, 83
city hall, journey from the classroom to, 72
civic participation and voting, promoting, 83
CMC. *See* California Mini-Corps
colonialism, 49, 62. *See also* coloniality
coloniality, 49, 61
colonialization, in U.S. P-20 educational systems, 240
community-based researchers and educators, 240
Community Cultural Wealth model, 50, 98
community/ies: change, 70; of color, 48, 51, 75; of practice, 11–12, 21; responsiveness, *58*
competence, cross-cultural, 26
confianza, 50
Consortium, 214–19; survey, 215; work to be done, 219–20
content instruction, limited access for ELLs, 213
Corps students' perceptions of language, 180–83
Coulter & Jiménez-Silva, 216
Council for the Accreditation of Educator Preparation (CAEP), 153
council woman, Latinx, 72, 76

counter-storytelling, as counter-narratives, 74
criminal justice system, disproportionate punishments of, 194
critical: identity development, 41; incidents, 32; inquiry, 21
critical consumers of information, teaching students to be, 82
Critical discourse analysis (CDA), 27
critical literacy, 9–10, 20–21
Critical Race Theory (CRT), 27, 74–75
CRP. *See* culturally relevant pedagogy
CRSH. *See* culturally responsive sustaining humanizing
CRT. *See* Critical Race Theory
crucial elements in the education of all teachers, 139–47
CSP. *See* culturally sustaining pedagogies
cultural: capital, 50; community knowledge, 75; competence, developing, 117–18; knowledge, shared, 34–35; models, 27–28, 39
cultural and linguistic competence, 50
culturally and linguistically minoritized students, growth trajectory of, 7
culturally relevant and culturally responsive pedagogy, 117
culturally relevant pedagogy, (CRP), 98, 117
Culturally Responsive Sustaining Humanizing (CRSH), 52, 61
culturally responsive teachers and teaching, 21, 49, 50, 153, 156, 157, 162
culturally sustaining, 47, 61, 215; pedagogies, (CSP), 50, 61, 98, 243
cultural wealth, *59*, 69–70, 175, 177
culture shock, 30, 69
Cummins, 8, 12
curriculum/a, 42, 43, 82, 101
cycle of unshifting perspectives and practices, 88, 92, 96–97. *See also* perspectives

Deferred Action for Childhood Arrivals (DACA), 136, 195
deficit ideologies, that shape educational policies, 241
deficit views or perspectives, 93–95, 97–98. *See also* perspectives
deportation, of Mexicans/immigrants, 4, 71
depression, 137–138, 223–26, 228–31, 234
development of positive dispositions toward difference, 161
dialogue, cultivating space for, 118
discourse/s, 27–28, 37, 40–41, 89; marker, 34; of post-truth, 48
discussions, classroom, of social justice, 43
disparities, 154, 155
distrust, between Latinx communities and leaders, 47–48
diversifying the teacher workforce, need for, 145
diversity, 55, 89, 154
DLBE. *See* dual language bilingual education
Dreamers, 193
dual language (DL): certificate, creation of, 217–18; programs, Hispanic, 29; schools, as spaces for ethnic identity formation, 27
dual language bilingual education, (DLBE), 26

EBLs. *See* emergent bilingual learners
educational leaders, 61–62
Educator Preparation Program (EPP), 153, 169
ELLs. *See* English language learners
emergent bilingual learners (EBLs), 8–9, 11–13, 21n1; restrictive language policies impacting, in AZ, 211; segregated from English-speaking peers, 213; socially constructed identities of, 12
engagement of difference, 113

engagement with Latinx populations, urgent need for, 109
"English for the Children", 9, 211, 213. *See also* Arizona, Proposition 203
English language learners (ELLs), 9, 13; classified, 89–91; Latinx, deficit view of, 95–96; negative stereotypes and tracking of, 90; over and under representation in Special Education, 90; stigmatized by classification, 89
English-only, 13; education policies, 26; movement, 213
epistemologies: Chicana, interpretation of standards grounded in, 157; dominant, 241–43
EPP. *See* Educator Preparation Program
equity, lessons learned on the journey toward, 59–61
ethnic: identification, developing positive, 41; studies, 42, 61–62
Eurocentric systems, as the norm, 26
exclusionary practices in higher education, 196

Familismo, 160–62, 169
fear, 47; of deportation, Latinx students', 127, 137; of other and of difference, 118
Fernandez, Patricia, 217
first-generation college student/s, 67, 69, 72, 77
First Generation College Student Workshop, 69
first language, students', as a problem, 113
Franquiz, 10
Freire, 10
funds of knowledge, 98, 161

Gandara, 146
growth in Hispanic population, and cultural, linguistic and ethnic diversity, 90

Harvard Graduate School of Education, 68

HB2281, 48
HHS *See* Hope High School
high school dropout rate of Latinx students, 90
Hispanic, xvi, 29; identifying as, 33–35; and Latinx, interchangeable use of terms, 88
home language, encouraging student use of, 102
Hope High School (HHS), 49, 51
House Bill 2064 (H.B. 2064), 9
House Consensus Bill 2005 (HCB 2005), 213

identifying as Latinx, 41
identity/ies, 8, 12, 15, 28, 37, 39, 166, 168–69; development/formation of, 11, 26, 37, 39; investment, perspective, 11–12; notions of, implications for teacher education practices, 168; politics, 25–26, 42, 127; text/s, 8, 20. *See also* social identity/ies
immigrant/s, 79, 87–89, 91; % of U.S. population, 109; and children of, portrayed as not belonging, 132; and linguistically diverse youth, learning amidst threats and discrimination, 7; students *vs.* "the real students", 94
immigration: in California, controversy over, 3; issues, Latinx pre-service teaches' connection to, 167
imposter syndrome, 68–69
incarcerated youth, stories of mistreatment of, 194
inequality/ies, 43, 240; personal accounts of, 43
insider/s, 28, 29, 39–41
insiders or outsiders, positioning as, 28, 39. *See also* status
inspiring marginalized students to advocate for themselves, 84
institutional capacity, building, to work with undocumented students, 200

INTASC. *See* Interstate Teacher Assessment Support Consortium
inter-institutional partnerships, for educator support, 147
Interstate Teacher Assessment Support Consortium (INTASC), standards, 154, 156
interviews, 30, 34–36
introspection, critical, 118–19
"Introspectives", 159
issues: of equity and access in education, 98; of social class, race, class, power and identity, students examine, 21

journey, as an undergraduate at UC Davis, 193–94

K-12 school settings, xv; role of dominant epistemologies in, 241

label/s: dehumanizing, 61; ethnic identity, 38, 41; identity, associated with race and language, 35; Latino/a, as a positive identity, 41; pan-ethnic identity, 27, 32–35, 37, 40; social identity, 32
lack of diversity and representation of Latinx at the collegiate level, 129
Ladson-Billings, 117
In Lak Ech, 51–52
language brokers, empowering adolescents as, 110
language nests, 173, 174. *See also* nidos de lengua
language/s: discrimination, 182; hybridized, 182; loss, intergenerational, 26
language use of EBLs and identity development, connections between, 11
LatCrit. *See* Latino/a Critical Race Theory
Latina, 32, 33, 36–39; first-generation, 68–69

Latino/a, 35–37, 39, 43n1
Latino/a Critical Race Theory (LatCrit), 27, 73–75
Latinx, xv, xvi, 7, 43n1, 47, 74–75, 84, 89, 120, 133, 168; pre-service teachers, 157; recruitment and retention in teacher education programs, 129; student enrollment in U.S. schools and colleges, diversity of, 133–35; students, low academic achievement of, variables to explain, 135; students, opportunity to thrive, xxii; students who want and do become teachers, supporting, 130; students/youth, 25, 27, 40–42, 50–51, 53, 80, 88–90; teachers, 84, 135–36; youth dropout rates, 128
leadership, as a form of resistance, 72, 84
lengua y comunidad, 175
linguistic and cultural capital, as part of the curriculum, 12
Lopez, 21

MAGA hats, 4
make a difference, 5
"Make America Great Again", 193
Maldonado-Torres, 49
marginalized communities, criminalization of, 72
MAS program. *See* Mexican American Studies (MAS) program
McIntosh, Peggy, essay on White privilege, 159
Measure 2, Massachusetts, 213
mental health: issues, related to Latinx youth, 223–24; services for marginalized communities, barriers to, 224; teachers' roles as allies in addressing issues of, 223; and trauma counseling, 80–81
mentors and teachers of color, 68
Mexican American Studies (MAS) program, 42, 48, 51
Mexican flags, 53, 55

microaggression/s, 48, 51–52
micro-spaces, 39, 40, 42
minoritized: communities, how racism and discrimination disempower, 239; students, struggle to be legitimized as change agents, 240
Multiple Choice Questions (MCQs) instrument, 227; survey results from pre-service teachers, 228–29

NAEP. *See* National Assessment of Educational Progress
names, gaining trust through learning to say, 59
narrative/s, 92, 95, 96; false, of colorblindness, 98
National Assessment of Educational Progress (NAEP), xvi, 91, 134
National Council of La Raza, 137–138
nationalism, and nativism, 82, 110
nido de comunidad, 174, 186–87
nidos de lengua, 173–74, 184–85
Noah, Trevor, 82

official knowledge, what counts as, 10, 153
Open Door national study-abroad, data for, 111
opportunity gap in education of ELLs, 92, 96–97
oppression, forms of, 75
ownership of meaning, 17

Paris and Alim, 10, 21, 216
pedagogies of the home, 157, 162
pedagogy, centered around students' experiences, 43
perspective/s, deficit, xvi, 96
perspectives, teachers', 93–95, 97–99, 113
Plyler v. Doe, 195
policies, nationalistic, implications for teacher education, 110
portrayal of Mexicans/Mexican Americans in the media, 89

positionality, 90
positioning, 21, 28, 109–11, 116, 156, 240
post-truth, 48, 70, 73–75, 153, 155–56
practices that highlight and value the community, teachers' engagement in, 70
pre-service teachers' preparation to address students' mental health issues, 224
pre-service teachers/s', Latinx, 156, 158–59, 161, 167, 169
President Biden, Joseph R., election of, xxi
prison industrial complex, work towards abolishing, 194
professional development, 43, 52, 84, 142, 216, 218; to disrupt negative attitudes and perspectives, 98; during the COVID-19 pandemic, 219; focused on asset-based mindsets, 216; to support teachers to work effectively with Latinx students, 138; training for student-depression-intervention, need for, 233; training to support undocumented immigrants in higher ed, 199, 205–6
Proposition 58, California, 185
Proposition 203, 9, 212–13. *See also* Arizona; English for the Children
Proposition 227, California, 185, 213

"raced epistemologies", 26, 42
racism, 88, 109, 239, 240
radical educator/s, 67, 70
recommendations for preparing teachers of Latinx and all students, 139–147
recruitment of diverse students into the teaching profession, 145
reflection, providing students space for, 100
relationships, as important, 240–41
research with Latinx undergraduates, 175–76
resistance, 72, 84, 162, 164–65, 169

resources supporting teachers/administrators of emergent bilinguals, 216–17
restorative justice, 79–80
restrictive language policies, in AZ, 212–13
retention of Latinx teachers, importance of, 146
rhetoric, anti-immigrant, racist, xv, 25, 42, 47, 71, 74, 83–84, 89, 127, 186, 241; hostile, experienced by students/faculty of color in higher ed, 128; Trump era, effect on the classroom, 81. *See also* Trump, Donald
roots discourse, of being Latino, 36, 37, 40

sanctuary: cities, 5, 71; classroom as a, 81; state, 71; state law, 3
SB54. *See* Senate Bill 54
school-prison-pipeline, 49
school/s: Alma Elementary, 12; Espada, 29–30, 34, 41–42; as microcosms of society, 25; North Bay Area High, 48; "two-way" bilingual or immersion, 29
SEI. *See* Structured English Immersion
self-awareness, role of in practicing anti-racist pedagogy, 102
self-study of diversity, authentic, 156
Senate Bill 54 (SB54), 3–5, 71
shifting school/classroom practices to support all students, 99
Silva, Alexandria and Kaveh, Yalda, Drs., 217
situated identities, 28, 39
social capital, 36
social change, 69, 84
social identity/ies, 21, 32, 40, 43
social justice, 72, 75, 78
social studies, 82
Southern Poverty Law Center (SPLC), xv
Space, for positive ethnic identification, 41

Spanish speakers, % of U.S. school-age students, 8
speech, derogatory, hateful, impact of, xvi, xvii
SPLC. *See* Southern Poverty Law Center
status as insider or outsider, 36
STEMSS CRUISE EL Project, 214
Structured English Immersion (SEI), 212, 213, 217–18
student/s: of color, 7, 49, 50, 240–41; immigrant, 79, 87, 113; undocumented, 87, 195–98, 200–206. *See also* Latinx
student teaching in the current challenging context, 131–32
study-abroad teacher education program, in Chili, 110, 111, 114–16
systems: of dominance, societal, 27; of subordination in society, 27; that support positive ethnic identity formation, 42

teacher education/preparation, 128, 138, 147, 157
teacher educator, 129
teacher leader/s, 72–76; as bridges, advocates, and role models of civic engagement, 84; Latinx, 73–74; from underrepresented communities, 73; as a way of thinking and being, 73
teacher leadership, 72–73, 79
teacher of color, as a mentor for students, 68
teacher/s: beliefs, about language and students' experiences, effect on their practices, 96, 98; beliefs, effect on expectations and on student's behaviors and achievement, 141; beliefs and attitudes, affected by appropriate training and education, 141; challenged by their own beliefs and perceptions of difference, 118; Latinx, risk of being deported and discrimination against, 136; reflection of their own cultural identity, perceptions, beliefs, and interactions, 118; who advocate for students and the teaching profession, 72–73; who are sociocultural conscious, 118; who serve as Latinx role models, 145; who teach Latinx students, demographics of, 135
Teachers of Language Learners Community (TL3C) Consortium, 214
teachers' preparation, 139, 141–45
teaching: career, negative perceptions of, in the United States, 139; force population, 90; of Latinx Students, effective, 51; and learning as political, 243; residency model, 145; trauma-informed, 144
Teaching in Chile program, explained, 110–11
tensions, 11, 87–88, 92, 240
terms, Hispanic and Latinx, use of, xvi
testimonio/s, 72, 74–76
transformation, xxii, 21
translanguage, awareness of need to, 167
Trump, Donald, xv, 8, 25, 71, 87–89, 98, 137
trust, 48, 59–60, 62
Tutors for Incarcerated Youth (TFII) program, 194

undocually trainings, 196–205
undocumented, 193, 195, 202–3, 205
Undocumented Student Resource Centers (USRCs), 196
UndocuScholars Project, 195, 198–99
unshifting practices and perspectives, 87–88
U. S. Census Bureau, 7

a vacuum of leadership and support networks, in AZ, 212
Valenzuela, Angela, 50
Vice-President Harris, Kamala, election of, xxi

vignettes, of deficit perspectives and anti-racist pedagogy in practice, 93–95, 99–102
Villegas and Lucas, 162
voice/s, 70, 213, 241; parents', finding theirs through decision-making, 100–101; and power for those who want to blame immigrants, 88; student/s', 56, 61, 62, 67, 69–70, 101, 156; young people's, centralizing, 52

waivers, for EBLs, 9
"we need to keep fighting the fight", 194
Wenger, 11–12, 15, 17, 20
whiteness, 35
white supremacy, 47, 48, 51
"Words matter", xvi
wraparound services and schools, 79, 146

writing, student, 8, 14, 16, 21

xenophobia, and response to, 47, 109–10
xenophobic responses, 4, 7

Yolo County Juvenile Detention Center, 193
Yosso, Tara, 50, 98, 175, 177, 216; community cultural background, 142
youth: black and brown, hyper-criminalization of, 53; centered as productive agents and contributors of knowledge, 243; participatory action research, 42

zero-tolerance policies, 49–50
zones of contact, 26, 40

About the Editors and Contributors

EDITORS

Margarita Jiménez-Silva is Associate Professor and Chair of Teacher Education at the University of California, Davis, and co-founder of Sisterhood for Equity Consulting. Prior to entering higher education, Professor Jiménez-Silva worked with newcomer students as a middle school math and science teacher. Her research focuses on preparing and supporting teachers to work with culturally and linguistically diverse learners, especially in addressing emergent bilinguals' linguistic and academic content development. More specifically, her research strands include teacher education pedagogy and curriculum, educational policy, and family/community engagement. She has coordinated curriculum and programs addressing the needs of emergent bilinguals both in the United States and internationally. Her most recent work focuses on developing pipelines of future bilingual teachers in ways that honor and build on their cultural and linguistic capital. Her research has been published by journals such as *Harvard Educational Review*, *Childhood Education*, and the *Journal of Research on Childhood Education*. She is co-editor (with Cathy Coulter) of *Culturally Sustaining and Revitalizing Pedagogies: Language, Culture, and Power* (Emerald Publishing, 2017). Her research has been supported by the National Science Foundation and the U.S. Department of Education. A graduate of Concordia University Irvine, she holds Master's and Doctor of Education degrees from the Harvard Graduate School of Education.

Janine Bempechat is Clinical Professor at Boston University, Wheelock College of Education and Human Development. Dr. Bempechat is a developmental psychologist with a deep interest in the socialization of achievement. She studies family, cultural, and school influences in the development of student motivation and academic achievement in low-income children and youth, both nationally and cross-nationally. Her most recent work focuses on the impact of parental educational messaging on adolescents' developing achievement-related beliefs and behaviors. Her research has been published in journals including *Child Development, Journal of Ethnographic and Qualitative Research, Teachers College Record*, and the *Journal of Youth and Adolescence*. She is the author of *Against the odds: How "at-risk" students exceed expectations* (Jossey-Bass, 1991) *and Getting our kids back on Ttack: Educating children for the future* (Jossey-Bass, 2000). She is coeditor (with Helen Haste) of *Civic concepts and civic culture: Challenges for American education* (Brill-Sense, forthcoming) and is coeditor (with David J. Shernoff) of *Engaging youth in schools: Evidence-based models to guide future innovations* (Teachers College Press, 2014). A former National Academic of Education Spencer Fellow, her research has been supported by the Spencer Foundation and the William T. Grant Foundation. A graduate of McGill University, she holds Master's and Doctor of Education degrees from the Harvard Graduate School of Education.

CONTRIBUTORS

Leticia Alvarez Gutiérrez is a first-generation, Purépecha, Xicana, associate professor in the Department of Education, Culture & Society at the University of Utah. She earned a master's degree in education at Harvard University and a Ph.D. at the University of Wisconsin-Madison. Dr. Alvarez Gutiérrez is a critical community-engaged scholar who grew up in a working-poor, mixed-status, immigrant household along the San Diego-Tijuana border. She attended school in both the United States and Mexico and entered school in the United States as a monolingual Spanish speaker. These experiences have shaped her research agenda, which includes focusing on the educational experiences of Latinxs as well as taking actions to dismantle inequities in the educational system for BIPOC students and families.

Evelyn C. Baca is Assistant Professor of Bilingual/Bicultural Education at Illinois State University. Her research explores the policies, practices, and discourses that influence culturally and linguistically diverse students across K-12 educational contexts. To date, her research has used varying lenses to explore language policy, bi/multilingual learning contexts, school reform processes, and educator preparedness to work with culturally and linguistically diverse students. Prior to receiving her Ph.D. from Arizona State University in Educational Policy & Evaluation, she taught Spanish and English as additional languages.

Carmen Cáceda is Professor of education and leadership at Western Oregon University. She earned a master's degree in Spanish literature and a Ph.D. in culture, literacy, and language from the University of Texas, San Antonio. Her research is focused on teacher candidates' beliefs, bicultural/bilingual practices, language and identity issues, and the preparation of EFL/ESL/bilingual teachers. Prior to graduate school, she taught English as a foreign language to middle and high school students in Lima, Peru.

Jaclyn Caires-Hurley is Assistant Professor of multicultural education and critical pedagogy in the College of Education at Western Oregon University, where she also chairs the office of justice, equity, diversity, and inclusion. She earned a Ph.D. in the social, multicultural, and bilingual foundations of education with an emphasis on educational equity and cultural diversity from the University of Colorado, Boulder. Prior to graduate school, she taught in Phoenix, Arizona. Her research includes examining the sociopolitical context of teaching and learning and documenting how we prepare pre-service teachers for anti-racist teaching.

Orlando Carreón is Lecturer/Supervisor at the University of California, Davis. He is the son of immigrant parents with roots in Guerrero, Mexico. His interests include teaching and researching within a decolonial and social justice framework to disrupt how discourses of race, culture, ideology, and power affect BIPOC communities. Current topics include effective teaching practices of Latinx Youth; Ethnic Studies; Teacher Education; and Culturally Sustaining Practices. Dr. Carreón has over 15 years of experience as an educator and is currently dedicated to develop Grow Your Own Teacher programs where local communities can create pathways for students to become teachers.

Ofelia Castro Schepers is Associate Professor in the Department of Elementary Education and Literacy at Metropolitan State University of Denver. She earned her Ph.D. in Educational Equity and Cultural Diversity from the University of Colorado, Boulder. Dr. Schepers's teaching and research focus on educational equity, educational access points, teacher retention, teacher secondary traumatic stress, and effective literacy practices for emerging bilinguals in dual language and general education classrooms and TIPCrit.

Jesus Cisneros is Associate Professor of Educational Leadership and Foundations at the University of Texas at El Paso. Cisneros takes a critical interdisciplinary approach to education policy and practice, providing a nuanced and complex understanding of identity, power, resistance, and oppression. His research moves gender, sexuality, and immigration status, and their conceptual margins, to the center of analysis in an effort to explore and understand the way politics and identity interact with various axes of inequality.

Ashley Coughlin is an instructional coach at a middle school in the Washington Elementary School district in Phoenix, Arizona. She has experience teaching bilingual education, special education, and general education as well as working with emergent bilinguals in Arizona's SEI programs. She holds a Masters in Curriculum and Instruction and a National Board Certification in English as a New Language. She was recently accepted to the Ph.D. program for Educational Policy and Evaluation at Arizona State University. Coughlin focuses on creating professional development in areas related to meeting the needs of diverse learners in content-area classrooms, weaving content into language acquisition classrooms, creating asset-based mindsets among educators, and involving families and community stakeholders in school communities.

Andrea M. Emerson is Assistant Professor of Early Childhood Education in the Division of Education and Leadership at Western Oregon University in Monmouth, Oregon. She holds Early Childhood–focused degrees in both Human Development and Family Studies and Curriculum and Instruction. She is passionate about educator preparation, early childhood play, relationship-based practices in early and higher education, and anti-racist education. She brings diverse personal perspectives to her teaching and research from her Colombian immigrant and white American family heritages.

Melody Esqueda is a third-year AP English and ELD teacher at Abraham Lincoln High School in East LA. She grew up in South East Los Angeles and always desired to give back to her community through education. As a first-generation college student, she received her B.A. in Narrative Studies from the University of Southern California and her Ed.M in English teaching at the Harvard Graduate School of Education. Her specialties include working with students from diverse populations, trauma-informed education, and anti-bias, antiracist (ABAR) education at the high school level.

Dr. Kenneth Fasching-Varner is Professor of Education in the College of Education at the University of Nevada, Las Vegas. Dr. Varner's areas of scholarly expertise and interest center on the intersections of identity and difference in globalized contexts, with attention to the language and literacy practices of individuals and communities. Dr. Varner examines the nature of White Racial Identity (WRI), Critical Race Theory (CRT), and Culturally Relevant Pedagogy, as well as the role of international education, neoliberalism, and educational foundations within global language and literacy contexts.

Laura M. Gomez is Adjunct Faculty member in the Social Sciences for both Glendale and Los Angeles Community College Districts. Dr. Gomez Gonzales teaches Ethnic and Chicano Studies, including History of the Mexican American, Latinos in the United States, Introduction to Chicano Studies, and Ethnic Minorities in the United States. She earned her Ph.D. from Arizona State University in Education Policy and Evaluation Program, and her M.A. and B.A. degrees in Chicana/o Studies from California State University, Northridge.

Karen Guerrero is Clinical Assistant Professor at Mary Lou Fulton Teachers College at Arizona State University. She is a National Geographic Explorer and educator with 20 years of K-12 classroom experience and 16 years of higher education teaching. She has worked with a variety of students from inner-city children to urban adults in both informal and formal education settings. Dr. Guerrero's work is in STEMSS learning and professional development for diverse learners. She holds an Ed.D. in leadership and innovation with a focus on teacher professional development and a Ph.D. in Philosophy of Education with an emphasis on eLearning.

Anne Ittner is an assistant professor of Literacy Education in the Division of Education and Leadership at Western Oregon University in Monmouth, Oregon, USA. Her research interests include literacy education for emergent bilinguals in elementary schools, literacy professional development, and teacher education. She is co-author (with L. Helman and K. McMaster) of *Assessing language and literacy with bilingual students: Practices to support English learners* (Guilford Press, 2020).

Jenny E. Jacobs teaches English and native Spanish literacy courses with newcomer bilingual high school students in Boston Public Schools, after over two decades of experience as an educator, teacher-educator, instructional coach, and researcher. Dr. Jacobs has lived and worked in the United States, Mexico, El Salvador, Honduras, and Spain, where she has pursued advocacy for and collaboration with immigrant youth and families, especially from Central America and the Caribbean, with a focus on equal access to high-quality reading and writing programs in their home language(s). She is also involved in local advocacy and organizing for educational justice.

Karen Kay is a senior at the University of California, Davis. As a first-generation Mexican American college student, she advocates for equity for underrepresented students. During her undergraduate education at Davis, worked with system-impacted youth and English language learners. She will begin a master's program in education in the fall of 2021 where she hopes to continue her work with underrepresented students learning English.

Christine Montecillo Leider is Assistant Professor of Applied Linguistics at the University of Massachusetts Boston. Her work focuses on teacher beliefs on language diversity, antiracist and culturally/linguistically responsive pedagogical practices, and policy and civil rights issues regarding teacher training and multilingual learners' access to education. Dr. Leider's work has been published in *Education Policy Analysis Archives*, *Journal of Multilingual Theories and Practice*, *International Journal of Bilingual Education and Bilingualism*, *TESOL Journal*, and *TESOL Quarterly*.

Joseph Luevanos is a senior at Santa Susana High School. He was a Boy Scout for twelve years and served as Senior Patrol Leader for Troop 689. He has served as volunteer tutor for students studying Biology, Chemistry, and Calculus, and has also volunteered for numerous community events including Juneteenth in Simi Valley, LGBTQ Pride Picnic, and Scouting for Food. He will pursue undergraduate studies at Northeastern University in fall, 2021.

Ruth Luevanos is National Board Certified teacher at a continuation high school in Reseda, California. She has worked in K-12 Title 1 public schools in Los Angeles for over 20 years. She regularly presents on strategies for engaging Latinx parents and supporting culturally and linguistically diverse students. She is a former board member for the California Council for Social Studies and chair of the Committee of Diversity and Social Justice. She is a former National Council for Geography Education Middle School Teacher of the Year and Teach Plus Fellow for Los Angeles. In 2018 she was elected to Simi Valley City Council for a four-year term.

Gabrielle Luu a second-year medical student at the University of Arizona College of Medicine-Tucson (UACOM-T). As a first-generation Vietnamese American college graduate and co-director of UACOM-T's First-Generation/Low-Income Club, she advocates for providing mentorship for first-generation medical and undergraduate students. During her undergraduate education at Arizona State University, her honors thesis focused on pre-service teachers' understanding of supporting K-12 students' mental health needs. She has presented her work at international conferences. Currently, she supports culturally responsive mental health services as a coordinator at a free psychiatry clinic for uninsured patients.

Patricia D. Quijada Cerecer is Associate Professor in the School of Education at the University of California, Davis. Dr. Quijada Cerecer is also the associate editor of the *Journal of American Indian Education (JAIE)*. She has worked with and learned from young people, community-based organizations, and educational systems to improve access to post-secondary institutions for Latinx/ Indigenous and Native American students and faculty. Dr. Quijada Cerecer uses Indigenous and critical race frameworks to examine issues related to place, sense of belonging, family community school partnerships, and the preparation of educational leaders. A graduate of the University of California, Riverside, she earned her master's degree from the Harvard Graduate School of Education and her Ph.D. from the University of Wisconsin-Madison.

Molly Ross is a K-12 SEI instructional coach in the Randolph, MA, Public School district. In this role, she supports mainstream and ESL educators to best meet the needs of our English learners through co-planning, modeling, and leading professional development opportunities. Previously, she has taught ESL and content classes for English learners to both elementary and middle school students. Ms. Ross is also an adjunct faculty member at Boston University where she teaches a course on how to support English learners in the content classroom. Additionally, she serves on the board of directors for Massachusetts of Teachers of Speakers of Other Languages (MATSOL) where she also leads a group of instructional coaches.

Nadeen T. Ruiz is Professor Emeritus at CSU Sacramento and Lecturer at the School of Education, University of California at Davis. Dr. Ruiz earned her M.A. and Ph.D. at Stanford University in bilingual education and linguistics. Formerly, Dr. Ruiz was Chair of Bilingual Multicultural Education at California State University Sacramento and Director of Elementary Education at Stanford University. Dr. Ruiz co-founded the Optimal Learning Environment (OLE) Project, a research and professional development program focusing on effective literacy instruction for emergent bilingual students in general and special education classrooms. Her other recent research areas include bilingual teacher preparation and transnational teacher education.

Megan Schantz is a middle and high school ESL teacher. She earned her bachelor's degree in bilingual education and her master's degree in Literacy Education, both from Boston University.

Samantha A. Smith is a first-generation community college transfer student from rural eastern California. She is pursuing a Masters in Public Policy at the Goldman School of Public Policy at the University of California, Berkeley, and is a research assistant at the School of Education at the University of California, Davis. Her research interests are focused on actionable research and policy analysis. Ms. Smith is currently investigating the urban/rural divide in access to resources within California and barriers to higher education among rural residents.

Eleonora Villegas-Reimers is Clinical Professor and Chair of the Department of Teaching and Learning at the Boston University Wheelock College of Education and Human Development. Dr. Villegas-Reimers has served as consultant to a number of international organizations including UNESCO and the Singapore National Institute of Education on matters related to education, teacher preparation, and education for democracy. Dr. Villegas-Reimers is a member of the Massachusetts State Department of Early Education and Care (DEEC) Board. She is a founding member of the Massachusetts Consortium for Socio-Emotional Learning in Teacher Education (SEL-TEd). She holds Master's and Doctor of Education degrees from the Harvard University Graduate School of Education.

www.ingramcontent.com/pod-product-compliance
Lightning Source LLC
Chambersburg PA
CBHW020112010526
44115CB00008B/794